SECOND EDITION

CONNECT TO YOUR CAREER
Job-Search Skills for a Digital World

Suzann Connell, MEd, PhD

Lead Faculty, Area Chair
English and Communications
University of Phoenix
Los Angeles, California

Julie Jaehne, MS

Adjunct Faculty, College of Education
University of Houston
Houston, Texas

Publisher
The Goodheart-Willcox Company, Inc.
Tinley Park, IL
www.g-w.com

09-CFU-429

Preface

Connect to Your Career is more than a text about how to get a job; it is a technology-driven 21st century reflection of how adults find and cultivate careers. Finding a job you enjoy is a long process, one that is outlined in this text.

The job-search process begins with writing a plan that will build a foundation on which your professional reputation will rest. Next, you will draft employment documents that position you as an outstanding candidate that will attract attention from employers. Then, you will sort through numerous job postings to weed out scams and occupations for which you are not qualified. Finally, after some effort, you will be prepared to apply for jobs that you will enjoy, make you feel fulfilled, and are in line with your career plans.

To facilitate your understanding of the job-search process, we designed *Connect to Your Career* with one overriding goal in mind: to help you understand how to use technology, such as social media, job-search websites, and digital devices, to connect to a career. Technology will be an essential part of your career search, so it is important to know how to leverage it to help you find the career of your dreams.

Upon completing this book, you will able to:

- Identify your skills, talents, and career strengths to develop a career plan.
- Practice job-specific and employability skills required by employers.
- Learn how to brand yourself as a professional in the workplace.
- Build, protect, and maintain a professional online presence that will lead to employment.
- Develop professional networks to assist you in the job-search process.
- Learn how to protect your identity and personal information while searching and applying for jobs online.
- Create résumés that highlight your strengths and present you as a qualified job applicant.
- Create cover letters that convince employers to grant you interviews.
- Apply for jobs online and in-person and manage the job-search process.
- Prepare for various types of job interviews, including virtual interviews.
- Understand how to behave professionally while participating in a job interview.
- Use post-interview techniques to help keep the job-search process in perspective.
- Develop an understanding of what employers expect so you can be successful at your new job.
- Learn what it means to be a professional and connect to your career.

Your new career will come first from planning and then acting. Appreciate the time that it takes to secure your future employment and enjoy the journey of creating new professional connections, sharing your insights on social media, and gathering professional followers. It is time for you to *Connect to Your Career!*

About the Authors

Suzann Connell is Lead Faculty/Area Chair, Communications and English, for the Department of Humanities at the University of Phoenix. She teaches both face-to-face and online courses. Her curricula include career-development techniques, professional communication, writing, media writing, podcasting, and blog writing. Additionally, Suzann is a freelance instructional designer with a diverse career. She uses the principles compiled and written in this text for each new career move. Suzann holds her undergraduate degree from the University of Michigan and her master degree in Instructional Technology from Pepperdine University. Her PhD is in the field of nutrition counseling.

Julie Jaehne has been an adjunct faculty member for 21 years at the University of Houston in the College of Education. Via distance learning, she has taught instructional technology courses and teacher certification courses. Julie also has extensive experience with the use of technology with kindergarten through 12th grade instruction. She is a published author of multiple computer application textbooks and tutorials. In addition, Julie is a Career Education consultant and adviser for community workplace initiatives. Julie holds a bachelor degree in business administration from Baylor University and a master degree in education with a concentration in occupational education from the University of Houston.

Student Resources

Student Text

Connect to Your Career is a technology-driven 21st century reflection of how adults find and launch a new career. It reflects a seamless integration of technology and social media to guide students as they self-assess and discover who they are as future employees. Technology is an essential part of the career-search process, so it is important for students to know how to leverage it to help them find the career for which they are looking.

G-W Online Textbook

The G-W Online Textbook platform gives students instant access to the textbook and resources with browser-based devices including iPads, notebooks, PCs, and Mac computers. Textbook pages look exactly the same as the printed text, and all materials are located on a convenient online bookshelf and accessible at home, at school, or on the go. A linked table of contents provides quick access to each chapter. A search tool enables the user to locate a specific topic or word within the text. Students can enlarge or compress a page or print individual pages for off-line reading.

Online Learning Suite

The G-W Online Learning Suite includes the G-W Online Textbook, Skills Review, Workplace Connection activity files, and a Career Assessment Inventory, creating a complete learning package. It is accessible through any Internet-enabled device, including computers, smartphones, and tablets. All instructional materials are found on a convenient online bookshelf and accessible at home, at school, or on the go.

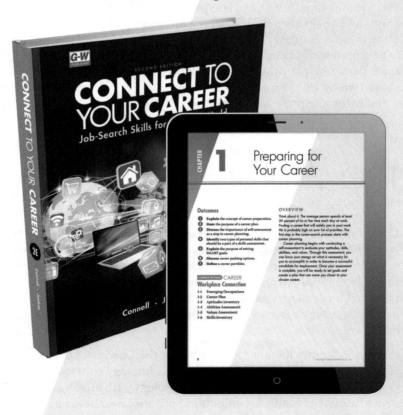

Instructor Resources

LMS Integration

Integrate Goodheart-Willcox content within your Learning Management System for a seamless user experience for both you and your students. LMS-ready content in Common Cartridge® format facilitates single sign-on integration and gives you control of student enrollment and data. With a Common Cartridge® integration, you can access the LMS features and tools you are accustomed to using and G-W course resources in one convenient location—your LMS.

In order to provide a complete learning package for you and your students, Common Cartridge® by G-W includes the Online Learning Suite (G-W Online Textbook, Skills Review, Workplace Connection activity files, Career Assessment Inventory) and Online Instructor Resources. When you incorporate G-W content into your courses via Common Cartridge®, you have the flexibility to customize and structure the content to meet the educational needs of your students. You may also choose to add your own content to the course.

QTI® assessment files are available within the Online Instructor Resources for import into your LMS. These pre-built assessments help you measure student knowledge and track results in your LMS gradebook. Questions and tests can be customized to meet your assessment needs.

Online Instructor Resources (OIR)

Online Instructor Resources provide all the support needed to make preparation and classroom instruction easier than ever. Available in one accessible location, support materials include answer keys, lesson plans, Instructor's Presentations for PowerPoint®, ExamView® Assessment Suite, and more! Online Instructor Resources are available as a subscription and can be accessed at school or at home.

Instructor's Resource CD

One resource provides instructors with time-saving preparation tools, such as answer keys, lesson plans, and other teaching aids.

Instructor's Presentations for PowerPoint®

Instructor's Presentations for PowerPoint® provide a useful teaching tool when presenting the lessons. These fully customizable slides help you teach and visually reinforce the key concepts from each chapter.

ExamView® Assessment Suite

ExamView® Assessment Suite allows you to quickly and easily create and print tests from a test bank of hundreds of questions. The components include the ExamView® Test Generator, ExamView® Test Manager, and ExamView® Test Player. You can have the software generate a test for you with randomly selected questions. You may also choose specific questions from the question banks and, if you wish, add your own questions to create customized tests to meet your classroom needs. Tests you create may be published for LAN-based testing or be packaged for online testing using WebCT, Blackboard, or ANGEL. The ExamView® software products are compatible with interactive whiteboard technology.

Focus on Your Career

Connect to Your Career will help students jump-start their futures in the competitive work environment of the 21st century. The unique approach of seamless integration of technology and social media presents content in a format that is clear, to the point, and realistic for the job-search process. The easy-to-read style and meaningful applications introduce behaviors for successful interactions while looking for the perfect career.

Outcomes

At the beginning of each chapter, a list of outcomes guide student learning as they read the material presented. Each outcome is aligned with the content headings, as well as with the summary at the end of the chapter. This alignment provides a logical flow through each page of the material so that students may build on individual knowledge as they progress through the chapters.

Workplace Connection

A list of Workplace Connection activities provides a preview of the personal self-assessment opportunities that appear at the end of each chapter. This list serves as a tool to enable students to plan accordingly for successful completion of the assignments. In addition, these activities are noted within the content to indicate the appropriate time to complete each one.

Career Portfolio

Career Portfolio activities provide guidance for creating a portfolio to use when exploring career opportunities. This process requires reflection on personal accomplishments and skills as students create documentation for final presentation. Completing this activity will help students prepare a professional product for the job application process.

What Employers Want

This special feature explores essential soft skills needed in today's workplace. Soft skills are the employability skills that help an individual find a job, perform in a job, and gain success in a career.

Social Media Slipup

An aspiring musician was looking for summer work in an effort to help offset some of the costs of his tuition for college. He was accepted to an expensive university that focused primarily on the performing arts. He was willing to take any job that came his way. Working during his time off would help him pay tuition, even if he did not particularly enjoy the work.

After countless job applications, and to help relieve some of the negativity brought on by his lack of employment, he wrote a song about why he felt he was being overlooked for jobs. Being a performing-arts student looking to build his portfolio, he recorded a video of himself singing it to post to his YouTube account.

In the video, he strummed his guitar and sang recently penned lyrics about the types of people who get hired instead of him. He described them using satirical language and criticized them. In his song, he suggested that most companies are only willing to hire people who "look the part" and not necessarily the "most deserving."

The video became somewhat of a hit on YouTube. It was viewed by thousands of people, most of whom had positive comments regarding the structure and composition of the song. Hundreds of people began sharing it across multiple social networking sites.

Eventually the video made its way to a university social networking page where it was seen by one of the student's professors. This professor had previously agreed to serve as a reference for the young musician, but changed his mind after seeing the video. The professor sent an e-mail to his student explaining that he saw the video and found it embarrassing. He then asked the student to remove him from his list of references out of concern to his own professional reputation.

Networking is an important part of the job search. It is about establishing references that can lead to potential career or job opportunities. Damaging a relationship of an important reference can create

Christian Kieffer/Shutterstock.com

The Best App for That

Monster.com Job Search

The *Monster.com Job Search* app allows you to stay connected to the job-search process when you are away from your computer. Easy access to your Monster account enables you to access and update your account as well as apply for jobs directly from the app. You can also receive notifications for jobs that fit your criteria as well as upload your résumé via Dropbox or Google Drive. In addition, you can have discreet communication with recruiters via the Message Center in the app.

Nontraditional Résumé

Not all résumés will follow a traditional résumé format. For example, if a person were applying for a job as a website developer, he or she may choose to create an online résumé to reflect his or her abilities with creating and maintaining a online presence. Similarly, design highlight Two c web-ba

Web-

When or per a web option then c from th of your browse similar matting your ré portfoli conven

Rath page, y résumé

and can be highly designed to include various types of content, such as images, sound clips, and video clips. A job seeker can use a web-based résumé to display his or her design abilities, technical skills, or other talents and experience. For example, a musician can post sound or video clips of past performances directly to his or her résumé website. Similarly, a web developer can include a demo of a program he or she created. There are many free templates available online that can help you get started.

Before you create this type of résumé, conduct research to make sure this format is appropriate for the job you seek. It is a good idea to have both a web-page résumé and résumé website available for potential employers. If you use a web-based résumé, add a link to it in your professional e-mail signature block.

Visual Résumé

A creative way to highlight your résumé is to create a visual résumé. A **visual résumé** is one that presents information in a **graphically** appealing format. An **infographic résumé** is a visual résumé in which the content is displayed using a combination of words and graphics to present information clearly and quickly. Others can view your information without having to read through many lines of text.

There are many websites that offer templates for visual résumés for free or at a minimal cost. This makes it practical for anyone to create a visually appealing

---

Summary

1. **Summarize the importance of personal brand.**
A personal brand is the way in which a person expresses identity and differentiates himself or herself from others. It describes what value a potential job candidate offers to an employer. A personal brand reflects a person's professional aptitudes, skills, abilities, personality, and values.

2. **List steps for creating a personal brand statement.**
Four steps that can be taken to create a personal brand statement are defining who you are as a professional, listing your soft skills and hard skills, creating short phrases describing how you work, and compiling the information to make a concise statement.

3. **Explain the purpose of a personal commercial.**
A personal commercial is a rehearsed introduction that includes brief information about a person's background and a snapshot of his or her career goals. Also known as an elevator speech, a personal commercial can be delivered in person, or a candidate can stand out from the crowd by filming a personal commercial, posting it online, and including the URL on employment documents.

Glossary Terms

personal brand	personal brand statement	personal commercial

Review

1. How can performing a self-assessment help when defining your personal brand?

2. When creating a personal brand statement, what types of words should be chosen?

3. How can you find brand keywords that will help you create your personal brand statement?

Social Media Slipup

Real-world examples illustrate the importance of mastering social media and creating a positive online presence. Impulsive postings and other negative online behavior can cost a job applicant a career opportunity. These cases exemplify the repercussions of *acting* before *thinking* when posting on social media.

The Best App for That

These helpful hints recommend smartphone apps that will make connecting to a career a more efficient process. Downloading apps can save time and make employment documents available when access to a laptop computer is not convenient.

End-of-Chapter

End-of-chapter material provides opportunity for review and application of concepts.

- A concise **Summary** reiterates the chapter outcomes and provides a brief review of the content for student reference.
- **Glossary Terms** identify vocabulary presented in the chapter to reinforce importance of career-ready terms that are needed in the job search.
- **Review** questions highlight basic concepts presented in the chapter so students can evaluate understanding of the material.
- **Application** activities challenge students to self-reflect on who they are as a potential job candidate.
- **Workplace Connection** activities provide opportunity for self-assessment as content is presented. A total of 54 activities invite students to record their personal reactions, research, and responses to scenarios encountered during the job application process. These activity files can be downloaded from the Online Learning Suite.

Organization

The text is divided into five units and 14 chapters to accommodate classes that are presented online or face-to-face. The units may be covered in any order that meets the requirements of the class. However, it is suggested that Unit 1 be the first unit introduced.

There are five specific units that follow a sequential progression of preparing for a career. Topics covered in these units include Career Planning, Online Presence, Job-Application Process, Landing a Job, and Your Career.

- Unit 1 focuses on career planning and the starting line in a person's job search. The content aligns with the real-world experience of conducting a self-assessment, writing a career plan, and creating a personal brand.
- Unit 2 explains the integration of the Internet and social media as tools for the job search. The creation of a positive online presence in the networking process, while learning to protect personal identity, is covered in detail.
- Unit 3 provides coverage of some of the most important aspects of a job search—résumés, cover letters, and job applications. The chapters also reflect approaches and methods for creating and tracking employment documents.
- Unit 4 prepares job seekers for interview preparation, execution, and reflection. This allows students to experience every aspect of a job interview, from scheduling and participating in an interview to assessing what was learned.
- Unit 5 emphasizes what to expect when a job is offered. Additionally, information is provided about how to make the most of the first job in a new career.

New to This Edition

The second edition of *Connect to Your Career* has been revised to reflect a more sequential presentation of the career-search process than in the previous edition. Additionally, the content in each chapter has been updated to reflect the ever-changing technological tools used in a job search.

The most noticeable change to this edition is the reorganization of the chapters. The workplace success chapters have been moved and appear in Unit 1 before the online presence and networking unit. These changes allow for a more logical order of creating a career plan that can be incorporated earlier in the job-search process.

In addition, two new chapters have been added which increases the length of the text to 14 chapters instead of 12. The additional coverage of branding and career success presents additional material that students need to understand before entering the workplace.

- Chapter 1 Preparing for Your Career provides students with insight regarding steps to begin planning for their future careers. Originally placed in Chapter 5 of the previous edition, this information was moved to the beginning of the text to better reflect self-assessment and the creation of a career plan as tools for success. Creating a career plan establishes the foundation for other skills as they are presented in the text. Career pathing is also included as a component of a career plan.
- Chapter 2 Workplace Success, formerly Chapter 4, now includes *digital citizenship*, which is explained in detail to prepare students for professional responsibilities surrounding Internet and computer usage in the workplace. This material serves as a refresher of the importance of respecting the Internet as a professional and the consequences that could be experienced if respect is not honored.

- Chapter 3 Personal Brand is a new chapter that explains personal branding and the importance of a 30-second elevator speech. Students have an opportunity to self-evaluate and start the creation of their personal brand, which will help form the reputation they build in the workplace. They also have an opportunity to write a personal brand statement that can be used on employment documents.
- Chapter 4 Your Online Presence is a combination of Chapter 1 in the previous text with additional new material. Instagram was added to expand coverage of social media accounts that can be used for online presence.
- Chapter 5 Networking for Your Career was formerly Chapter 3. This material has minor updates and revisions.
- Chapter 6 Protecting Your Identity was Chapter 2 in the previous edition. It was moved to more accurately reflect the progression of events that happens in this unit. New, updated content is included that discusses public Wi-Fi hotspots, ransomware, session hijacking, and securing a computer or mobile device.
- Chapter 7 Résumés was formerly Chapter 6. Minor updates were made to reflect current practices for résumé creation.
- Chapter 8 Cover Letters was formerly Chapter 7. Minor updates were made to reflect current practices for cover letter creation.
- Chapter 9 Applying for Jobs was formerly Chapter 8. Updates were made to include the creation of a job-tracking spreadsheet to be used when applying for jobs.
- Chapter 10 Preparing for the Interview was Chapter 9 in the previous edition. Discussion of mock interviews was moved to this chapter for a more logical flow of material. Minor updates were made to the remainder of the chapter.
- Chapter 11 The Interview was Chapter 10 in the previous edition. Minor changes and updates were made.
- Chapter 12 Evaluating the Interview was Chapter 11 in the previous edition and remains largely intact. However, an additional visual aid was added to outline commonly used post-interview techniques.
- Chapter 13 Your First Day on the Job is a hybrid chapter comprised of various information from chapters in the previous edition and new information, such as onboarding.
- Chapter 14 Starting Your Career is a new chapter that introduces the importance of performing as a professional in the workplace. Understanding workplace expectations, as well as learning to work with multigenerational coworkers, is much-needed preparation for those who will be entering the workforce.
- New Social Media Slipup feature illustrates realistic examples of job applicants who failed to properly use social media. Impulsive postings and other negative online behavior robbed them of career opportunities. These cases exemplify the repercussions of acting before thinking when posting on social media.
- Totally revised Career Portfolio features have been expanded to cover specific details important to the creation of a career portfolio. This information will guide students as they build a polished portfolio that they can use when applying for positions.
- Enhanced end-of-chapter activities challenge students to self-reflect on topics introduced in the chapter. Retrospection helps to focus on what qualities or skills an individual needs to develop to prepare for a career.
- Revised checklists throughout the chapters serve as job-search management tools to help organize and prioritize important tasks. Creation of a job-tracking spreadsheet and development of a Sunday Evening plan are examples of ways job seekers can remain focused and successful.
- Connect to Your Career activities have been renamed *Workplace Connection*. These are improved and moved from placement in the content to the end of the chapter. A total of 54 activities invite students to self-assess and record their personal reactions, research, and responses to scenarios that will be encountered during the job-application process.

How to Use This Text

The *Connect to Your Career* text and accompanying digital resources will help you begin a successful career-search process. The text presents proven strategies that use technology as a tool to find the career that is the correct fit for you. You will be guided through the steps of planning your career, establishing your online presence, protecting your online identity, and networking in the 21st century. Integrated in this technology-centric approach are traditional résumés, as well as nontraditional résumés, that are sure to capture the eye of an employer.

As you make your way through the chapters, try to relate each topic to how it applies to you. By following these suggestions, you can make the most of your career preparation experience.

- Read the outcomes listed in the chapter opener. Each outcome is tied directly to the headings within the content. In addition, they are repeated in the chapter summary and applied in the end-of-chapter activities. The connection of outcomes throughout the content helps you focus and apply important information as you read each chapter.

- Pay attention to the illustrations. Each illustration is strategically created to highlight important information. By studying these, you will extend your learning and improve retention and application of the content.

- Learn how to brand yourself as a professional in the workplace. Develop a personal brand statement, as well as a 30-second elevator speech. By doing so, you will succinctly create a snapshot of who you are as a job candidate. This exercise will help you prepare as you interview, as well as network, with individuals who can help you land a job.

- Begin the process of creating a personal career portfolio. Career Portfolio activities in each chapter provide guidance to create a portfolio for use when exploring career opportunities. This process requires reflection on your accomplishments and skill sets. Completing this activity will help you build confidence and identify who you are as a potential employee. It will also give you a head start on the career-search process.

- Write your résumé. The résumé is one of the most important documents you will create in your job-search journey. You will have opportunities to begin the process as you progress through the second half of the text. On-going revisions will lead to a document suitable for submission with a job application on completion of the course.

- Note the *Connect to Your Career* boxes placed strategically at the end of major sections of content. A total of 54 activities provide practical, realistic, and interactive exercises that enable you to apply the concepts that you learn to your own job-search experience. Digital versions of these activity files are available on the Online Learning Suite.

- Complete the end-of-chapter activities. By doing so, you will be able to self-assess your learning. This self-reflection is important to helping you determine who you are as a potential employee.

Reviewers

Goodheart-Willcox Publisher would like to thank the following individuals for their honest and valuable input in the development of *Connect to Your Career*.

Laura Alfano, JD, MEd, Vice President of Curriculum, Vista College, Richardson, Texas

Dorothy Anderson, Automotive Instructor, College of the Desert, Palm Desert, California

Arin Baynard, Career Development Coordinator, Seminole State College, Sanford, Florida

Dr. Larry A. Connatser, Assistant Professor/VCE Specialist, Virginia State University, Petersburg, Virginia

Christy S. Dunston, Assistant Director, University Career Services, University of North Carolina at Chapel Hill, Chapel Hill, North Carolina

Jeffrey A. Evans, Automotive Associate Instructor, Ivy Tech Community College, Indianapolis, Indiana

Nicole A. Graves, Assistant Professor, Family and Consumer Science Education, South Dakota State University, Brookings, South Dakota

Mindi Heitland, School-to-Work Coordinator, Waukee Schools, Waukee, Iowa

Anne Landon, Career Adviser, Lycoming College, Williamsport, Pennsylvania

Diane Klemme, Professor/Family and Consumer Sciences Program Director, UW–Stout, Menomonie, Wisconsin

Shauna Maher, Lead Instructor–Introduction to Computers and Information Literacy and Communications Skills for the Workplace, Chattahoochee Technical College, Marietta, Georgia

Amelia Maness-Gilliland, PhD, Career Planning and Management Professor/Adjunct Faculty, Colorado Technical University, Schaumburg, Illinois

Kevin G. Mess, Professor/Computer & Information Technology Department's Linux Server Administrator, College of Southern Nevada, Las Vegas, Nevada

Dr. Sandra Poirier, Professor, Middle Tennessee State University, Murfreesboro, Tennessee

Paul D. Shuler, PhD, Program Director, Texas Higher Education Coordinating Board, Austin, Texas

Marci Stone, Director of Career Services, Fortis College, Salt Lake City, Utah

Catharine Weiss, Professor of Fashion Merchandising and Fashion Communications & Promotions, Lasell College, Newton, Massachusetts

Julie A. Willits, Academic Adviser, The Pennsylvania State University, University Park, Pennsylvania

Amy Wolfgang, Leadership & Career Coach & Co-owner, Wolfgang Career Coaching & Coaching 4 Good, Austin, Texas

Brief Contents

Contents

UNIT 4 Landing a Job

UNIT 5 Your Career

Career Planning

Chapter 1 Preparing for Your Career
Chapter 2 Workplace Success
Chapter 3 Personal Brand

Why It Matters

Success in the workplace requires early and diligent planning. Understanding the job-search process can help you pursue the career path that you have set out to follow. However, a lack of direction and focus will hinder your ability to search for, locate, and apply for jobs that will lead to a fulfilling career.

The job-search process requires that you assess your aptitudes, abilities, personality, and values as you apply for positions. Evaluating your soft skills and hard skills will help you market yourself and become a successful candidate for employment. In addition, establishing your personal brand will help identify who you are as a job candidate. After your evaluation is complete, you will be ready to create a career plan that can take you one step closer to your goals. Each of these activities can help you market yourself and become a successful candidate for employment.

1 Preparing for Your Career

Outcomes

1. **Explain** the concept of career preparation.
2. **State** the purpose of a career plan.
3. **Discuss** the importance of self-assessment as a step in career planning.
4. **Identify** two types of personal skills that should be a part of a skills assessment.
5. **Explain** the purpose of setting SMART goals.
6. **Discuss** career pathing options.
7. **Define** a career portfolio.

CONNECT TO YOUR CAREER

Workplace Connection

1-1   Emerging Occupations
1-2   Career Plan
1-3   Aptitudes Inventory
1-4   Abilities Assessment
1-5   Values Assessment
1-6   Skills Inventory

OVERVIEW

Think about it. The average person spends at least 30 percent of his or her time each day at work. Finding a career that will satisfy you in your work life is probably high on your list of priorities. The first step in the career-search process starts with career planning.

Career planning begins with conducting a self-assessment to evaluate your aptitudes, skills, abilities, and values. Through this assessment, you can focus your energy on what is necessary for you to accomplish in order to become a successful candidate for employment. Once your assessment is complete, you will be ready to set goals and create a plan that can move you closer to your chosen career.

Career Preparation

Finding a satisfying, fulfilling career that balances your work life with your home life is a goal that most of us seek to accomplish. Like other goals we strive to achieve, preparation is the key to success. In order to find a satisfying career, you must adequately prepare for it. *Career preparation* is a journey that differs from person to person. However, most successful job candidates have certain similarities in common, including learning to define the difference between a job and career and understanding how to create a well-developed career plan.

A **job** is short-term employment for compensation. At different times in a person's life, jobs help to pay bills, offset school costs, and meet other financial obligations. These jobs can often serve as stepping stones toward future employment goals. However, in college, it becomes time to make plans for long-term employment.

A **career** is a long-term progression in one particular field with opportunities for growth and advancement. It is a lifetime endeavor that utilizes particular skills and expertise. A career generally requires more education than a job, and during your working years, it may change multiple times. Evaluating career opportunities that are right for you can be an overwhelming task that requires long-term planning. You spend most of your waking hours at work, so decisions made regarding employment should not be taken lightly.

In your educational experience, you may have been introduced to career pathways that categorize various jobs common in the workplace. As shown in Figure 1-1, *career pathways* are broad categories that focus on specific skills and competencies for various types of jobs. These pathways are a part of the 16 career clusters that are centered on related career fields. Within each pathway, specific industries are referenced. Selecting a career involves choosing the career pathway that is best suited to your aptitudes, skills, abilities, and values, and then selecting an industry within it.

With each passing decade, employment trends evolve. It is your task to try to predict future employment options in the career field of your choice. One of the ways to analyze the future employment outlook is to compare yesterday's job trends with current market advertisements. The federal government, as well as many individual states, compile and publish data for emerging occupations. **Emerging occupations** are new occupations that have developed or changed due to technological or other advancements. For example, in the past, an office clerk filed hard-copy papers into file cabinets. That job has changed to an emerging occupation for IT professionals who clean up and defragment files stored on a computer or build and maintain a database of the same information. A list of emerging occupations is listed in Figure 1-2.

The **Occupational Information Network (O*NET)** is an occupational resource that provides descriptions of in-demand industry areas in emerging occupations. O*NET OnLine is a tool job seekers can use for career exploration and job analysis.

The US Department of Labor is another resource for job seekers. Through the Department of Labor, users can view job information, hourly standards for jobs, wage information, and occupational safety information. According to the Department of Labor, in-demand occupations are vital to our economy's health.

CONNECT TO YOUR ❯ CAREER

Complete 1-1 Emerging Occupations, pg 19

Career Plan

A **career plan** is documentation of where a person is today in the job-search process and where he or she would like to be over the course of a career. The benefits of creating this plan include self-reflection, goal setting, and a commitment to complete ongoing tasks.

The Best App for That

Glassdoor

The *Glassdoor* app is a job-search-and-recruiting app that includes a database of company reviews, salary information, and more. Job seekers can search the database to find anonymous reviews from former employees of companies. Former employees often share information about salaries paid at those companies, what it is like to work there, and other inside information that only employees can provide. Employers can post job openings, a company profile, and other information to use for recruiting new employees. From this information, job candidates can apply for a position directly through the app.

FIGURE 1-1

Career pathways are broad categories that focus on specific skills and competencies for various types of jobs.

Career Pathways	
Agriculture, Food & Natural Resources Food Products and Processing Systems Plant Systems Animal Systems Power, Structural & Technical Systems Natural Resources Systems Environmental Service Systems Agribusiness Systems	**Hospitality & Tourism** Restaurants and Food/Beverage Services Lodging Travel & Tourism Recreation, Amusements & Attractions
Architecture & Construction Design/Pre-Construction Construction Maintenance/Operations	**Human Services** Early Childhood Development & Services Counseling & Mental Health Services Family & Community Services Personal Care Services Consumer Services
Arts, Audio/Video Technology & Communications Audio and Video Technology and Film Printing Technology Visual Arts Performing Arts Journalism and Broadcasting Telecommunications	**Information Technology** Network Systems Information Support and Services Web and Digital Communications Programming and Software Development
Business Management & Administration General Management Business Information Management Human Resources Management Operations Management Administrative Support	**Law, Public Safety, Corrections & Security** Correction Services Emergency and Fire Management Services Security & Protective Services Law Enforcement Services Legal Services
Education & Training Administration and Administrative Support Professional Support Services Teaching/Training	**Manufacturing** Production Manufacturing Production Process Development Maintenance, Installation & Repair Quality Assurance Logistics & Inventory Control Health, Safety, and Environmental Assurance
Finance Securities & Investments Business Finance Banking Services Insurance	**Marketing** Marketing Management Professional Sales Merchandising Marketing Communications Marketing Research
Government & Public Administration Government National Security Foreign Service Planning Revenue and Taxation Regulation Public Management and Administration	**Science, Technology, Engineering & Mathematics** Engineering and Technology Science and Math
Health Science Therapeutic Services Diagnostic Services Health Informatics Support Services Biotechnology Research and Development	**Transportation, Distribution & Logistics** Transportation Operations Logistics Planning and Management Services Warehousing and Distribution Center Operations Facility and Mobile Equipment Maintenance Transportation Systems/Infrastructure Planning, Management, and Regulation Health, Safety, and Environmental Management Sales and Service

Goodheart-Willcox Publisher; Information source: www.careervision.org

FIGURE 1-2

Emerging occupations are new occupations that have developed or changed due to technological or other advancements.

Emerging Occupations

- ambulance driver and attendant (except EMT)
- audiologist
- cartographer and photogrammetrist
- commercial driver
- genetic counselor
- hearing aid specialist
- home health aide

- information security analyst
- interpreter and translator
- nurse practitioner
- occupational therapy aide
- occupational therapy assistant
- operations research analyst
- ophthalmic medical technician
- personal financial advisor
- physical therapist

- physical therapy assistant
- robotics engineer
- statistician
- sustainability specialist
- transportation security screener
- wind turbine service technician

Goodheart-Willcox Publisher

A career plan enables you to reflect on your progress, practice setting goals, and create a roadmap to accomplish those goals. It is not a static document and should be reviewed and updated at least twice a year.

A well-developed career plan contains all goals and milestones a person hopes to achieve within a given time period. These goals can range from the creation of a résumé or portfolio to establishing a retirement plan. Items listed in a career plan are called *action items*, as

they all require some type of action on the part of the person who created it.

Common action items in a typical two- to four-year career plan are shown in Figure 1-3. Notice these items fall into general categories, such as academic, job-search, and career-research goals. An individual will decide which categories are more important and the point they are in their career search. For some, making money to purchase items like a car and house may be a category.

FIGURE 1-3

Items listed in a career plan are called action items and are typically categorized as academic, job-search, or career-research goals.

Action Items for Career Plan	
Year 1	**Year 3**
• Monitor and maintain a strong grade point average (GPA)	• Evaluate satisfaction with current job
• Evaluate skills, abilities, and aptitudes	• Update career portfolio
• Establish short-term job goals and long-term career goals	• Investigate corporations to gain long-term employment
• Determine which courses are required to meet career goals	• Attend employee workshops
• Create a résumé	• Review existing and potential employee benefits including 401(k) plans
• Create online career profiles	• Map out future career goals
• Visit online resources such as O*NET Online	**Year 4**
• Target a specific job to obtain	• Write a statement of career for the next 10 years
• Use social media for professional networking	• Set a goal for financial independence
Year 2	• Determine which long-term assets to acquire, such as housing
• Continue to update online career profiles	• Evaluate professional life in comparison with your personal goals
• Update résumé to reflect current career position	• Network as a professional in field of expertise
• Recruit current coworkers for professional references	• Determine if additional academic training or certification is necessary
• Expand knowledge of technology and learn new software	
• Set goals for position titles and salary increases	

Goodheart-Willcox Publisher

Once you have drafted action items that are important for your future, you can start writing your actual career plan. There is no right or wrong way to format this document. Figure 1-4 shows an example of a template you could use to get started.

Before creating a career plan, it is helpful to first conduct a self-assessment and skills assessment, and then set SMART goals. You will continue revising the career plan as you achieve your goals and set new ones.

CONNECT TO YOUR CAREER

Complete 1-2 Career Plan, pg 20

Self-Assessment

One of the first tasks in the creation of a career plan is to complete a self-assessment. A *self-assessment* is a measurement of an individual's actions or attitudes as they relate to student and career performance.

Conducting a self-assessment enables a person to focus on career direction and provides information about his or her natural aptitudes, abilities, personality, and values. Discovering this information can help identify job opportunities that result in successful and gainful employment.

Aptitudes

An **aptitude** is a characteristic that an individual has developed naturally. When a person has an aptitude for something, he or she learns it easily and performs it well. Some aptitudes are *cognitive*, or mental. Other aptitudes are *physical*. For example, some college students have an aptitude for math, while others have an aptitude for ballet. Within both the cognitive and physical categories, aptitudes manifest themselves in

familiar areas, such as art, computers, logic, mechanics, music, socialization, or writing. Different jobs require different aptitudes.

Read the job posting in Figure 1-5. In this job posting, the employer is looking for a candidate with a strong mechanical aptitude. At times, employers ask for a specific aptitude as opposed to formal training.

One key to job success is to find work in an area that matches your aptitudes. Understanding your aptitudes can provide clues regarding how to begin the job-search process. In order to plan a career, experts suggest selecting opportunities that match your strongest characteristics. Natural interests often match career goals. For example, aptitudes for one or more of the following are common:
- drawing
- mathematics
- repairing machines
- sports
- writing

Successful professionals who are experts in their fields likely found work that matched their natural tendencies or aptitudes.

Various tests can help identify your aptitudes and natural interests. An *informal aptitude test* helps distinguish your personality and skill set. These tests are usually available online through a simple Internet search. The results of these tests, while informal, can often point a person in the direction in which he or she will likely find interesting and rewarding work. They can also be excellent practice for formal aptitude tests.

Formal aptitude placement tests, such as the SAT or ACT college placement exams, are used to measure overall achievement and compare performance to others. The ASVAB (Armed Services Vocational Aptitude Battery) is another example of an aptitude test. In this situation, the United States Military administers the exam to students who are enlisting. They use the results to classify enlistees for training opportunities.

A career plan template can be used to gain a head start on the development of a career plan.

Career Plan: Year 1			
Career Item	Specific Action to Take	Target Completion Date	Actual Completion Date

Goodheart-Willcox Publisher

FIGURE 1-5

An aptitude is a characteristic that an individual has developed naturally. At times, employers ask for a specific aptitude as opposed to formal training.

Quality Maintenance Technician II

Company Name: Sears Import

Job Type: Full Time   **Required Travel:** Frequent

Duration: Permanent   **Salary:** Commensurate with experience

Location: Banning, California, USA

Job Description
The Quality Maintenance Technician II (QMTII) will provide unit-level support for maintenance and safety standards, to include the performance of preventive maintenance checks, and review of in-store maintenance procedures as assigned, in full-line stores and off-mall stores. The QMTII assists the assigned stores in maintaining the standards and disciplines needed to provide a high level of customer satisfaction while minimizing energy usage. The person seeking this position should be a self-starter, be proficient in completing tasks in the required time frame, and have a strong mechanical aptitude. Daily travel is required. This position reports to the District Facilities Manager.

Goodheart-Willcox Publisher

Experiences from the past can indicate direction for the future. People who started new jobs but quit soon after their hiring dates were likely working in a position that did not match their aptitudes. Some people begin a job or career and then realize that it was not as they had imagined. To effectively plan for a career, consider your interests. Working in a field that interests you will increase your chances for a happier, more fulfilling work experience. For example, students are likely to get better grades in the classes with subjects they find interesting than in the classes they find boring. The subjects you found interesting can lead to possible career directions. Finding enjoyable work begins with finding interesting work.

placement is one in which a person's aptitudes, skills, and abilities align with one another. Examples of must-have abilities in job postings often include the following:
- assist others with little or no direction
- effectively handle multiple projects
- implement visual designs
- speak multiple languages
- think logically
- work long hours without tiring

It is important to determine your abilities when it comes to performing all the requirements of any job before applying. Even if all of the qualifications match on paper, a missing ability may mean it is necessary to continue looking for other opportunities.

CONNECT TO YOUR ▸ CAREER

Complete 1-3 Aptitudes Inventory, pg 21

CONNECT TO YOUR ▸ CAREER

Complete 1-4 Abilities Assessment, pg 21

Abilities

Your aptitudes and skills are just the beginning of what employers seek. An employer will list a variety of abilities as part of a job posting. An **ability** is a mastery of a skill or the capacity to do something. Having aptitudes and skills is supported or limited by your abilities. For instance, a college student who has a musical aptitude and skills to reinforce it might not have the ability to perform under pressure in musical concerts. An ideal job

Personality

Personality is the unique blend of qualities that predict attitudes, values, and work habits, such as dependability, loyalty, and natural motivation. Your personality is tied to how you think and relate to others around you. In order to gain insight to your personality type for the purpose of career exploration, consider taking a personality assessment. Personality assessments can guide you as you explore potential career areas of interest.

There are multiple personality assessments on the market. One of the most popular assessments is called the Myers-Briggs Type Indicator (MBTI). The *Myers-Briggs Type Indicator (MBTI)* measures a person's psychological preferences in making decisions and his or her view of the world. The assessment measures a person's preferences toward extroversion versus introversion; sensing versus intuition; thinking versus feeling; and judging versus perceiving.

Understanding one's personality preferences is a good way for a person to explore the type of career for which he or she is best suited. For example, if a person is introverted with a preference toward logical, step-by-step instructions, he or she is probably not well suited for a career in broadcasting, but rather engineering or computer programming. Taking a personality test can help determine these preferences.

Employers often rely on personality tests in order to predict job success for potential candidates. Although these tests are not always perfect indicators of workplace success, employers use them to select candidates who fit the position best. Before you start your career, it is wise to begin your own personality assessment so that you can investigate the type of career that works best for you.

Values

Values are principles and beliefs that a person considers important. They are the things that matter most to an individual. A value represents what a person believes and how he or she chooses to work and live. Values affect every part of life, including relationships and work decisions. Some values change with time, and others remain constant. Values that are not likely to change can be used as guideposts or directional markers toward a great career match.

Examples of values include believing in working hard or the importance of caring for others. Other examples of values include:
- accountability
- commitment
- growth
- inner harmony
- trust
- work-life balance

All people have values, but many have not taken the time to identify them. It is possible for two people to have the same values. Values are important principles in working relationships and environments. It is important to identify your values in order to focus on finding a career that aligns with them.

Complete 1-5 Values Assessment, pg 22

Skills Assessment

A skills assessment is another step in creating a career plan. A **skill** is something an individual does well. Unlike aptitudes, which come naturally, skills develop over time. However, skills fluctuate in their level of intensity. For example, skills can be gained by repetition or lost when not used. People are not born with skills. Instead, skills must be practiced and require consistent work. For example, a person who practices piano every day and then stops for an entire year will likely lose at least *some* piano-playing skills. A skills assessment should take into consideration both *soft skills* and *hard skills*.

Soft Skills

Soft skills are applicable skills used to help an individual find a job, perform in the workplace, and gain success in any job or career. They involve behaviors that a person uses to relate to others, and they are not easy to measure. Soft skills are also called *employability skills* or *foundational skills*. These skills often transfer from job to job. Examples of soft skills include leadership, charisma, tact, personal and professional time management, conflict resolution, and professionalism.

Employers include skills as part of specific job requirements. They select words that best describe the skills required for the position they are looking to fill. These words are known as keywords. **Keywords** are words that specifically relate to the functions of the position for which the employer is hiring. For example, an employer might post an advertisement including keywords that describe someone who has developed time-management skills. Another employer might post an ad for someone with social skills. *Social skills* are soft skills that enable a person to work well with others.

Hard Skills

Hard skills are measurable, observable, and critical skills necessary to perform the required, work-related tasks of a given position. They are *job-specific skills* that a person is required to perform as an employee. Some hard skills include software and technology skills, speaking or writing in a foreign language, keyboarding, programming, and graphic design. All of your skills are marketable commodities. Figure 1-6 lists examples of soft skills and hard skills that employers look for in today's job market.

Technology skills are of special importance in today's workplace. It is almost guaranteed that you use a great deal more technology than your parents did when they were your age. You might not realize that the technology you use to communicate with friends, such as social media, texting, taking photographs, and conducting

FIGURE 1-6

Soft skills are applicable, transferrable skills; hard skills are critical skills necessary to perform work-related tasks.

Soft Skills		Hard Skills	
• active listening • effective communication • flexibility • integrity • motivation • patience	• problem-solving • self-confidence • teamwork • time management • trustworthiness	• accounting • carpentry • computer programming • data analysis • graphic design • machine operation	• manufacturing • marketing • nursing • welding • writing

Goodheart-Willcox Publisher

research, translate into proficient and employable skills. In addition to a host of technology tools at your disposal, you probably rely on apps to navigate directions, check the weather, or even purchase movie tickets.

Do not take your technology skills for granted. Completing a technology skills assessment can help you as you create a career plan. A *technology skills assessment* is a process in which an individual documents software and other technology skills that he or she possesses. It begins with identifying specific technology and then determining your level of skill with it. The assessment reveals the technology you use on a daily basis and the knowledge you possess about it. You will use this information with your current proficiencies as part of the data you gather to organize your job search. It also helps identify gaps that you need to fill during the next two to four years. This gives you an opportunity to research what is needed in your career so that you may identify new skills that will be necessary for you to be successful. This assessment will also be of importance when the résumé-writing process begins. A sample technology assessment is illustrated in Figure 1-7.

FIGURE 1-7

A technology skills assessment is a process in which an individual documents software and other technology skills that he or she possesses.

Technology Skills Assessment						
	Current Proficiency Level			Desired Level of Accomplishment		
Technology	Novice	Experienced User	Expert	Novice	Experienced User	Expert
Facebook		X				X
Instagram	X				X	
LinkedIn	X					X
Microsoft Word	X				X	
Pinterest	X				X	
Twitter		X				X
Tumblr	X				X	
YouTube	X				X	
WordPress	X					X

Goodheart-Willcox Publisher

CONNECT TO YOUR ▶ CAREER

Complete 1-6 Skills Inventory, pg 23

SMART Goals

Another step in career planning is to create SMART goals. A **SMART goal** is a goal that is specific, measurable, attainable, realistic, and timely, as shown in Figure 1-8. SMART goals help students ground themselves in the reality of earning an income after college graduation.

Specific

Goals should be specific and easily understood. For example, "I want to get a job" is not a specific goal. Stating "I want to have a job in finance" is a more specific goal. Specificity makes it easier to track progress and understand what you need to do in order to achieve your goals.

Measurable

Goals should be measurable. Otherwise, you may never be able to determine if you have actually achieved them. For example, a goal stated as "I want to determine if I'm capable of scoring above average on the MCAT" is difficult to measure. How can you determine your capability to pass a test? Restating your goal as "I want to score between 490 and 510 on the MCAT" is easier to measure; you will know if you achieved your goal when you complete the test.

Attainable

Goals should be attainable. For example, a goal for a college graduate should not be "I want to get a job as a partner at an established law firm." That goal is not attainable until after years of practicing law. Setting unattainable goals can have negative effects on a person's self-worth and self-esteem. Focus on what you are able to accomplish now, and build your goals around it.

Realistic

Goals should be realistic. It is not realistic to expect high-level careers right out of college, nor is it realistic to expect career advancement after only a few months on the job. Setting realistic goals goes hand in hand with setting attainable goals. For example, working in Manhattan as an entry-level accountant clerk and making $30,000 annually may be attainable, but it is probably not realistic given the cost of living in Manhattan. Try to keep in mind what you have the ability to achieve and what you can realistically achieve, and develop your career goals based on that realization.

Timely

Goals should have beginning and ending points. Establishing a time frame is a vital element of goal-setting. It allows you to keep track of where you are in achieving your goals, and it allows you to prioritize tasks. For example, if your goal is to gain acceptance to graduate school in the next three years, you may not have to start applying to schools for two years. Instead, you can focus on preliminary tasks, like taking preliminary exams and researching programs.

Career Pathing

Career pathing, not to be confused with career pathways, is a strategy an employee can use to determine personal career development. Through career pathing, an individual may be able to

- work toward promotions and move up within a company;
- make a lateral move within a company to learn new skills and talents;
- change employers; or
- change careers.

Navigating a career is much like following directions on a GPS. Your career preparation, planning, and responses to employers' requirements will take many turns each year.

FIGURE 1-8

A SMART goal is one that is specific, measurable, attainable, realistic, and timely.

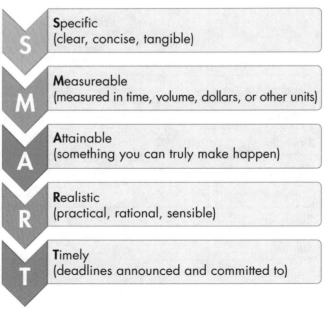

SMART Goals

Specific
(clear, concise, tangible)

Measureable
(measured in time, volume, dollars, or other units)

Attainable
(something you can truly make happen)

Realistic
(practical, rational, sensible)

Timely
(deadlines announced and committed to)

Goodheart-Willcox Publisher

Self-confidence is being certain and secure about one's own abilities and judgment. Self-confident people believe in their abilities to perform in a given situation. They know what they are good at, and they trust their instincts. Self-confidence is affected by *self-talk*, which is the practice of talking to one's self. Positive self-talk includes reinforcement of one's appearance to abilities and boosts a person's self-confidence. Negative self-talk disparages a person and reduces self-confidence.

Today's workforce is one that changes regularly. No matter which career you target, you will find shifts in how to prepare for it. The good news is that there is an unlimited array of job possibilities in many career fields and unlimited ways to gain skills to reach them. Learning about career ladders and career lattices can help you as you progress in your career.

Career Ladder

Many who find a career decide to stay with one company and climb something referred to as a career ladder. A **career ladder** is a sequence of work in a career field, from entry to advanced levels. Each career level is typically categorized by skill or education level, as shown in Figure 1-9.

FIGURE 1-9

A career ladder is a sequence of work in a career field, from entry to advanced levels.

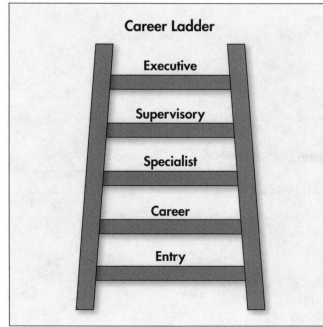

Career Ladder

Executive

Supervisory

Specialist

Career

Entry

Goodheart-Willcox Publisher

Entry-Level Position

An *entry-level position* is the first career step for those seeking on-the-job experience. This is the best place to start for those who have little to no experience or prior training in a desired career field. Positions at this level are often introductory with less salary than the other career levels.

Career-Level Position

A *career-level position* requires preparation and skills as listed by the employer for a particular job or position. This may be where you are as a college student. Many students may qualify for career-level positions after they serve as interns, volunteers, or apply for a position as college graduates.

Specialist-Level Position

A *specialist-level position* means that an employee has worked in a specific career field for at least a few years. He or she may be able to apply for a better position in a company or navigate to a different corporation in order to provide expertise. A specialist-level position is task centered. In other words, this position does not require managing or supervising other employees.

Supervisory-Level Position

A *supervisory-level position* is typically reserved when specialists have the requisite people skills and specific work knowledge to manage other employees well. These are typically employees who have a wealth of knowledge and experience or have been with the company for an extended period of time. This level of employment carries significantly increased responsibility and, for many jobs, presents a ceiling above which an employee may never climb.

Executive-Level Position

An *executive-level position* is the highest level in a career ladder or lattice. Executive-level duties include all of the above as career experience and also the ability to plan, organize, and manage a company. This level is reserved for presidents, vice presidents, and officers of the company.

Career Lattice

For some people, climbing a career ladder may not be the path to their ultimate career. Many individuals prefer lateral moves along with vertical moves. These moves can be seen in a career lattice. A **career lattice** is a series of lateral and vertical moves in one career field. The biggest distinction between a career ladder and a career lattice is that while a ladder refers only to the upward mobility of an employment field, a lattice also accounts for lateral transitions.

Imagine you are employed as a mechanic for an independently owned automotive repair shop. If you accepted a job with the same title working in the repair shop of a nationwide automotive dealer, you would not be moving up to a higher level of employment, but laterally to the same job in the same industry, but with a different company. There are many reasons to consider a move like this. For example, companies with larger employment totals may have more opportunities for advancement or higher wages. Additionally, the new job may not require any additional skills, but may yield new knowledge and experience that can be valuable in the future. By using a career lattice strategy, employees can achieve continued growth and career development throughout a lifetime. A visual representation of a career lattice is shown in Figure 1-10.

Career Portfolio

A **portfolio** is a compilation of materials that provide evidence of a person's qualifications, skills, and talents. As you begin planning your career, it is a good idea to start creating a portfolio. When you apply for a job, you will need to demonstrate to others how you are qualified for the position.

Showcasing examples of work you have completed or awards you have received is one way to communicate your qualifications. As a part of the portfolio-creation process, collect and save all documentation that demonstrates your accomplishments. Include copies of certificates, recommendation letters, and diplomas. If you have published articles or written other material that are exemplary of your writing, include those also. In addition, gather evidence of academic or work projects you have completed. These items are testimonials that strengthen your position as a potential employee.

FIGURE 1-10

A career lattice is a series of lateral and vertical moves in one career field.

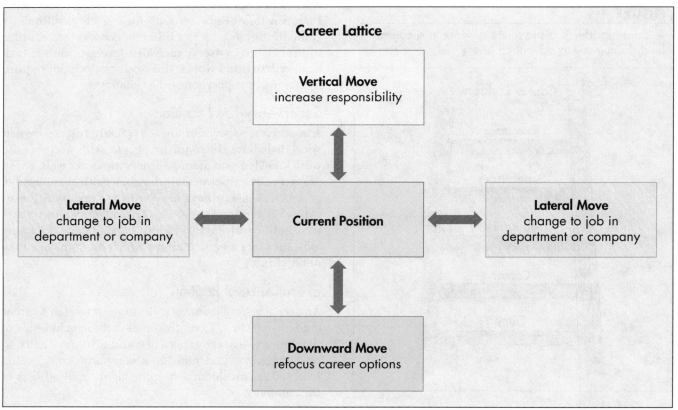

Goodheart-Willcox Publisher

It will be helpful to select documents that position you as a great candidate for a potential job. Examples of information to consider adding to your portfolio include the following:

- causes where you have active involvement
- certifications and diplomas
- courses related to your desired job or career
- honors and awards
- internships
- leadership positions in organizations or jobs
- letters of recommendation
- outstanding test scores
- patents
- references
- résumé
- volunteer work

Organization and presentation of a portfolio is necessary. Two common types of portfolio formats are print and electronic. For print portfolios, the creator hand carries the portfolio to job interviews to provide potential employers a chance to review pertinent work samples. Print portfolios are effective for original certificates, achievement awards, grade transcripts, and résumés.

An *electronic portfolio* contains data and content in digital form. Some common tools used to create an electronic portfolio are Microsoft Word, Microsoft PowerPoint, YouTube, Prezi, or WordPress. It is a best practice to develop your portfolio using familiar software, rather than spend time learning a new program. You may use a flash drive or CD that you leave behind with the interviewer, or you may use a hosting service.

Career Portfolio

Andrey_Popov/Shutterstock.com

Overview. When applying for a job, one way to demonstrate your qualifications is to present the interviewer with a portfolio. A *portfolio* is a selection of related materials that you collect and organize to demonstrate your job qualifications, skills, and talents. For example, a certification showing you have completed your Microsoft Office Specialist training could help you get a job at a local newspaper. A portfolio is a *dynamic document*, which means it should be reviewed and updated on a regular basis.

Artists and other communication professionals have historically presented portfolios of their creative work when seeking jobs or admission to educational institutions. However, portfolios are now used in many professions. Figure 1-11 lists types of portfolios and potential uses for each. It is helpful to identify which type is appropriate for the industry in which you are applying for a position.

Commonly used formats for a portfolio are print and electronic. Job seekers will need adequate copies of a portfolio in both formats when applying for a position.

A *print portfolio* is a hard-copy version that can be carried to an interview. It can be presented in a three-ring binder with divider tabs or any other method that works for you.

An *electronic portfolio* is a digital version of a print portfolio. It can be saved to cloud-based storage services, flash drives, or CDs. There are many creative ways to present a digital portfolio. One option is to create an electronic presentation with slides for each item. Websites are another option for presenting a digital portfolio. Another option is to place the files on a CD. The method you choose should allow the viewer to easily navigate and find items.

As you collect materials for your portfolio, you will need an effective strategy to keep the items clean, safe, and organized for assembly at the appropriate time. Structure and organization are important when working on an ongoing project that includes multiple pieces. Photocopy each document that you want to include and file the original in a safe place for future reference. Never include an original document in a portfolio. A large manila envelope works well to keep hard copies of documents, photos, awards, and other items safe. File folders also work well.

1. Review *Types of Portfolios* listed in Figure 1-11, and select the one that is most appropriate for you.
2. Consider and plan for the technology that might be needed for creating and scanning documents for an electronic portfolio. You may need access to desktop publishing software, scanners, cameras, and other digital equipment or software.

Some websites offer online portfolio-hosting services, some of which are free and others for which there is a charge. Alternatively, you may choose to create your own web page to post your portfolio. Through just one link, a potential employer has the opportunity to spend time looking through portfolio contents as desired.

An electronic portfolio has several advantages over a print portfolio. Electronic portfolios:
- provide virtually unlimited space for documentation
- can be viewed any time
- can be updated or edited quickly and efficiently
- demonstrate technology skills

Developing a portfolio is an ongoing process, so do not be concerned if you are uncertain about what to add. In most cases, people have more information and documentation than they realize. The goal is to keep it simple and relevant. Portfolios that are cluttered with too much data are often ignored.

Types of professional portfolios vary, as shown in Figure 1-11. For example, if you are interested in pursuing work as a photographer, you will want a portfolio to display your photography skills. If your potential career involves writing, then much of your portfolio will highlight your written work. Select the type of portfolio you prefer to create to match your career goals.

FIGURE 1-11

A portfolio is a selection of related materials an individual collects and organizes to show his or her qualifications, skills, and talents.

Types of Portfolios	
Portfolio Type	**Potential Uses**
Showcase	Document high grades, awards, achievements, and milestones, as well as photography, video captures for musical performances, and public speaking
Process	Display progressive growth in academic skills highlighted with reflection pieces, such as original blogs, articles, or commentaries
Documentation	Demonstrate sustained academic success or work performance accomplishments
Hybrid	Display a combination of showcase, process, and documentation portfolios and include feedback from professional third parties
Dossier	Exhibit an instructor's preparedness and effectiveness in the classroom, also referred to as a *teaching portfolio*
Professional	Display specifically work-related accomplishments, company workshops, or training programs completed successfully, along with valuable skills used on the job

Goodheart-Willcox Publisher

Summary

 Explain the concept of career preparation.
Career preparation is a journey that differs from person to person. It includes learning to define the difference between a job and career and understanding how to create a well-developed career plan. Selecting a career involves choosing which career pathway is best suited to a person's aptitudes, skills, abilities, and values, and then selecting an industry within it.

 State the purpose of a career plan.
A career plan is documentation of where a person is today in the job-search process and where he or she would like to be in two to four years. It is a road map to accomplish those goals and should be reviewed and updated at least twice a year.

 Discuss the importance of self-assessment as a step in career planning.
Self-assessment is an important aspect of career planning because it allows a person to focus a career search to industries that match his or her aptitudes, abilities, personality, and values. Conducting a self-assessment enables a person to focus on career direction and provides information about his or her natural aptitudes, abilities, personality, and values.

 Identify two types of personal skills that should be a part of a skills assessment.
Two types of personal skills that should be evaluated as a part of a skills assessment are soft skills and hard skills. Soft skills are applicable skills used to help an individual find a job, perform in the workplace, and gain success in any job or career. Hard skills are measurable, observable, and critical skills necessary to perform required, work-related tasks of a position.

 Explain the purpose of setting SMART goals.
The purpose of setting SMART goals is so a person can set achievable goals. Generic, vague goals are difficult to measure, but SMART goals are specific, measurable, attainable, realistic, and timely. By setting SMART goals, a person can better ground himself or herself in the reality of making an income after college graduation.

 Discuss career pathing options.
Career pathing, not to be confused with career pathways, is a strategy an employee can use to determine personal career development. Career pathing options include earning a promotion, making a lateral move within the company, changing employers, or changing careers.

 Define a career portfolio.
A portfolio is a compilation of materials that provide evidence of a person's qualifications, skills, and talents. Showcasing examples of completed work or awards received is an effective way to communicate one's qualifications when searching for a job.

Glossary Terms

ability	emerging occupations	personality
aptitude	hard skills	portfolio
career	job	skill
career ladder	keywords	SMART goal
career lattice	Occupational Information	soft skills
career plan	Network (O*NET)	values

Review

1. Differentiate between a job and a career.

2. Identify steps an individual can take to evaluate career opportunities.

3. Summarize the development of a career plan.

4. Describe the importance of self-assessment in career planning.

5. What is an aptitude? How can aptitudes lead to job success?

6. What is an ability? How does it differ from an aptitude or skill?

7. Explain two types of personal skills that should be a part of a skills assessment.

8. Explain the purpose of setting SMART goals.

9. What is *career pathing*?

10. Explain the purpose of a portfolio.

Application

1. List examples of resources that could be helpful as you evaluate career opportunities.

2. Explain how jobs you have had up to this point in your work life will benefit and help you reach your career goal.

3. List your personal aptitudes, skills, abilities, and values that could translate into a career.

4. Consider your strongest natural aptitude. To what type of occupation does it lend itself?

5. Without ability, aptitudes and skills are limited. What are some ways for a person to develop his or her abilities?

6. What new abilities must you develop in order to work at your dream job or career?

7. Taking your own personality into account, what types of careers do you think you should seek?

8. What does a typical career ladder for your chosen career look like? What type of skills and experience will you need to move up the career ladder? How long would you expect to stay at each level?

9. A career lattice allows employees to move up, down, or horizontally in their careers. If moving in your career lattice required you to take a step back and learn a new skill, how would you reconcile the fact that you are not actually moving "up"?

10. List examples of documents you would include in your portfolio.

CONNECT TO YOUR CAREER
Workplace Connection

1-1 Emerging Occupations

Use O*NET (www.onetonline.org) to research emerging occupations. Consider your aptitudes, skills, abilities, and values when researching the occupations. Select two occupations that interest you.

Occupation 1:

Occupation 2:

Record notes on details of the emerging occupations you selected.

	Occupation 1	Occupation 2
Industry		
Job description		
Tasks associated with job		
Salary range		
Required educational level		
Technology used in position		

What aptitudes, skills, abilities, personality traits, and values do you have that make you well suited to these careers?

Which one of the two emerging occupations you researched would you be more likely to pursue? Explain why.

1-2 Career Plan

Refer to Figure 1-3 to brainstorm ideas for action items you may include in your career plan. These items will serve as a foundation as you begin developing your plan.

Create a table, similar to the one that follows, for each year that will be encompassed by your career plan. Use the template in Figure 1-4 as an example. This will help keep your information organized.

Career Plan: Year 1			
Career Item	Specific Action to Take	Target Completion Date	Actual Completion Date

Career Plan: Year 2			
Career Item	Specific Action to Take	Target Completion Date	Actual Completion Date

Career Plan: Year 3			
Career Item	Specific Action to Take	Target Completion Date	Actual Completion Date

Career Plan: Year 4			
Career Item	Specific Action to Take	Target Completion Date	Actual Completion Date

This plan should be revisited and may evolve as you progress through this text. Keep in mind there is more than one way to write a career plan. Create and maintain a document that works best for you.

1-3 Aptitudes Inventory

Create a list of common aptitudes with which you are familiar. Examples include persuasion, photography, science, and studying. Rank your top five personal aptitudes 1–5, with the number 1 aptitude as the strongest.

Aptitude #1:

Aptitude #2:

Aptitude #3:

Aptitude #4:

Aptitude #5:

Which one of your top five aptitudes would you most want to demonstrate to an employer? Why do you think this is important for career success?

Conduct an Internet search using the phrase *career aptitude tests*. For example, CareerColleges.com offers a free career assessment. Select one aptitude test, and complete it. After completing the test, take a screen capture of the results or record the results in this document. What did you find out about yourself?

1-4 Abilities Assessment

Recall your top five aptitudes from Activity 1-3. How do these translate into your abilities? For example, you may have an aptitude for persuasion, which may translate to an ability to sell products to customers. List your top five aptitudes and an ability that you have developed for each.

What other aptitudes do you have that could be developed into new abilities?

Consider other abilities you have. Which of these would be desired qualities an employer might look for in a candidate?

1-5 Values Assessment

There are many examples of recognized values, such as ambition, family, and integrity. Make a list of 10 values that are important to you. Rank each value in your list with the most important one marked as number 1.

Value #1:

Value #2:

Value #3:

Value #4:

Value #5:

Value #6:

Value #7:

Value #8:

Value #9:

Value #10:

How do you think your personal values will affect your job search and your future career?

1-6 Skills Inventory

The following words are examples of soft skills: attitude, ethics, hard working, innovation, loyalty, and reliability. List and rank your strongest soft skills 1–5, with the number 1 skill as the strongest.

Soft Skill #1:

Soft Skill #2:

Soft Skill #3:

Soft Skill #4:

Soft Skill #5:

Describe why your top-ranked skill is your strongest soft skill.

The following words are examples of recognized hard skills: computer literacy, graphic design, mathematical skills, and research skills. List and rank your strongest hard skills 1–5, with the number 1 skill as the strongest.

Hard Skill #1:

Hard Skill #2:

Hard Skill #3:

Hard Skill #4:

Hard Skill #5:

Describe why your top-ranked skill is your strongest hard skill.

2 Workplace Success

Outcomes

① **Identify** two sets of workplace skills.

② **Describe** workplace ethics.

③ **Explain** digital citizenship.

④ **Discuss** the value of certification.

OVERVIEW

Workplace success is, in a sense, determined by the employee, not the employer. For the most part, an employee can be successful simply by having the appropriate skills and following company policy. Additionally, employees can ensure a successful working experience by incorporating good digital citizenship.

In some industries, certification is essential in order to qualify for employment or to stay employed. Certification confirms that an individual has acquired knowledge and mastered skills for a specified area. Earning certification can also help to not only ensure workplace success, but possibly help project a career forward, as well.

Workplace Skills

Employers look for potential employees who can help make their companies successful. There are many criteria used to sort through the hundreds of résumés submitted for open positions. Employers often first look for a potential employee with the required educational background and experience. For example, an employer looking to fill a nursing position will confirm that the candidate is educated and trained as a nurse. The applicant's degree and work experience will also be reviewed to confirm the individual has the appropriate workplace skills. *Workplace skills* are skills a person must have in order to be successful in a career. Two general sets of skills that constitute a person's workplace skills are job-specific skills and employability skills.

Job-specific skills are the critical skills necessary to perform the required work-related tasks of a given position. These are usually acquired through work experience, education, and training. Without them, an individual would be unlikely to perform the job successfully.

As you apply for jobs, potential employers will ask questions related to your employability skills. *Employability skills* are applicable skills used to help an individual find a job, perform in the workplace, and gain success in a job or career. Employability skills are also known as *foundation skills* or *transferrable skills*. You have likely already acquired many of these skills in school. However, some of these skills are gained through life experience, such as working at a job or interacting with others in social situations. These skills are not specific to one career, but rather transferrable to any position a person may have throughout his or her life. Foundation skills can be categorized as basic skills, thinking skills, people skills, and personal qualities.

Basic Skills

Basic skills are fundamental skills necessary to function effectively in society. These skills include reading, writing, speaking, listening, mathematics, and technology skills. They also include understanding how to apply these skills in a given situation.

- *Reading* involves acquiring meaning from written words and symbols to evaluate their accuracy and validity. Reading skills allow you to locate information from various sources, including books, images, and the Internet. Reading also helps you comprehend and evaluate material to ensure understanding and form judgments.
- *Writing* is using written words to express ideas and opinions. Writing skills enable you to communicate effectively on paper or while using a computer. It also requires you to edit and revise written communication for accuracy, emphasis, and intended audience.
- *Speaking* is communicating ideas verbally. Speaking skills enable you to present information clearly, maximize word choices, control tone, and adjust your message for your audience.
- *Listening* is hearing what others say and evaluating their messages for information. When you use listening skills, you pay attention to what other people are saying and understand the points being made.
- *Mathematics* is the study of numbers and their relationships. Mathematical skills enable you to use numbers to evaluate information and detect patterns so decisions can be made.
- *Technology skills* are skills that enable a person to operate a computer, mobile device, or other electronic component. These include the ability to use social media, software, and basic computer systems.

Thinking Skills

Thinking skills are skills that enable a person to solve problems. Even if a person is unable to find a solution, thinking skills help him or her assess a situation and identify options. Examples of thinking skills include decision making, creative thinking, problem solving, visualization, and reasoning.

- *Decision making* is the process of analyzing a situation and evaluating possible outcomes in order to choose the best solution. Decision-making skills enable you to weigh pros and cons in order to solve problems.
- *Creative thinking* involves developing or designing unusual or clever ideas about a given topic or situation. When you use creative-thinking skills, you develop unique or different ways to solve a problem.
- *Problem solving* is implementing a solution in the most efficient manner. Problem-solving skills help you carry out a plan or implement new processes to achieve a desired outcome.
- *Visualization* is the ability to form mental images. Visualization skills allow you to imagine how something will function or appear prior to an actual process.
- *Reasoning* is the ability to combine pieces of information or apply general rules to specific problems. Reasoning skills enable you to reach conclusions based on what you already know.

People Skills

People skills, also called *interpersonal skills*, are skills that enable people to develop and maintain working relationships with others. They help people communicate and work well with each other. These skills are necessary to complete job duties and ensure a positive working environment. In general, people skills have a significant impact on relationships with coworkers.

Examples of people skills include social perception, negotiation, leadership, teamwork, collaboration, respect, and diversity.

- *Social perception* is the awareness of others' feelings and understanding of why they may act a certain way. Socially perceptive people exhibit kindness and understanding. However, it is important to balance social perception with the ability to assert yourself politely and professionally when appropriate.
- *Negotiation* is discussing various positions of an issue and reconciling any differences of opinion. The key to negotiating is being able to pinpoint common goals among each position. This prepares everyone to argue facts from his or her point of view and reach an agreement.
- *Leadership* is the ability to influence or inspire other people. In the workplace, leaders encourage others and coordinate activities to reach goals.
- *Teamwork* is the cooperative efforts by individual team members to achieve a common or shared goal. Being a team member of a company work group is similar to playing on a sports team. Success is measured in terms of the team's achievement, not the achievements of the individual team members.
- **Collaboration** is the act of working together with another person to accomplish a goal. In order to collaborate effectively, individuals must be willing to compromise. To **compromise** is to come to a mutually agreed-upon decision.
- **Respect** is the feeling or belief that someone or something is good, valuable, and important.
- **Diversity** is the representation of different backgrounds, cultures, or demographics in a group. This includes age, race, nationality, gender, mental ability, physical ability, and other qualities that make an individual unique. Work environments are usually diverse, and employers expect their employees to recognize and appreciate the diversity within their organization.

Personal Qualities

Personal qualities are the characteristics that make up an individual's personality. Employers look for employees who are flexible and can adjust in a positive manner to work situations as they change. This includes being professional, having a positive attitude, and, above all, being ethical. Examples of personal qualities include self-esteem, self-management, and responsibility.

- *Self-esteem* is the level of confidence a person has in his or her abilities.
- *Self-management* is the ability to work independently without supervision.
- *Responsibility* is being trusted to complete duties or tasks.

CONNECT TO YOUR CAREER

Complete 2-1 Workplace Skills, pg 36

Workplace Ethics

Employers set many expectations for their employees. Perhaps one of the highest expectations is that employees will be ethical. **Ethics** are the moral principles or beliefs that direct a person's behavior. Ethics often conform to accepted standards of right and wrong. *Workplace ethics* are principles that help define appropriate behavior in a business setting.

Ethical behavior calls for honesty, fairness, reliability, respect, courage, tolerance, civility, and compassion. These and other qualities make our lives with each other peaceful and safe. Unethical behavior is considered wrong and is sometimes illegal. It includes actions such as cheating on an exam, stealing office supplies from an employer, surfing the Internet on company time, or returning merchandise to a store for a refund after using it.

Many companies have documents in place that outline ethical behavior. A *code of conduct* is a document that dictates how employees are to behave while at work or when representing the company. For example, some businesses do not allow their employees to wear clothing that has derogative comments that could be offensive to those with whom they work. A *code of ethics* is a document that dictates how business should be conducted. Its goal is to institute a value system for the company that will enable employees to make sound ethical decisions. For example, some businesses do not allow their employees to accept gifts from clients.

Unethical and illegal behavior includes discrimination and harassment. **Discrimination** is the unfair treatment of an individual based on his or her race, gender, religion, national origin, disability, or age. **Harassment** is any unsolicited conduct toward another person based on his or her race, gender, national origin, age, or disability. Harassment can take many forms including inappropriate jokes, teasing, physical interactions, threats, insults, and intimidation. It can also include the displaying of offensive images, gestures, or objects.

CONNECT TO YOUR CAREER

Complete 2-2 Workplace Ethics, pg 38

Social Media Slipup

An aspiring musician was looking for summer work in an effort to help offset some of the costs of his tuition for college. He was accepted to an expensive university that focused primarily on the performing arts. He was willing to take any job that came his way. Working during his time off would help him pay tuition, even if he did not particularly enjoy the work.

After countless job applications, and to help relieve some of the negativity brought on by his lack of employment, he wrote a song about why he felt he was being overlooked for jobs. Being a performing-arts student looking to build his portfolio, he recorded a video of himself singing it to post to his YouTube account.

Christian Kieffer/Shutterstock.com

In the video, he strummed his guitar and sang recently penned lyrics about the types of people who get hired instead of him. He described them using satirical language and criticized them. In his song, he suggested that most companies are only willing to hire people who "look the part" and not necessarily the "most deserving."

The video became somewhat of a hit on YouTube. It was viewed by thousands of people, most of whom had positive comments regarding the structure and composition of the song. Hundreds of people began sharing it across multiple social networking sites.

Eventually the video made its way to a university social networking page where it was seen by one of the student's professors. This professor had previously agreed to serve as a reference for the young musician, but changed his mind after seeing the video. The professor sent an e-mail to his student explaining that he saw the video and found it embarrassing. He then asked the student to remove him from his list of references out of concern to his own professional reputation.

Networking is an important part of the job search. It is about establishing references that can lead to potential career or job opportunities. Damaging a relationship of an important reference can create additional obstacles in a job search that job seekers may struggle to overcome.

Digital Citizenship

Digital citizenship is the standard of appropriate behavior when using technology to communicate. Good digital citizenship focuses on using technology in a positive manner rather than using it for negative or illegal purposes. People who participate in the digital society have a legal responsibility for their online actions, whether those actions are ethical or unethical.

Company Equipment

Company equipment is designated for business-related functions, not for personal use. Office equipment includes desktop computers, phones, and photocopy machines. This equipment is provided to employees to improve efficiency. In many cases, it would be impossible for an employee to perform his or her job without it.

Many businesses have codes of conduct that outline employee guidelines for visiting websites and rules for downloading to company computers. These rules protect the business' computer system and its private information.

Company-owned mobile devices, such as smartphones or tablets, are also company property and should *not* be used for personal reasons. Company policies for appropriate communication and workplace behavior should be followed at all times.

Software Downloads

It is unethical and illegal for an employee to download software that has not been purchased and registered by the employer. When buying software, a license is purchased. A *license* is the legal permission to use a software program. All software has terms of use that explain how and when the software may be used. *Piracy* is the illegal copying or downloading of software, files, or other protected material. This includes scanning or downloading images or music.

Career Portfolio

Pressmaster/Shutterstock.com

Objective. Before you begin collecting information, it can be beneficial to write an objective for your portfolio. An *objective* is one or two complete sentences that state what you want to accomplish.

When creating an objective, first focus on your short-term and long-term goals. A short-term goal is a goal you would like to achieve in the next one to two years. A long-term goal is a goal you wish to accomplish in the next five to ten years. By focusing on your goals, you will be able to write a descriptive objective for your portfolio.

When writing your objective, include enough details so that you can easily judge when it is accomplished. Consider this statement: "I will demonstrate to a potential employer that I am a good candidate for an open position." Such an objective is too general. A better, more detailed one might read, "I will create a well-organized portfolio by September 1 to use in my search for an entry-level accounting job."

1. Create a word-processing document with the heading "Portfolio Objective." Then create two subheadings, one that says "Short-Term Goals," and another that says "Long-Term Goals." List your goals under their respective headings. These goals are the goals to focus on when writing your objective.
2. Next, write your portfolio objective based on those goals. Keep in mind that this objective will likely change as your ideas and goals evolve during the portfolio creation process.
3. Place this document as the first page of your portfolio to guide you as write your objective. This is your working document, so remember to remove it when you organize the final product.

Intellectual Property

Intellectual property is something that comes from a person's mind, such as an idea, invention, or process. Intellectual property laws protect a person's or a company's inventions, artistic works, processes, and other original material. Any use of intellectual property without permission is called **infringement**.

A **copyright** acknowledges ownership of a work and specifies that only the owner has the right to sell the work, use it, or give permission for someone else to sell or use it. The laws cover all original work, whether it is in print, on the Internet, or in any other form or media. You cannot claim work as your own or use it without permission. **Plagiarism** is claiming another person's material as your own, which is both unethical and illegal.

Proprietary information is any work created by company employees on the job that is owned by that company. Proprietary information may be referred to as *trade secrets* because it is confidential information a company needs to keep private and protect from theft. Proprietary information can include many things, such as product formulas, customer lists, or manufacturing processes. All employees must understand the importance of keeping company information confidential. The code of conduct may explain that company information may only be shared with permission from human resources. Sharing proprietary information with people outside the company is unethical and, possibly, illegal.

Netiquette

Netiquette is etiquette used when communicating electronically. Netiquette includes accepted social and professional guidelines for Internet communication. It applies to e-mails, social networking, blogs, texting, and chatting. For example, it is unprofessional to use texting language in a business environment. Always proofread and spell-check e-mails before sending them. When communicating electronically, it is important to follow the same common courtesy used in face-to-face discussions.

CONNECT TO YOUR CAREER

Complete 2-3 Digital Citizenship, pg 38

Certification

The workplace is more competitive today than in recent history. Some jobs require a candidate to have a professional certification in order to be employed. **Certification** is a professional status earned by an individual after passing an exam focused on a specific body of knowledge. The individual generally prepares for the exam by taking classes and studying content that will be tested. Certification programs are usually sponsored by associations or vendors. There are many types of certifications in most industries and trades, as shown in Figure 2-1.

For example, a financial planning agency might require a financial planner to be certified as a qualification for the job. Other employers may prefer, but not require, certification. An individual may have a degree in accounting and be employable with that degree alone. However, some accounting firms may favor hiring accountants who are certified public accountants (CPAs).

The Best App for That

Job Compass

The *Job Compass* app helps you search for jobs in a given radius using your mobile device. Once downloaded and launched, Job Compass will use the GPS in your phone to display a map of available jobs relative to your phone's current location. If you are not in the area in which you wish to look for employment, you can key a city or zip code in the search bar and set a search radius of 5, 10, 25, 50, or 100 miles from your desired area. You can also search using job keywords to narrow your results.

FIGURE 2-1

Certification is a professional status earned by an individual after passing an exam focused on a specific body of knowledge.

Certifications by Industry	
Administrative Certified Professional Secretary (CPS) Certified Administrative Professional (CAP)	**Internal Auditing** Certified Internal Auditor (CIA) Certification in Control Self-Assessment (CCSA)
Automotive ASE Certified Medium/Heavy Truck Technician ASE Master Certified Automobile Technician	**Manufacturing** Certified Manufacturing Technologist (CMfgT) Certified Engineering Manager (CEM)
Financial Planning Certified Financial Planner (CFP)	**Project Management** Project Management Professional (PMP) Certified Associate in Project Management (CAPM)
Health Support Certified EKG/ECG Technician (CET) Certified Nurse Technician (CNT)	**Real Estate** Certified Commercial Real Estate Appraiser (CCRA) Certified Residential Specialist (CRS)
Hospitality Certified Hospitality Accountant Executive (CHAE) Certified Hospitality Supervisor (CHS)	**Workplace Safety** Certified Environmental Health and Safety Management Specialist (EHS) Certified Safety Auditor (SAC)
Human Resources Professional in Human Resources (PHR) Senior Professional in Human Resources (SPHR)	**Workplace Skills** National Career Readiness Certificate (NCRC)
Information Technology Cisco Certified Network Professional Microsoft Certified Systems Administrator Sun Certified Java Programmer	

Goodheart-Willcox Publisher

There are certifications that must be renewed on a regular basis. For example, if you earned one of the many certifications sponsored by Microsoft, the certification is only valid for one specific version of software. When the next version is released, you must take another exam to be certified for the update.

Other certifications require regular continuing education classes to ensure individuals are current with up-to-date information in the profession. These classes are known as *continuing education* for which *continuing education units* (CEUs) are earned. If you are a teacher, your school system may require that you earn a specified number of CEUs every year to keep your teaching certification up-to-date.

Some certifications are not subject-specific but attest that the individual has employability skills. These certifications confirm that the person who earned the certificate possesses the skills to be a contributing employee. The focus of these certifications is on workplace skills. Individuals who earn this type of certification have demonstrated they possess the qualities necessary to become an effective employee.

CONNECT TO YOUR CAREER

Complete 2-4 Certification Options, pg 39

Benefits of Certification

Hundreds of applications are submitted to employers each day for a limited number of open positions. Many criteria are used to screen these submissions, and certification has become one of them. For employers, certification takes the guesswork out of determining whether a candidate is qualified for a position. Anyone can say that he or she has a skill, but a certification confirms it. The certificate earned proves the holder met the required qualifications. Employers no longer have to rely on a candidate's evaluation of his or her own skills.

For the employee, certification offers many of the following advantages:
- Certification is often voluntary. Those who seek it demonstrate ambition and dedication to a career.
- Certification provides personal achievement and accomplishment. Working to be recognized in your career area results in a sense of pride.
- Certification may give you priority when interviewing for jobs as well as when being promoted on the job.
- Certification may increase your salary. Some companies offer higher salaries for those who are certified.

Becoming certified in your career area can allow your résumé to stand out from others. Hundreds of job seekers applying for the same position may all have similar work experience and education. However, certification proves that you have the skills needed on the job, and this distinction can put you at the top of the list of acceptable candidates. Research certification options in your chosen career field or areas of interest to decide if a certification is right for you. There might be many available in your career field. Conducting research can help you decide which is best for you and your career plans.

Certifications look great on a résumé, and earning certifications can help an individual gain valuable skills that can transfer to a career. The table in Figure 2-2 depicts how academic skills can be transferred to a career.

How to Earn Certification

To earn certification in a specified area, it is important to prepare for the exam you select. There are several ways to accomplish this goal. One way is to take formal test-prep classes that cover important topics tested on the exam. These classes are usually offered at local colleges, universities, and businesses. Some classes are offered online. Be prepared to pay a fee for attending these classes.

The materials used in these classes are specifically developed to prepare individuals for the exam. The organization offering the certification may also publish training materials used for exam preparation.

FIGURE 2-2

Skills developed through earning a certification can be transferred to a person's career.

Transferrable Skills		
Skill	**Application in School**	**Application at Work**
accepting constructive criticism	Accepting instructor feedback on work	Accepting employer's feedback on work
clarification	Asking instructor to explain assignments	Asking employer to explain assignments
communication	Talking to instructors, advisers, counselors, etc.	Discussing career-related changes with human resources or employer
networking	Working on group projects or finding help from peer tutors	Building professional relationships
positive thinking	Avoiding negativity toward assignments and instructors	Avoiding negativity in a job search and career development
reading	Reading and understanding class texts	Reading and understanding employee handbook
research	Finding academic articles for research papers	Finding industry-related standards
social interaction	Socializing with friends	Socializing with coworkers
teamwork	Joining clubs and working in groups	Joining company-sponsored teams and working with coworkers
time management	Completing and submitting assignments on time	Meeting deadlines
tolerance	Engaging in a diverse learning environment	Working in a multicultural company
writing	Completing written assignments or essays	Writing work-related documentation such as procedures

Goodheart-Willcox Publisher

Alternatively, companies working with the certification organization may prepare study materials.

Another way to prepare for the exam is to purchase exam-preparation materials from a bookstore or online. There are many books available for those who wish to study without taking a formal class.

In addition to training materials, practice tests are often available as preparation tools. For each type of certification area, the test will usually have a specific format. Typical test formats include matching, multiple choice, or short answer. Before you take an exam, be aware of the test format so that you are not surprised on exam day.

Practice exams are an effective way to prepare. Many of these practice tests are available online. If you are taking a formal class, practice tests will more than likely be a part of the curriculum.

A certification exam is usually administered by an official testing organization. These testing organizations have been approved by the certification sponsor. Do not take a certification exam at a location that is not an official test center. It will be necessary to pre-register for the exam, and in most cases, there will be an exam fee. Be prepared to show identification, such as a driver's license, when you arrive for the test.

Summary

Identify two sets of workplace skills.
Two general sets of skills that constitute a person's workplace skills are job-specific skills and employability skills. Job-specific skills are critical skills necessary to perform the required work-related tasks of a position. These are usually acquired through work experience, education, and training. Without them, the individual would be unlikely to perform the job successfully. Employability skills are applicable skills used to help an individual find a job, perform in the workplace, and gain success in a job or career. Employability skills are also known as *foundation skills* or *transferrable skills* and can be categorized as basic skills, thinking skills, people skills, and personal qualities.

Describe workplace ethics.
Workplace ethics are principles that help define appropriate behavior in a business setting. Specific information regarding how employees are to behave and business conducted is typically outlined in the company's codes of conduct and ethics.

Explain digital citizenship.
Digital citizenship is the standard of appropriate behavior when using technology to communicate. This extends to use of company equipment, downloading and use of software, handling of intellectual property, and practicing netiquette.

Discuss the value of certification.
Certification attests to workplace skills that an individual possesses. For the employer, certification helps identify qualified employees. For the employee, it confirms that the individual can perform in a given position.

Glossary Terms

basic skills	discrimination	people skills
certification	diversity	personal qualities
collaboration	ethics	plagiarism
compromise	harassment	proprietary information
copyright	infringement	respect
digital citizenship	intellectual property	thinking skills

Review

1. What are *workplace skills*?

2. Where are you likely to have gained foundation skills?

3. How are foundation skills categorized?

4. List and describe examples of personal qualities.

5. Describe *workplace ethics*.

6. Differentiate between a code of conduct and a code of ethics.

7. Explain *digital citizenship*.

8. What is *netiquette*?

9. Why is it important to an employer that an employee be certified?

10. How can certification help an individual compete for a position?

Application

1. List examples of job-specific skills you anticipate needing for your chosen profession.

2. Identify someone you know who has been working in his or her industry at least five years. Interview this person to learn more about employability skills. How have these skills helped him or her advance in the workplace?

3. Transferrable skills are skills that you have acquired in school or working in another career field. Consider the skills you have gained throughout your life. Describe how the skills you learned in one situation, such as in school or at a part-time job, can transfer to your chosen career field.

4. Basic skills are necessary to perform nearly any job. Basic skills include reading, writing, speaking, listening, mathematics, and technology skills. Write two to three sentences describing how each of these skills is important in your chosen career field.

5. People skills enable a person to work with others successfully. Select one or two people skills from the bulleted list provided in this chapter that you feel you need to improve. Describe how you can improve the skills you select as you progress through your job search.

6. Employers look for positive personal qualities in job candidates. Explain why self-esteem, self-management, and responsibility are important qualities for an employee.

7. All employees are expected to work in an ethical manner while representing their given companies. Describe the types of ethical decisions you may encounter in your profession.

8. Imagine you have created a process for your company that saves time and money. If you accepted a position at a different company, should you be able to take that process with you? Why or why not?

9. Why do you think netiquette is an important part of workplace success?

10. List required certifications for your career. Include the agency or company that issues the certification as well as any other pertinent information you need to know. If your occupation does not require certification, list certifications that can help make you more marketable as a job candidate in your field.

2-1 Workplace Skills

Workplace skills are the job-specific and employability skills a person must have in order to be successful in a career. List examples of workplace skills you think may be necessary in your desired industry. Using a scale of 1–10 with 10 being highest, rate your ability to perform each skill.

Workplace Skill #1:

Workplace Skill #2:

Workplace Skill #3:

Workplace Skill #4:

Workplace Skill #5:

Workplace Skill #6:

Workplace Skill #7:

Workplace Skill #8:

Workplace Skill #9:

Workplace Skill #10:

As your job search progresses, you will decide the type of position for which you will apply. The job may have a specific title, such as teacher. Alternatively, you may be looking for a position in a functional area, such as marketing. Marketing positions have many job titles, such as marketing assistant, marketing manager, or promotions manager, to name a few. Write down the job title or area for which you are interested.

Job postings list the skills qualified applicants are expected to have. Often the skills listed include job-specific skills as well as employability skills. Use the Internet to locate three job postings in your area of interest. List the job-specific skills mentioned in each posting. Next, list the employability skills requested.

	Job-Specific Skills	Employability Skills
Job #1		
Job #2		
Job #3		

Which of the employability skills in the job posting do you consider to be most important for those particular jobs? Write a paragraph that supports your opinion.

2-2 Workplace Ethics

A *code of conduct* identifies the manner in which employees should behave while at work or when representing the company. Conduct a search on the Internet using one of the job titles you listed in 2-1 and the phrase *code of conduct*. Describe the type of information you find regarding a code of conduct for your desired occupation.

List potential ethical situations you may encounter in your desired occupation and how you intend to approach them.

Ethical Situation #1:

Ethical Situation #2:

Ethical Situation #3:

2-3 Digital Citizenship

As a professional, you will be expected to demonstrate appropriate behavior while using technology at work. Technology at work is not intended for an employee's personal use. Company equipment, software downloads, and intellectual property should be respected. Provide examples of appropriate and inappropriate usage for each of the following.

Company Property		
Description	**Appropriate Use**	**Inappropriate Use**
computers		
customer data		
e-mail		
fax machines		
Internet access		
iTunes		
photo and document scanners		
photocopiers		
printers		
proprietary information from the Internet or print		
social media, such as Facebook		
software downloads		
telephones		
Wi-Fi access		

Netiquette is a professional requirement in the workforce. Most work is completed on a computer, so it is imperative that employees understand and practice netiquette. Create a list of netiquette examples that should be required by employees. Next to each, explain why that behavior is necessary.

Netiquette Behavior #1:

Netiquette Behavior #2:

Netiquette Behavior #3:

Netiquette Behavior #4:

Netiquette Behavior #5:

2-4 Certification Options

Conduct an Internet search for a list of certifications in your industry. List available certifications in the left column of the following table. In the right column, explain how each certification could help further your career.

Certifications in My Industry	
Certification	**How it will further my career**

Which certification are you most interested in obtaining and why?

What will be required of you to earn this certification?

3 Personal Brand

Outcomes

1 **Summarize** the importance of personal brand.

2 **List** steps for creating a personal brand statement.

3 **Explain** the purpose of a personal commercial.

OVERVIEW

As a professional in the workplace, the way you conduct yourself plays a part in establishing your reputation. Your reputation is also known as your *brand*, which is who you are, how you differentiate yourself from others, and how others see you.

By completing a self-assessment, you will have a better idea of your strengths and weaknesses. The self-assessment process will help you understand what you think your reputation *is* as a professional and how *you* see yourself. You can then use personal branding to establish the reputation you *want* as a professional and the way you want *others* to see you. Personal branding can help you build a reputation that helps you fulfill your goals and achieve success in a career.

Your Personal Brand

As a professional, you will work to develop your personal brand. A **personal brand** is an individual's reputation. It is a concept that defines a person's professional aptitudes, skills, abilities, personality, and values. Your brand is who you are, how you differentiate yourself from others, and how others see you.

When you think of Oprah Winfrey's brand, you probably associate it with books, philanthropy, and media. Her reputation is built upon being consistent and delivering engaging and relatable media across multiple platforms. That is the power of a brand—it immediately communicates a person's or company's qualities.

Just as Oprah developed her brand, or reputation, you are doing the same, even if you are not aware of it. Each time you meet a deadline or behave in a courteous manner, those around you are forming an opinion of who you are. You have complete control over how you project your brand and what your reputation will be over the course of your career.

In Chapter 1, you completed a self-assessment, which will help you have a better idea of your strengths and weaknesses. The self-assessment process is one of many important tools that will help you understand what you *think* your reputation is as a professional and how you see yourself. You can then work on your personal branding to create the reputation you *want* as a professional and the way you want *others* to see you. Personal branding can help you build the reputation, or brand, that you desire and will help you be successful in a career.

CONNECT TO YOUR CAREER

Complete 3-1 Personal Brand, pg 49

Personal Brand Statement

A **personal brand statement** is one sentence that describes what a potential job candidate offers an employer. It reflects the aptitudes, skills, abilities, personality, and values a person will provide to a company in exchange for an agreed-upon salary. It is, in a sense, a tagline or slogan designed to sell a company on the idea of hiring that person. The goal of a personal brand statement is to leave an employer with an idea of how an individual would contribute to the company.

A brand statement clarifies your most important values. Consider an individual who possesses time-management skills. His or her brand statement may use keywords such as *efficiency* and *expectations*. For example, a brand statement could include the following, "A professional who consistently implements customer-driven solutions while being held to the highest expectations."

Businesses often use slogans and logos as a branding strategy to convey their company values. For example, Apple used the slogan "Think different" in advertisements to make their customers feel as though the use of Apple products set them apart from the rest of the world. A person can convey value and identity by exhibiting his or her personal brand through a brand statement.

Creating a Brand Statement

A personal brand statement should be concise, using the keywords that best reflect how you want to be known in your industry. The number of keywords in a brand statement should be limited for maximum effect, and you should brand yourself as the professional you want to become, not necessarily the professional you are at the moment. Examples of brand statements are listed in Figure 3-1.

FIGURE 3-1

A personal brand statement is one sentence that describes what a potential job candidate can offer an employer.

Personal Brand Statements
• A creative problem-solver who can combine mathematics skills and science expertise to help develop sustainable energy sources.
• A writer who is able to blend communication and critical-thinking skills to illustrate solutions to common problems.
• A driven team player who uses leadership skills to motivate others and exceed goals.
• A customer-service professional with excellent communication skills committed to market-driven collaboration and idea sharing in an effort to continue 100 percent customer satisfaction.
• A product development coordinator with impeccable time-management skills dedicated to prioritizing promotion of outside-the-box thinking to stay competitive in tomorrow's marketplace.
• A production manager who implements soft skills to continually promote client-based, customer-directed deliverables while maintaining the highest standards.

Goodheart-Willcox Publisher

The Best App for That

Hootsuite

Once you establish an online presence, it is important to stay active by posting information that promotes you as a professional. However, updating multiple social media accounts can be time consuming when done individually. The *Hootsuite* app is a social media dashboard that organizes and presents information in an easy-to-read format. A dashboard is an interactive management tool. Hootsuite enables you to update and manage many social networks from a single interface, streamlining and easing the process of keeping your networks up to date.

When writing a personal brand statement, choose words that best describe your aptitudes, skills, abilities, personality, and values. These words will become your *brand keywords* and help create a memorable statement. You can find keywords to use by researching the industry in which you would like to work and looking for terms that reflect the core of the occupations in that industry. For example, school administrators typically seek teachers who have passion, enthusiasm, sensitivity, empathy, and a sense of humor. Including these keywords makes it more likely your brand statement will yield employment opportunities. The creation of a personal brand statement can be accomplished in four steps.

Step one: The first step in writing a personal brand statement involves defining yourself. What is your reputation? Consider what other people say about you and how they would define you, and list as many descriptive adjectives as you can. For example, you may list educator, thinker, manager, problem solver, or hard worker as words that describe you.

Step two: The next step is to list your skills. Focus on soft skills and hard skills you possess that are relevant to your industry. For example, if your goal is to work in advertising, identify skills you possess that will help you obtain a job in an advertising field. These skills will help paint a picture of your background and demonstrate your value to an employer.

Step three: The next step is to create short, descriptive phrases that describe how you work, what you are capable of accomplishing, and what you can offer an employer. What sets you apart from the rest of the workforce? Why should a company hire *you* over another applicant? For example, you may work with urgency to deliver results despite obstacles. Include that description in your list of phrases.

Step four: The final step is to compile the words and phrases you have listed to create a succinct statement that provides an overall description of you as an employee. Using the examples given in each of the previous steps, a personal brand statement could be "A creative problem solver with copywriting experience who works with urgency and grace under pressure to deliver results, even when obstacles present themselves."

Applying a Brand Statement

After you are comfortable with your brand statement, use it whenever appropriate. This means adding it to your career-search tools including your résumé, cover letter, professional social media accounts, and portfolio. Your brand statement is your slogan, and you are advertising yourself. Just as notable individuals use their personal branding to reach their audiences, you can use your brand to further your career and expand your network.

CONNECT TO YOUR CAREER

Complete 3-2 Personal Brand Statement, pg 50

Personal Commercial

During the job-search process, there will be many opportunities to communicate your brand. One of the first applications of your personal brand should be developing a personal commercial. A **personal commercial**, also known as an *elevator speech*, is a rehearsed introduction that includes brief information about a person's background and a snapshot of his or her career goals.

It is suggested that a 30- to 60-second commercial is an appropriate length. Keep your commercial brief, as if you could recite it while on an elevator going from one floor to the next with professional contacts. Chances are you will not recite your speech verbatim. However, there is value in being prepared with a concise message that promotes who you are and your abilities. A commercial makes the most of the few seconds you may have when you meet a potential networking contact.

Career Portfolio

antoniodiaz/Shutterstock.com

Skills and Talents. Employers evaluate candidates based on their qualifications, including their skills and talents. For example, the ability to communicate effectively, adapt, and perform under pressure are qualities that employers seek in job applicants. These types of qualities are often called soft skills. *Soft skills* are applicable skills used to help an individual find a job, perform in the workplace, and gain success in any job or career. They are also called *employability skills* or *foundational skills*.

Employers also look for candidates who have skills necessary to be successful in a position, such as the ability to use software programs or machinery. These abilities are called hard skills. *Hard skills* are measurable, observable, and critical skills necessary to perform required, work-related tasks of a position. They are also referred to as *job-specific skills*.

Depending on the position for which you may be applying or interviewing, your talents may be criteria an employer uses to evaluate your qualifications. Do you have a special talent in an area such as art, music, or design?

You have collected documents to demonstrate your skills. One way to document your talents is to create a video. For example, if you are an artist, create a video that shows your completed works. If you are a musician, create a video with segments from your performances. If you plan to feature other people in your video, be sure you have their permission to do so.

1. Create a word-processing document that lists your skills. Use the heading "Skills" along with your name. Make one section for soft skills and another section for hard skills. Next to each skill listed, write a description of an assignment and explain how your skill was involved in completing it. Include documentation that supports your skills. Attach notes to the documents to identify each item and state why it is included in the portfolio. For example, a note on a newsletter you wrote might say, "Newsletter that illustrates desktop-publishing skills."

2. If you have talents you want to showcase, create a visual presentation that will reflect what you want the employer to see. Use an appropriate name to label your presentation, such as the phrase "Talent Video" and your name.

Developing a Personal Commercial

When developing a personal commercial, it is important to be succinct and clear in your purpose. Your listener must understand why you have created this commercial and what your career goal is. If your goal is to network for a job, include the

- title of the job you are seeking;
- skills required for the job that you possess; and
- general location of your target geographical area.

There are situations in which you may be seeking advice or guidance rather than networking for a specific job. You may be searching for a person who can educate you on potential career choices or skills necessary for a future job possibility. If your goal is to network for advice, include

- a clear example of what kind of advice or information you are seeking;
- the specific topics you want to discuss; and
- your availability to meet.

A personal commercial, like a personal brand statement, can be created by performing the following steps.

Step one: Review your personal brand statement. Your brand statement is who you are and reflects your professional qualities, values, and goals. It will be the basis of your elevator speech.

Step two: Summarize your education, soft skills, and hard skills. Write a brief paragraph that identifies highlights of your education. It may be the type of degree you earned, area of concentration, or school you attended. Review the earlier self-assessment you made of your soft skills and hard skills. Select one or two of each that demonstrate your best skills.

Step three: Determine exactly what you are seeking from the networking contact you may meet in the elevator on other impromptu situations. You may be looking for a job or looking for information about an industry. The elevator speech is a networking tool for finding information and making a connection with someone who can help you in your career.

Step four: State your motivations for your career direction. It may be that you want to inspire others through teaching or learn all you can about technology so you can make a future career decision.

Step five: Write your elevator speech. As you summarize the material, remember that your brand statement is your guiding force. Figure 3-2 illustrates the narrative for a 30-second commercial. Notice that the first column shows a personal brand statement that is used as the basis for the commercial.

CONNECT TO YOUR CAREER

Complete 3-3 Personal Commercial, pg 51

Rehearsing a Personal Commercial

In order to be prepared when an unexpected networking opportunity presents itself, it is necessary to practice your personal commercial. Rehearsing your commercial will help you achieve the goal of making a positive impression on the person with whom you are speaking. If your commercial is not polished and ready to present, a career opportunity can be missed.

Begin by practicing in front of a mirror and rehearsing your speech. Do not read your commercial word-for-word even while you are practicing. The goal is to make the interaction conversational and comfortable for the person with whom you meet. Time your commercial and remember to keep it within 30 to 60 seconds.

When you are satisfied with the content and delivery of your commercial, ask a friend or family member to record you as you deliver it. Ask for feedback from your listeners, and record it multiple times until you are satisfied with the final product.

You may decide to post the final version of your commercial to a website such as YouTube or Instagram. The link to the video can then be added to your résumé, e-mail, or portfolio.

FIGURE 3-2

A personal commercial is a rehearsed introduction that includes brief information about a person's background and a snapshot of his or her career goals.

Personal Brand Statement	Personal Commercial
A marketing professional who is dedicated to creating jaw-dropping promotions.	I am Susan Roskowski, an assistant marketing product manager **<current job title>** with a degree in marketing communications from Baylor University. I am located in the greater Houston area **<target geographical area>** and looking for a career in an advertising agency **<job title goal>**. My skills include writing promotions that capture the attention of the target audience based on their demographics **<hard skills required for the job>**. I am proficient at ad creation and social-media marketing. I am flexible and skilled at working with others **<soft skills required for job>**.

Goodheart-Willcox Publisher

Summary

 Summarize the importance of personal brand.
A personal brand is the way in which a person expresses identity and differentiates himself or herself from others. It describes what value a potential job candidate offers to an employer. A personal brand reflects a person's professional aptitudes, skills, abilities, personality, and values.

 List steps for creating a personal brand statement.
Four steps that can be taken to create a personal brand statement are defining who you are as a professional, listing your soft skills and hard skills, creating short phrases describing how you work, and compiling the information to make a concise statement.

 Explain the purpose of a personal commercial.
A personal commercial is a rehearsed introduction that includes brief information about a person's background and a snapshot of his or her career goals. Also known as an elevator speech, a personal commercial can be delivered in person, or a candidate can stand out from the crowd by filming a personal commercial, posting it online, and including the URL on employment documents.

Glossary Terms

personal brand	personal brand statement	personal commercial

Review

1. How can performing a self-assessment help when defining your personal brand?

2. When creating a personal brand statement, what types of words should be chosen?

3. How can you find brand keywords that will help you create your personal brand statement?

4. List and describe the steps for creating a personal brand statement.

5. Provide examples of ways a personal brand statement can be applied once it is created.

6. What is an appropriate length for a personal commercial?

7. What are three items that should be included in your personal commercial if you are looking for a job opportunity?

8. What three items should your personal commercial contain if you are seeking information or advice?

9. List and describe the steps for creating a personal commercial.

10. What are some recommendations for practicing a personal commercial?

Application

1. What is your *current* reputation as a professional? Why?

2. What do you want your *future* reputation as a professional to be?

3. What can you do now to work toward your future reputation?

4. Make a list of words that your friends use when they describe you. What are you known for?

5. List examples of keywords you will you use when you create your personal brand statement.

6. In what ways will you apply your personal brand statement when searching for a career?

7. How is your personal brand statement different from your personal commercial?

8. How can you incorporate your personal brand statement into your elevator speech?

9. You should be prepared to network at all times. Why do you think you might need more than one rehearsed personal commercial?

10. What benefit do you think you would gain by recording a video of your personal commercial and posting it on YouTube?

CONNECT TO YOUR CAREER
Workplace Connection

3-1 Personal Brand

Conduct an Internet search using the phrase *personal branding*. Read about the importance of a personal brand and how a personal brand statement can help you market yourself. Record your findings in the space that follows.

How would others describe your personal brand?

What do you want your personal brand to be, and what can you do to reach that goal?

3-2 Personal Brand Statement

Use the four-step process described in this chapter to build a list of qualities and characteristics that will be included in the development of your personal brand statement.

Step one: Define yourself and your reputation.

Step two: List your hard and soft skills.

Step three: What sets you apart from other workers?

Step four: Compile your brand statement.

3-3 Personal Commercial

Conduct an Internet search using the phrase *elevator speech*. This phrase is often used interchangeably for *personal commercial*. Read about expectations for a personal commercial. Using your research, list a set of guidelines you can follow when creating your personal commercial. For example, how long it should be, how many words it should include, etc.

Guideline #1:

Guideline #2:

Guideline #3:

Guideline #4:

Guideline #5:

Using the guidelines you established in the first part of this activity, follow the five-step process outlined in the chapter to draft a personal commercial that you can use in your job-search activities.

Step one: Review your personal brand statement.

Step two: Write a paragraph that highlights your education and skills.

Step three: Summarize what actions you are looking for from your networking contact.

Step four: Succinctly summarize your career motivation.

Step five: Write your elevator speech.

Practice your commercial for a friend or family member. Consider the feedback they give you to improve your speech. After you have perfected your speech, record a video of yourself delivering it so that you may post it to your social media sites.

UNIT **2** Online Presence

Why It Matters

The landscape for finding a job in the twenty-first century has experienced a change. Jobs are harder to find, there are fewer jobs available, and the competition is fierce. The Internet drives the job-search process, and savvy career seekers learn how to use it as a strategic tool to reach an employment goal.

Online job-search strategy starts with creating and developing your online presence. When employers search for your name on the Internet, will they find positive or negative information? After you have established your online presence, you can use it to develop a professional network that will help you make connections in the workplace. However, remember to always be cautious with your Internet activity as protecting your identity is an important aspect that should not be ignored in the job-search process.

4

Your Online Presence

Outcomes

1. **State** ways a job seeker can create a positive online presence.

2. **Explain** the importance of a professional e-mail account.

3. **Describe** how a LinkedIn account can be used in the job-search process.

4. **Describe** how a Twitter account can be used in the job-search process.

5. **Describe** the use of Instagram as a job-search tool.

6. **Explain** the importance of positive thinking during the job-search process.

CONNECT TO YOUR CAREER

Workplace Connection

4-1 Online Presence

4-2 Professional E-mail Account

4-3 LinkedIn Account

4-4 Twitter Account

4-5 Instagram Activity

4-6 Positive Thinking

OVERVIEW

The first step in the career-search process starts with your online presence. People learn many things on the Internet—current events, news, weather, social issues, and much more. Potential employers will explore the Internet to see what they can find about you. Although your name might not be the subject of millions of search engine trends, your name and the online results that it returns are important considerations during your job search.

An online presence can help to inform professionals in your field about your skills, qualifications, and talents. Additionally, it can reveal information about your character based on the websites associated with your name. How will you stack up against other candidates?

Creating Your Online Presence

One of the first steps in the job-search process is to evaluate your online presence. An **online presence** is what the public can learn about a person from viewing his or her Internet activities. In today's workforce, an online presence can influence success for a job seeker in the career-search process. Hiring managers often conduct independent research on job applicants to determine if the interview process should move forward.

Most people retain Facebook, Twitter, and Instagram accounts to socialize and maintain relationships with friends and family. These are important aspects of online communication. However, since the Internet can reveal private information to unapproved parties, a potential employer may be able to view private exchanges without the account owner's knowledge or consent. Discretion should be used when posting to social websites, as these activities might appear when a search is conducted for your name.

Most personal social media sites offer privacy customization so the user can designate who can and cannot visit specific pages. Privacy settings for personal accounts should be set so that potential employers, or the public, cannot view personal photos or information of the owner of the account. Photos or comments posted online will become part of a person's digital footprint. A **digital footprint** is a data record of all of an individual's online activities. Items posted to the Internet cannot be completely hidden or deleted. What is posted online today could risk personal and professional opportunities in the future.

Most employers enter an applicant's name in a search engine to see what the online presence reveals about the person. This search will yield a positive, negative, or nonexistent online presence. It could also reveal a shared online presence if someone else has an account with the same name. Figure 4-1 lists each type of online presence.

A *positive online presence* can lead to employment opportunities. This occurs when a hiring manager enters a name into a search engine and discovers results such as links to well-written articles, a professional portfolio, or memberships to business networking sites. As a result, an employer's impression of a potential employee can be positively influenced, even before an interview.

A *negative online presence* can harm an individual's professional reputation and minimize a person's chances for potential job interviews. Inappropriate photos, improper behavior, or lewd remarks on social media sites can eliminate a person from employment opportunities.

A *nonexistent online presence* denotes lack of technology skills, abilities, or lack of motivation or proactive thinking. It implies that a person does not stay up to date in today's society which can be a reflection of who the person might be as an employee.

Entering your own name into a search engine is the best way to evaluate your personal online presence. If the results are anything but positive, consider what you can do to reflect a more positive image. If the results are nonexistent, consider participating in positive activities that will get your name in circulation.

If the search results show multiple accounts by other people with a shared name, consider examining the results. A hiring manager will likely not know what you look like, so it is possible for the wrong profile to be selected, which may generate a poor first impression of you. If possible, think of how to differentiate your name in your online accounts. This can be accomplished by using a middle initial, for example. This way you have a unique online presence when someone conducts an Internet search for your name.

CONNECT TO YOUR ▶ CAREER

Complete 4-1 Online Presence, pg 69

FIGURE 4-1

An online presence is what the public can learn about a person from viewing his or her Internet activities.

Types of Online Presence	
Positive	Search engine results reflect your professional accomplishments.
Negative	Search engine results reflect activities that negatively impact your chances of getting hired.
Nonexistent	A search engine returns no results that match your name.
Shared	Search engine results are an exact match to your name; however, the results are not about you, but about someone with your same name.

Goodheart-Willcox Publisher

Professional E-mail Account

Before beginning the career-exploration process, a professional e-mail account should be created to keep your personal and professional activities separate. This e-mail account should be used during the job-search process. Businesses use e-mail to communicate available jobs and schedule interviews with job candidates. A separate e-mail account will enable you to manage communication for the job-search process and other professional business. Examples of e-mail addresses are shown in Figure 4-2.

Recruiters and human resource departments may sort job applicants by names that appear in the e-mail address. An e-mail address is a reflection of the owner of the e-mail account. An employer expects to see an e-mail contact by his or her name, not an unprofessional e-mail address. For that reason, consider using your first name and last name separated by a period. If your name or a variation of it is not available from the selected provider, try using your first initial and last name or other combinations that reflect your legal name. If all combinations fail, consider switching providers. For example, if you do not find the name you prefer from Gmail, try opening a Yahoo e-mail account instead.

A secure password is needed for an e-mail account. A **secure password** is a code used to access a private account or other private information, such as an e-mail account or computer network. A secure password is between 6 and 20 characters long and a combination of letters, numbers, and special characters. The safest password combinations are those that are unpredictable. Examples of password strategies and examples are shown in Figure 4-3.

Less secure, predictable passwords often contain the following data:
• address
• birthday or anniversary date
• common words
• favorite numbers
• repeated numbers or numbers in a sequence
Unauthorized users should not be able to easily identify or guess your password. To protect your identify, never share a password with others.

After you have created your e-mail account, the next step is to create a signature block. A **signature block** is the full name, phone number, and e-mail address of the owner of the account. All e-mail accounts have a field that automatically adds a signature each time a new e-mail is created or a response is made to a previous message. You may choose to include a job title under your name in your signature block. If you do not have a permanent position, you can designate a job title that describes your skills, such as *Instructional Design Consultant*, until you find a permanent position. Or, you may choose to use your brand statement. Figure 4-4 shows examples of professional signature blocks. It is important to use a readable font style and size.

CONNECT TO YOUR CAREER

Complete 4-2 Professional E-mail Account, pg 71

LinkedIn Account

Networking plays an important role in the career-search process. **Networking** is talking with people and establishing relationships that can lead to career growth or potential job opportunities. It is the process of creating new contacts with a goal of giving and receiving support while building relationships. In order to build and expand your professional network, it is essential to learn to network online.

LinkedIn is a professional social networking site that provides static communication regarding business and employment opportunities. This professional networking site is used by more than 400 million people in the global workforce for purposes of making new contacts and building business relationships. It is limited to closed groups and individual contacts. LinkedIn offers users space for posting and finding jobs that might not be advertised publicly.

FIGURE 4-2

A professional e-mail account should be created to keep personal and professional activities separate.

Sample E-mail Addresses	
Personal E-mail Address	**Professional E-mail Address**
hockeystar@gmail.com	kevin.jones@ymail.com
sassy55555@yahoo.com	carol_smith@gmail.com
totallyrockin_thehouse@yahoo.com	jdouglas@rocketmail.com

Goodheart-Willcox Publisher

FIGURE 4-3

A secure password is a code used to access a private account or other private information.

Password Strategy 1	
Start with a memorable sentence.	I will exercise more.
Remove the spaces and punctuation.	Iwillexercisemore
Capitalize or lowercase an unexpected letter.	iwilleXercisemore
Create a memorable, unique misspelling.	iwilXercisemor
Add numbers and symbols.	#iwilXercisemor2

Password Strategy 2	
Start with a memorable sentence.	My brother was accepted to Stanford University in 2013.
Use only the first letter of each word in the sentence.	M b w a t S U i 2013
Remove the spaces and punctuation.	MbwatSUi2013
Capitalize or lowercase unexpected letters.	mBwatSUi2013
Add a symbol.	#mBwatSUi2013

FIGURE 4-4

A professional signature block includes a person's full name, phone number, and e-mail address in a readable size and font.

Signature Blocks

Shelley Jones
Junior Accountant
(212) 555–1234
sjones@e-mail.com

Rakesh Singh
Lab Assistant
(623) 555–4023 | rsingh@e-mail.com
http://www.websiteurl.com

John Smith
Assistant Developer, Point n' Click Web Design
(312) 555–3997 | johnsmith@e-mail.com
Twitter: http://www.twitter.com/johnsmithweb

Tinicia Henson
Social Media Associate | AgriCo
(215) 555–1601 | hensont@e-mail.com
LinkedIn: http://www.linkedin.com/in/tiniciahenson
Twitter: http://www.twitter.com/TiniciaAgriCo
Instagram: http://www.instagram.com/AgriCoProducts

LinkedIn's basic account type is a freemium model. *Freemium* means you can take advantage of basic services without paying. When first joining LinkedIn, the freemium model is a good choice. As your career advances, you might wish to purchase account upgrades which provide premium services and features. There are several upgrade plans from which to select.

The advantage of establishing an account on LinkedIn is that the site promotes your profile through search engine optimization. **Search engine optimization (SEO)** is the process of indexing a website so it will rank higher on the list of returned results when a search is conducted. When someone searches for a person who has a LinkedIn account, that person's name will appear either at the top or near the top of the search results list.

Create an Account

In order to use LinkedIn, an account must be created. To do this, navigate to www.LinkedIn.com in your browser. Where prompted, provide your first and last name, professional e-mail address, and desired password. Select the **Join now** button. LinkedIn will send a notification to the e-mail address you provided. Confirm that you received the e-mail by selecting the link inside the body of it. The link will return you to the LinkedIn website, where you may begin populating your account.

Career Portfolio

Makistock/Shutterstock.com

Certificates. A certificate is a document that serves as evidence of completion of an activity, training, or other accomplishment. For example, a certificate might show that you have completed a training class. Another one might show that you can key at a certain speed.

Certificates are sometimes awarded to an individual as proof of receipt of scholarships, grants, or other recognition. Those who served in the military will probably have certificates that reflect awards, ranks, or other honors that were earned.

Diplomas are certificates and should be a part of a portfolio. If you are still in college, you may choose to include your high school diploma. If you have graduated from college, only include college diplomas. It is assumed you have graduated from high school.

Some certificates provide evidence of specialized training without a degree being granted. These programs are designed for individuals who are not seeking a degree but are looking to update their current skills or taking courses specifically for employment. *Certification* is a professional status earned by an individual after passing an exam focused on a specific body of knowledge. Some jobs *require* certification. For example, information technology specialist positions may require industry-specific hardware or software certifications. Real estate careers require passing a certification exam, as do teaching positions. Already having and displaying a certification makes it more likely you will be seriously considered for the position.

1. Collect certificates of accomplishment that you have earned that are not associated with a degree or certification. You can arrange them in order of importance or dates earned.
2. Collect college diplomas, proof of certification, and other examples that relate to educational or military accomplishments. These should also be arranged in a logical order.

Once your account is created, LinkedIn generates a URL address, or link, that navigates directly to your page. You will have a chance to customize the URL if you prefer not to use the default provided. After your LinkedIn URL is created, you can add it to your e-mail signature block and résumé.

CONNECT TO YOUR ▶ **CAREER**

Complete 4-3 LinkedIn Account, pg 71

Create a Profile

A **profile** is information that describes who a person is in his or her professional life. An account profile is not just personal information, but a career snapshot and part of an individual's professional online presence. Potential employers can use this information to learn more about a person's professional background. Therefore, an account profile should reflect career activities separate from family, friends, and personal social connections.

Your LinkedIn account profile is a web page where you will describe your background, career history, education, and skills. As you complete your profile, LinkedIn will track your progress. Be diligent and make sure your profile is 100 percent complete.

There are multiple sections of an account profile, and not all of these sections will apply to every user. For example, if you have not earned a certification, then that section should be left blank when creating the profile. Four important sections that should always include information in a LinkedIn profile are the headline, summary, experience, skills and endorsements, and education sections.

Headline

The headline includes four parts: your full name, title, geographic location, and industry. After you have input your name, enter your title. This is an opportunity to position yourself as you want others to see you. If you have a job, it is appropriate to use your current title and name of your employer, such as *Personal Banker at Southwest Mutual and Savings Bank*. If you do not have a permanent position, you can designate a job title that describes your skills, just as you did in your e-mail signature block.

This is also a good opportunity to publish your brand statement. As you begin completing the title, LinkedIn will offer suggestions for pertinent words that might help you to make an appropriate choice. Some examples of titles are as follows:

- Accountant's Apprentice
- Hotel Concierge
- Lab Assistant
- Bank Teller

Next, add your geographic area and your industry. This information helps employers who are searching for candidates in a specific geographic location.

Finally, upload a professional photo to your account. As part of an account profile, it is acceptable to display a work-appropriate photograph. If a professional photograph is not available, consider asking a friend or family member take one that can be used temporarily. The following tips can be helpful when taking a professional photo:

- Dress appropriately to present a professional appearance.
- Have the photo taken from the shoulders to the top of your head. This type of photo is referred to as a *headshot*.
- Be aware of what is displayed behind you when you have your picture taken so that nothing detracts from your face.
- Avoid busy patterns in your attire and in the background.
- Smile showing your teeth.

Summary

The summary section is where you can describe your professional background and help define how you want to be known in your industry. This is also a good place to include your brand statement or your personal commercial. Think of your summary as an employer's first introduction to your qualifications. A summary should:

- consist of three to five short paragraphs;
- use keywords that illustrate your value;
- reflect who you are as a professional;
- be an authentic representation of you;
- be written in a way that reflects your conversational tone; and
- be error-free.

Vague words, such as "smart" or "energetic," should be avoided for your LinkedIn descriptors, while concrete words will help market your talents. Your summary should not be boring, but rather invite the reader to continue looking at your profile.

Experience

The experience section of the profile is where work history is listed similarly to the way it is listed on a résumé.

Provide detail for each work experience, even if the experience was a volunteer position. Providing detailed information about the types of work you have experienced can help the employer see you as a preferred job candidate.

Skills and Endorsements

The next step in completing a profile is to add skills. The skills area begins with your most important skills and is followed by other expertise you may possess. There is no limit to the skills you can add, so include as many as you feel necessary. However, do not list skills you do not have. Your connections will be able to *endorse*, or verify, that you have the skills listed. This certifies to employers that you may be a viable candidate.

Education

Similar to a résumé, there is an opportunity to enter educational degrees and experience. Schools and training programs can be added individually, and you can include courses taken and degrees or certifications obtained at each one. This information can be specific or general depending on what you want your network and potential employers to know about your educational background.

Connections

The purpose of creating a profile is to share who you are as a professional. The best way to accomplish this is to make connections. **Connections** are people in an individual's network who are added only by invitation. By accepting your invitation, your connections agree to share their network with you. Those who are connected can view each other's profiles without limits. However, those not connected will only have a limited view of each other's profiles. If you are not connected, your name may not be found by an important contact. Therefore, it is advantageous to gain as many connections as possible.

LinkedIn users connect by sending invitations to other LinkedIn members. You can search for a person you know on LinkedIn by using the search function. Once you see the profile for which you are looking, select the **Connect** button to send an invitation. On the full website, a window will open containing standard text inviting the person to connect. This is an opportunity to read the invitation and customize before sending. When sending a connection invitation on a mobile device, touch the **Connect** icon next to the profile of the person with whom you would like to connect. You will not be able to customize a message to be sent along with the connection invitation on the mobile app.

LinkedIn discourages spamming or sending invitations to total strangers. Members have the option to report unwarranted connection invitations to LinkedIn.

Social Media Slipup

A young nursing student recently graduated with an excellent history of volunteer experience and clinical hours, as well as a list of well-respected references. However, after applying for every available nursing position in the area, she had no luck finding employment.

Frustrated by the lack of job leads, she registered and paid for services of a career-counseling service that helps job seekers find employment. The first meeting with the case worker included a review of her transcripts, résumé, and volunteer experience. He determined she was good candidate for a nursing position and was surprised she had not had opportunities. His conclusion was that lack of opportunity was due to a higher-than-average number of people applying for similar jobs with more experience.

The case worker then entered her name into an Internet search engine. He came across a publicly accessible social media page for a person with her exact name. However, when he saw the photo, he realized it was not her.

The page contained negative information that would discourage an employer from reaching out to her. Since potential employers generally do not know what a candidate looks like, she was likely suffering from mistaken identity.

He immediately called the applicant and revealed what he found. He advised her to establish multiple social media accounts and use a middle name or initial in her profile name to differentiate herself from the person with the same name. This would help build a professional, positive online presence to help in her job search. He also suggested that the name on her résumé be adjusted to match those accounts. Once employers were able to identify her and see her qualifications, opportunities for interviews became a reality.

Before applying for jobs, it can be in your best interest to evaluate your personal online presence. If the search results show multiple accounts by other people with a shared name, think of ways to differentiate your name. This will help you have a unique online presence when an employer conducts an Internet search for you.

Connections are categorized as first, second, or third degree.

- A *first-degree connection* is a direct connection, mutually agreed upon by you and another LinkedIn member. You are able to view the entire profile of someone who is your first-degree connection, and that person can see your entire profile.
- A *second-degree connection* means you are not directly connected to the other member, but you have a first-degree connection in common. You have a limited view of the profiles of your second-degree connections. You can connect with these users by clicking the **Connect** button.
- A *third-degree connection* is someone who is connected to one of your second-degree connections. You have a limited view of the profiles of your third-degree connections.

No connection means that LinkedIn did not detect any association from your profile, work experience, or education that you have in common with the other member.

Another way to communicate with other members is via messages from your LinkedIn inbox. The *LinkedIn inbox* is LinkedIn's proprietary version of e-mail that will permit private communications with any connection in your network. It is possible to send a message to those with whom you are not connected, but you have to either upgrade your account or pay a fee per message. This is done to eliminate spamming.

Groups

Once your profile is complete, you can join a variety of groups. LinkedIn groups provide users with a way to connect, and sometimes share information with, other members. There are two basic types of groups, standard and unlisted. A *standard group* is a group that appears in LinkedIn search results, allows group members to invite others to join, allows members to view content, and will display the group logo on its members' profiles. An *unlisted group* is a group that does not appear in search results. Its members can invite others to join and display the group logo on its members' pages.

LinkedIn users must request permission to join either type of group. If you have sent a request to join a group, a group manager will receive and review your request. You will receive a notification if you have been given permission to join. LinkedIn connections can be built by joining groups and contributing to discussions. Some groups are for exchanging information, while others are for recruiters and hiring employees. Once you join a group, you can send invitations to connect to others in the same group without being considered a spammer. One of the first groups to join, especially when unemployed, is a job seekers group. It is suggested to select a group that is appropriate for your desired employment industry.

Posting to LinkedIn

You can update potential employers and your network regarding your professional pursuits from LinkedIn's homepage. These updates are unlike Facebook or other social sites where it is acceptable to express emotions or your view on the day's activities. Instead, the goal of a LinkedIn status update is to promote yourself in your professional life. Some examples of appropriate status updates include your activity on the site, such as becoming a member of a group or sharing a link to a news article relevant to your industry.

Twitter Account

Twitter is an online news and social networking site for professionals and nonprofessionals to communicate in real time. Since Twitter communication occurs in real time, it can be much faster than e-mail. The purpose of networking on Twitter is to follow available job posts, as well as people's ideas, stories, opinions, and information. Twitter is a place where employers post jobs and job seekers visit to find employment opportunities.

Twitter communication consists of user-driven postings called *Tweets*. There is no limit to how often a user can Tweet, but each Tweet is limited to 140 characters. This makes Twitter-based communication a form of microblogging. A **microblog** is short communication limited to a certain number of characters per post. The 140-character limit not only necessitates brevity, but encourages users to make succinct, memorable posts, as well.

CONNECT TO YOUR CAREER

Complete 4-4 Twitter Account, pg 72

Create an Account

To join Twitter, you must sign up for an account by navigating to www.Twitter.com. Locate the New to Twitter box and select the **Sign up** button. Provide your full name, professional e-mail address, and a secure password. After you have entered the necessary information, you will select another **Sign up** button. Similar to other accounts you have created, you will receive an e-mail confirmation. Select the link inside the body of the e-mail to confirm your Twitter account.

After you register, you can choose to see people you know who have already joined Twitter. If you choose to do this, provide your e-mail contact list to connect with people in your professional network.

Twitter accounts can be set as public or private. Tweets from public accounts are viewable by anyone, even those without a Twitter account. In order to view Tweets from a private account, a user must request and gain permission from the account owner.

Create a Profile

Creating a profile on Twitter differs from creating a profile on LinkedIn. A Twitter profile consists of just two details: a username and bio. The remainder of the user's Twitter page serves to display that user's Tweets. Even though a Twitter profile contains less information than that of LinkedIn, create it in a way that highlights who you are as a professional. This includes uploading a professional photo. In an effort to stay recognizable across networking platforms, consider using the same photo used for your LinkedIn account.

Username

Twitter allows its users to create a unique username or use an e-mail address as a username. Usernames on Twitter are unique in that they feature the @ symbol as a prefix. Create a professional-sounding username on Twitter so recruiters will follow your posts. Although you are limited in the number of characters in a username, you have creative license. For your professional Twitter account, focus on including your legal name with an occupation, professional designation, or geographic area. This helps make it memorable and marketable. Consider the following examples:
- name with profession, such as a writer: @BobbyCross_Writer
- name with professional designation, such as MBA: @CrandallJonesMBA
- name with general location, such as NYC: @AmyMackNYC

Bio

A Twitter bio is similar to a LinkedIn headline. In their bios, users display information about who they are and what they do. A Twitter bio is limited to 160 characters, which is about three lines of copy, so consider using your personal brand statement here. Using keywords is important because if people search for those keywords on Twitter, your account will appear in the search results. You may also include a link to your portfolio, website, or blog, providing those who view your profile with a direct link to your work.

Followers

Where LinkedIn has connections, Twitter has followers. **Followers** are Twitter members who view another user's Tweets in their own Twitter feed. When you post a new Tweet, your followers will see it first. Users are permitted, and often encouraged, to follow as many public profiles as they choose. Those who have public Twitter accounts can be followed by any user at any time. The account owner will receive notification of a follower, but the follower does not have to receive permission.

By changing an account's settings to private, the account owner will have the ability to approve or deny who follows his or her Tweets. In order to follow someone with a private profile, a user must send a request to the user in question and wait for approval. For both public and private profiles, an individual has the option of "blocking" a particular user. Users cannot view profiles from which they have been blocked.

Posting to Twitter

If you are a Twitter user, create an account for professional use to Tweet about topics relevant to your industry. Write your Tweets in a way that promotes your personal brand and encourages others to read your posts. To build a professional following, Tweet your comments about an article you read, a project you are directing, or a course you have completed. This allows you to brand yourself as a potential leader in your field. A successful Twitter user is one who Tweets regularly and focuses on his or her intended audience.

Tweets can be used to create a dialogue with other users. When Tweeting to a specific user, include the person's username with the @ symbol in your Tweet. For example, if you would like to direct a Tweet to Marie, begin the Tweet with @Marie. Marie will then receive a notification and be directed to your Tweet. This convention is only appropriate when communicating on Twitter.

Gaining popularity on Twitter can be achieved through the consistent use of hashtags. A **hashtag** is a searchable keyword that links users to all Tweets marked with the same keyword. This means that if a user searches for a specific hashtag that is included in your Tweet, then your Tweet will appear in the search results. Hashtags can be placed anywhere in a Tweet. Any word can be turned into a hashtag by adding the pound symbol (#) immediately before the word with no space between the symbol and the word. A string of words can also be turned into a hashtag using the same process. To make multiple words into a hashtag, precede the phrase with the pound symbol and remove spaces between each word. Some examples of hashtags include the following:

- #careermanagement
- #careers
- #consultingjobs
- #greenjobs
- #hireme
- #ITjobs
- #jobpostings

When appropriate, include a link to your portfolio, website, or blog in a Tweet. Because there is a limited number of characters for each Tweet, users can incorporate links by reducing the length of long links using URL shortening services, such as TinyURL. These services create shortened versions of long URLs for free. Alternatively, Twitter automatically shortens URLs that are copied and pasted into a Tweet. Using a shortened URL will help direct followers to your blog or website and still have room to add a message.

Twitter can be a good place to search for employment. In fact, Twitter outpaces online job-search sites with more than half a million Tweets each month for job listings alone. Searches can be conducted for available jobs that have been advertised in Tweets by using the hashtag #jobpostings.

Instagram Account

Instagram is a mobile-centric media-sharing site that allows users to share pictures and videos publicly or privately. Although originally designed as a social networking tool, job seekers use it as a powerful tool to help establish and maintain an online presence and establish a personal brand.

Similar to other social and professional networking sites, you will need to create an account, password, and perform other basic tasks to activate a profile. It is recommended to use your Twitter profile name for your Instagram account name. This makes it easier for people to find you on Instagram, and it ensures that any item in which you are tagged on Instagram will also show in your Twitter feed.

Just as you did with your LinkedIn and Twitter accounts, upload a professional photo and create a bio. There are only 150 characters allowed for the bio, so it is a great place to record your personal brand statement. When you are finished creating your account, you will be ready to link your account to your other professional accounts such as LinkedIn and Twitter, which can be accomplished through your account settings.

As a career self-promotion tool, you can upload photos that highlight professional accomplishments such as a picture of an award or honor. Instagram is a great way to build a portfolio of videos and photos that demonstrate skills and talents that will catch the eye of an employer. A good way to demonstrate your talents to a potential employer is to post before and after photos of a project. This gives an immediate snapshot of your skills and what you are capable of accomplishing.

You can also upload short videos that allow an employer to see how you work in your chosen industry. For example, if you are a welder, you can upload a video of work being done on a project to illustrate your ability with a given tool or material.

After you have uploaded a photo or video, you can use a hashtag so it can be found by other users. Similar to Twitter, users can search for a specific hashtag, and all posts with that tag will be listed under the search results. For example, if you are an artist, you could tag a photo with #sunset, so anyone looking for a picture of a sunset can find your works by searching #sunset.

When looking for a business to which to apply for a position, a search for a company can be conducted in the same manner as other social media sites. By locating photos of a company of interest to you, you will be able to observe the culture and other characteristics of that business. This can help identify whether you are a good fit for the company before you apply.

You can include your Instagram link in your professional correspondence, portfolio, e-mail signature, LinkedIn profile, and Twitter profile. This helps to increase the number of people who view your profile.

As with professional networking sites, you can follow others and encourage them to follow you. When others reach out for communication, etiquette requires you to respond quickly and professionally. While regular activity is important, it is not essential to post something new every day. It can be helpful to establish a routine to make sure you stay current and your information does not become stale.

CONNECT TO YOUR CAREER

Complete 4-5 Instagram Activity, pg 73

Positive Thinking

Connecting to a career is a long-term adventure and should be approached as such. It will not be over in one day, or even in one week. Often, it will take months, and sometimes years, to find a career with which you connect.

It is up to you to make the adventure a pleasant one. The first step is to determine that the experience of creating a plan, gathering documentation, and completing all of the necessary steps to get in front of a hiring employer are doable.

The Best App for That

LinkedIn

The *LinkedIn* app enables you to update your profile, send messages to your connections, and send connection requests directly from your mobile device. When you find a job posting that interests you, you can apply through LinkedIn using the information found in your profile. Or, if you prefer, you can navigate to the website of the company listing the job advertisement. Once you begin a job search, this app will make additional job suggestions for you based on your search history. It will also provide data for you to review when someone looks at your profile.

The way you approach the career-search process reveals who you are as a potential employee. This means you must finish what you start and submit your best work, not mediocre work. Finish each lesson, each question, and take the time to explore additional resources and links provided in this text. At this stage, you are working as your own boss. However, you will only accomplish what you decide to accomplish.

Be positive during the job-searching journey. Concentrate on qualities you possess that other candidates may not. Believe you are the right person for each job for which you apply, and maintain positive thoughts throughout the process. The following represents common positive thoughts on which a person should focus on during a job search:

- I have capabilities that other candidates do not.
- I am a self-starter.
- I demonstrate critical-thinking skills.
- I have great judgment skills.
- I have awesome people skills.
- I can do this job.
- I will be able to find the work that I enjoy.
- I am a valuable employee.
- I could get hired by multiple employers.

Searching for a job can be a tedious process. Not every attempt will lead to an interview or job offer, but continue to be optimistic. Negative experiences can lead to negative thoughts. If this occurs during the job-search process, manage your emotions carefully. Examples of some common negative thoughts include the following:

- I do not know what I want to do for a living, so I should not do anything now.
- I do not want to take time to gather documentation.
- Many college graduates cannot find jobs; I will not either.
- School is a waste of time.
- Who would hire me?
- What if I am required to dress up for work when I hate dressing up?
- What if an employer finds out I was fired at a previous job?
- What if a new boss does not appreciate my work?

Self-talk is internal thoughts and feelings about one's self. Negative self-talk messages sometimes invade the thoughts of job candidates. In order to change negative self-talk to positive, start believing that an employer would like to have you as an employee.

CONNECT TO YOUR CAREER

Complete 4-6 Positive Thinking, pg 73

Summary

 State ways a job seeker can create a positive online presence.
A positive online presence can be established through the creation of well-written articles or blog posts, a professional portfolio, or memberships to professional networking sites.

 Explain the importance of a professional e-mail account.
A professional e-mail account is essential so a person can keep professional activities separate from personal activities. Most businesses use e-mail for employment-related communication. A professional e-mail address from a domain such as Gmail or Yahoo that contains or reflects the applicant's legal name is expected by an employer. An unprofessional e-mail address will almost certainly be eliminated at the beginning of the application process.

 Describe how a LinkedIn account can be used in the job-search process.
LinkedIn is a professional social networking site that allows job applicants and companies to communicate. It offers applicants space for posting résumés, skills, qualifications, and other important information to help them seem viable as a job candidate. It also offers companies space to post jobs that may not be advertised publicly. Staying active and updated on LinkedIn can not only help a person network with people in his or her industry, but find new employment, as well.

 Describe how a Twitter account can be used in the job-search process.
Twitter is a microblogging site in which users can communicate with their Followers in real time. Often, employers will post job openings to their Twitter feeds before posting to a publicly accessible job-search website. This gives Twitter users an advantage. Users can search hashtags such as #hireme, #careers, and #jobpostings to find recent employment opportunities that have been posted to the website.

 Describe the use of Instagram as a job-search tool.
Instagram is an online mobile-centric media-sharing site that allows users to share pictures and videos publicly or privately. When used correctly, Instagram can enhance a person's credibility as a potential employee by offering proof of abilities through photos and videos. When an employer views a person's Instagram feed, he or she should be able to get an idea of what that person is capable of achieving. Users can also search for businesses on Instagram to which they can apply to gain knowledge about the culture and atmosphere of the company.

 Explain the importance of positive thinking during the job-search process.
Finding and connecting to a career will take months, and sometimes years. Due to the long-term nature of this process, it is important that a person stays positive and focus on qualities that other candidates may not have. Practicing positive self-talk, while learning to avoid or ignore negative self-talk, is key for an individual to maintain an optimistic outlook.

Glossary Terms

connection	microblog	search engine optimization (SEO)
digital footprint	networking	secure password
follower	online presence	self-talk
hashtag	profile	signature block

Review

1. Explain the importance of a professional online presence.

2. List and explain the steps to create a professional e-mail account.

3. Explain the importance of networking during a job search.

4. Why is search engine optimization an important aspect of LinkedIn?

5. List and explain the steps to create a LinkedIn account.

6. Differentiate three types of connections on LinkedIn.

7. List and explain the steps to create a Twitter account.

8. How can Twitter be used in the job-search process?

9. How can Instagram be used as a career self-promotion tool?

10. Evaluate the importance of positive thinking during the job-search process.

Application

1. When considering you for a job, why do you think it is appropriate for a potential employer to take into account what he or she reads about you online?

2. Describe the privacy settings for each of your social media accounts. How will these settings affect your career search?

3. What may be considered negative online presence to one employer may not be considered negative to another. Create a list of characteristics that most employers would consider negative online presence and explain your reasoning for each.

4. Review the e-mail addresses listed in Figure 4-2. How might an employer perceive applicants with these e-mail addresses?

5. What elements did you add when you created a signature block for your e-mail account? How does your signature block strengthen you as a job candidate?

6. Search for jobs in your field using the search feature in LinkedIn. Notice that some of the same words are used in job posts from different employers. List ten of these repeated words that could be important in your job search.

7. Search for LinkedIn profiles of people you know. What ideas did you gain for your own profile?

8. What are some reasons why recruiters Tweet about available jobs as opposed to uploading the information to a job board?

9. You will have a chance to add media such as work samples to your Instagram profile. What would be appropriate for you to add to your profile?

10. Explain how you practice positive self-talk in situations that could be perceived as negative.

CONNECT TO YOUR ▶ CAREER
Workplace Connection

4-1 Online Presence

Enter your name in the following search engines: Google, Bing, Ixquick, Yahoo, and Spokeo. If you find you have a shared online presence, try entering your name and city to narrow the results. What entries were displayed when you entered your name? Record the top four entries for each search engine.

Google.com

  1.

  2.

  3.

  4.

Bing.com

  1.

  2.

  3.

  4.

Ixquick.com

  1.

  2.

  3.

  4.

Yahoo.com

1.

2.

3.

4.

Spokeo.com

1.

2.

3.

4.

Search engines do not always display the same results. Compare and contrast your findings from each search engine. What information is the same from one search engine to the next? What information is different?

Similar Information:

Different Information:

An interviewer will attempt to visit social media profiles of job seekers to find information. What type of information or photos should be removed or changed before the interviewing process begins?

4-2 Professional E-mail Account

If you have not already done so, create a professional e-mail account. Once an account is established, read the Terms of Service. If you already have an account established, visit the web site and read the terms again. What did you learn?

Since many users never read the user terms of agreements, they do not realize that e-mail is owned by the host company. Potentially, the e-mail provider has access to read or track communication sent and received without the user's permission. Do you think this is a violation of privacy? Explain why or why not.

List the URL for your e-mail provider here and add it to your favorites or bookmark it in your browser.

URL:

4-3 LinkedIn Account

If you have not already done so, create a LinkedIn account by completing the Getting Started information on the LinkedIn website. Once an account is established, read the Terms of Agreement. If you already have an account established, visit the web site and read the terms again. What did you learn?

1. Create a LinkedIn headline, including your full name, title, location, and industry. If you do not have a permanent position, write a title that succinctly describes your skills. You may choose to include your brand statement. Write your headline in the space provided.

2. Complete the other sections of the profile. Review your account profile. Make certain it is 100 percent complete.

3. LinkedIn automatically creates a URL for your profile. Customize the link to fit your needs, and write the URL in the space provided.

4. Download the app on your smartphone or tablet.

4-4 Twitter Account

If you have not already done so, create a Twitter account by completing the Sign Up for Twitter information. Once an account is established, read the Terms of Service. What did you learn?

Write your chosern user name for your professional Twitter account here.

1. Create a bio for your Twitter account. It should be a professional description that you want professionals to see. Consider including your personal brand statement. Keep in mind you will only have 160 characters. Write your Twitter bio in the space provided.

2. Download the Twitter app to your smartphone or tablet device.

What will you Tweet about to look for employment? What hashtags do you plan to use?

4-5 Instagram Activity

1. If you have not already done so, download, install, and open the Instagram app. Select **Sign up with e-mail or phone number** and follow the instructions to create your account. Alternatively, you can open an Internet browser and navigate to www.Instagram.com. From there, enter your mobile number or e-mail address, name, and desired username and password in the respective form fields and select **Sign Up**. Remember to upload a professional photo and create a bio.

2. Add your Instagram profile URL to your e-mail signature.

Using Instagram's search feature, search for businesses in your industry. Select a few profiles and browse through the images and videos they have posted. What did you learn about each company?

What in these companies' posts makes you think you would enjoy working for any of these companies?

Based on what you have seen from other Instagram profiles from those in your industry, what type of photos or videos do you think you will upload?

4-6 Positive Thinking

Freewriting is an activity in which you write down thoughts and ideas without stopping. Consider thoughts you might have as you enter the career-search process. Freewrite about yourself as a job candidate for three minutes. Write down positive thoughts as you practice self-talk. Note only positive qualities.

Next, write down the negative thoughts that might cross your mind as you begin the job-search process. How will you overcome those negative thoughts?

5 Networking for Your Career

Outcomes

1 **Discuss** the importance of professional networking.

2 **Describe** important etiquette necessary while networking.

3 **Define** professional reference.

OVERVIEW

Networking is a term used frequently in the workplace to describe the action of talking with people and establishing professional relationships. Anytime people interact, they are networking. It can happen virtually anywhere: in an office, on a train, or at a conference. Expanding your list of professional contacts who may be able to assist you in advancing your career is an important element in a job search. Sometimes, who you know can be just as important, if not more, than what you know.

Networking for your career can be done formally by attending meetings or events or informally through conversations with someone you meet at work or at a social event. These professional relationships can also be established through e-mail communication or through professional social media accounts. *Any* communication that leads to career discussions can yield a new member of your professional network.

Professional Networking

As you begin your job-search process, you will find that the more people you know, the greater your odds will be for finding job leads. *Networking* is talking with people and establishing relationships that can lead to potential career or job opportunities. You probably already have a personal network that includes your friends and family. These are the people with whom you socialize and build personal relationships.

As you begin your career, you will develop a professional network. A **professional network** consists of people who support an individual in his or her career and other business endeavors. Consider asking the career development director at your school or your favorite instructor to be part of your professional network. These people have come to know you during your formal education. Through your interactions with them, they may have become mentors or other respected sources of advice. Call on these individuals to help guide you through the career-search process.

Networking requires confidence and the ability to market one's self. Tentativeness is a networking obstacle. When others ask, let them know your career goals. This may lead to an opportunity to share your career-search activities. When stating your career goals, clearly communicate your skills and expertise, as well. Clear and concise self-promotion is critical for professional networking. There is no value in networking with others if they are unclear about your career potential and goals.

Networking can help you find jobs that may not be advertised to the public. Knowing someone at a company who has information about a job opening can lead to contact with a hiring manager. A person in your professional network may help you get an interview or give you good advice about a company that may lead to a job opportunity.

Conducting informational interviews is an important networking activity that can provide insight into your profession. **Informational interviewing** is a strategy used to interview and ask for advice and direction from a professional, rather than asking for a job opportunity. This can lead to networking opportunities and better prepare you for the job-search process. By talking with someone in your desired field, you can learn more about what is expected, types of jobs available, and other inside information about an industry.

Resist becoming a self-centered network that only *receives* information. Networking involves supporting others. Therefore, your support and assistance should be reciprocated when possible. Self-centered networkers face the chance of being rejected. Networking begins at the pre-career stage and becomes a permanent part of socialization. Your network will evolve and might include thousands of individuals over your lifetime.

Face-to-Face Networking

Face-to-face networking can begin anywhere you meet with individuals or groups of people. An opportunity to connect with someone who can share information that may help you in your career should never be discounted. Informal opportunities might start with people in your social network. By initiating a conversation about career topics, you may find that you are connected by a mutual friend to someone who may eventually become part of your professional network.

Before you begin face-to-face networking, consider creating business cards. Professionals are accustomed to giving and receiving business cards when introduced to a potential career contact. This exchange eliminates the need to record a person's contact information that might be needed for future communication.

You can model a business card from a professional in your field or conduct online research to find a format that is appropriate for you. The business card in Figure 5-1 can be used as an example. Your full name should be placed on the first line followed by a job title that describes your skills, such as *Instructional Design Consultant*. Without a title, the person to whom you give the business card may not remember the field or type of position in which you are interested. The job title is followed by a phone number and e-mail address. To protect your personal information, avoid including a physical address. If you have a LinkedIn account, the URL for your page should be included, as well. In addition, you might choose to use your personal branding statement.

Attending meetings, such as an alumni or professional-association event, is a good place to network.

FIGURE 5-1

A business card should include important contact information.

Betty Hernandez

Instructional Design Consultant

(605) 555-3462 | b.hernandez@e-mail.com
www.linkedin.com/in/bettyhernandez
www.hernandezinstruction.com

A driven team player who uses design skills to fulfill customer needs.

Goodheart-Willcox Publisher

You can begin by researching organizations that reflect your career goals. For example, if you are a marketer, check the American Marketing Association website for meetings open to the public. These activities provide opportunities to meet people in your profession.

Before attending a scheduled meeting with someone in person, prepare a list of questions regarding the industry and job. This not only helps you organize your thoughts and gain information, but reinforces your professionalism, as well.

Online Networking

Networking is not limited to face-to-face opportunities. In fact, it will be necessary to connect with others online, as well. This can be accomplished through professional social media accounts, such as LinkedIn, Twitter, or Instagram, among others.

When using LinkedIn, you can send connection invitations to people with whom you wish to network. Commenting on and sharing posts from your connections can amplify your network through exposure to second-degree connections. Joining industry-specific groups on LinkedIn can also yield new network members. A group membership status can help make introductions and establish new connections. You can also upload your résumé to your account so people who view your profile can also view your résumé.

When Tweeting to your network, Tweet often about topics in your career and industry, and use hashtags related to your industry to help widen your exposure. Similarly to LinkedIn, Twitter users can amplify their professional network by sharing Tweets of people they follow.

Networking on Instagram can be as simple as viewing the posts of those in your network. When you make new networking relationships, it is acceptable to ask for their Instagram accounts so you can follow their Instagram profiles. As they post photos that interest you or are related to your industry, like and comment on those photos. This is one of the fastest ways to strengthen your networking relationships. Commenting on the posts of those you follow can expose you to other followers of that account, potentially leading to new contacts and networking members. The more you comment, the more exposure you will gain.

Some of the best professional networking tools are available as apps. It may be worth the effort to download, install, and use these apps to network with others in your industry. Examples of popular networking apps include Shapr, which matches users with people who have similar interests, locations, and professional experiences so they can meet in real life; CityHour, which connects users to professionals in similar industries and allows them to schedule face-to-face meetings; and Meetup, which allows users to schedule meetings and automate notices regarding those meetings.

Online networking only works if you are active online. In order to be taken seriously with your job search, it will be necessary to check your professional social-media pages every day for updates. Just as when networking with someone in person, practice good manners when networking online. This includes thanking people for their comments when it is appropriate and responding promptly and professionally when people wish to connect with you.

Networking Etiquette

Etiquette is the art of using good manners in any situation. There are rules of networking etiquette that should be followed, both in person and online. Your professional reputation will be molded by the way you treat others.

Respect is an important part of networking etiquette. When you are reaching out to connect with others, only invite people with whom you are familiar. It is inappropriate to cold-call strangers and invite them to be a part of your network or send unsolicited connection requests online.

When networking, try to be brief and polite. It is considered rude to dominate a person's time with long conversations either in person or online. Remember, you are making an impression with a person who can potentially help build your career.

It is acceptable to let others know that you are seeking employment, but remain sensitive to each person's reaction when you do so. If a person does not respond offering a known job opportunity, quickly close the topic with a phrase such as, "If you hear of anything, please let me know," and move the conversation in a new direction. If a person responds positively, it is acceptable to send an e-mail that reminds him or her of the details of the conversation and include your résumé.

The Best App for That

CityHour

CityHour is a networking app that connects users to other professionals and allows them to arrange in-person meetings. CityHour synchronizes with your LinkedIn profile, enabling you to quickly find contacts in and out of your network who are open to face-to-face networking. Using the app, you can connect and schedule meetings with others who are in a 50-mile radius and available within a two-hour window. Other tools in the app, such as CityHour location, calendar integration, and in-app chatting make it an easy-to-use networking program.

In-Person Etiquette

On the day you will be meeting with a person who could become a member of your network, select attire that will match the appropriate dress code for the appointment and company while reflecting who you are as a professional. It is acceptable to arrive early for a meeting, but no more than 15 minutes prior to your scheduled meeting time. It is not acceptable to arrive late. Plan to come to the meeting alone; bringing an uninvited guest is considered unprofessional. If you rely on someone else for transportation, instruct the person to wait in the vehicle for the duration of your visit.

Prior to entering the building, mobile devices should be silenced or turned off and placed out of sight. Once you meet with your networking contact, it is appropriate for you to initiate a firm handshake while introducing yourself. Maintaining eye contact is important not only during the handshake, but throughout the rest of the meeting. A lack of eye contact can make you seem rude and uninterested.

During conversation, good communication skills should be used. This means avoiding slang or unprofessional language. You should not monopolize the conversation. It is important to demonstrate your interest in not only the job and information, but in the person with whom you are talking. Your focus and attention should be on the person and what he or she is saying.

When the meeting has ended, offer one of your business cards, and ask for one in return. It is a good idea to make notes on each business card you have collected. These notes can be as simple as a physical feature or detail you learned about the person, or they can consist of what a typical day in that position entails. Before leaving, initiate another handshake and thank your networking contact for meeting with you.

A follow-up e-mail should be sent thanking the person for his or her time. This reinforces your professionalism and acknowledges the conversation you have had. It will also keep your name on the radars of the people with whom you met, which could potentially lead to further networking or career opportunities.

CONNECT TO YOUR › CAREER

Complete 5-1 Business Cards, pg 84

Online Etiquette

Etiquette is equally important for online communication as it is for face-to-face contact. Positive, professional communication leads to positive online networking experiences. Writing negative posts that rant or vent about an individual or company is ill-advised. If you are communicating via e-mail, follow the rules of grammar and proper formatting. Negative or poorly written online communication could influence a potential hiring manager to eliminate you as a job candidate.

People value their time, and professional networking is no exception. It is appropriate to send e-mails asking for job-search strategies or leads. However, do not flood a person's account with comments, questions, and other communication. One or two skillfully worded questions or comments spread over a period of time are enough to grab someone's attention. When a person does not reply immediately, it is best not to persist. Not everyone checks his or her professional accounts for updates every day. It may be a matter of time before a response is received. However, lack of communication may imply that he or she is not interested in communicating. If one person does not reply, find someone else who can be beneficial.

Although networking online can provide many new insights into the careers of people, remember to respect their privacy. Avoid sending e-mails to strangers inviting them to join your network. Sending unsolicited e-mails, connection requests on LinkedIn, and other online communications to people you do not know is unacceptable. This could be perceived as spam. If there is a person you do not know but want to add to your network, ask for an introduction from someone in your network who knows that person.

Career Portfolio

Dragon Images/Shutterstock.com

References and Recommendations. A *professional reference* is a person who is ready and willing to recommend an individual for a job, if requested. It is a person who knows your skills, talents, or personal traits and is willing to recommend you for a job, community service position, or other capacity. These individuals will likely be members of your network. Someone you know from your personal life, such as a youth-group leader, can also be listed. However, you should *not* list relatives. Consider which references can best recommend you for the position for which you are applying and always get permission from the person before using his or her name.

A *letter of recommendation* is a letter in which a person in your network assesses your qualities and abilities to perform in a specific capacity. It highlights your achievements in your academic or professional career and is usually written by an instructor, supervisor, or someone else who is familiar with your qualifications for a given job or application. The purpose of the letter is to advocate for you as a candidate for a position. A letter of recommendation will probably be written by a person who also agrees to serve as a reference for you. Two or three letters of recommendation are sufficient.

1. Ask several people from your network if they are willing to serve as a reference for you. Create a word-processing document with the names and contact information for those individuals. Use the heading "Personal References" and your name. Each entry should include complete contact information for the person. This page should follow your résumé when you are organizing your portfolio for presentation.
2. Ask several people from your network if they are willing to write a letter of recommendation for you. Writing the letter can, and should, take some time, so plan in advance. When organizing your portfolio, it is suggested that these letters follow your personal references document.

Professional References

It is important to identify a professional network so that you can compile a list of three to five professional references. A **professional reference** is a person who knows an applicant's skills, talents, or personal traits and is willing to recommend him or her. These are people who can comment on your qualifications, work ethic, and personal qualities, as well as the work-related aspects of your character.

To cultivate a list of references, select people from your network who are familiar with your professional strengths. Ask them if they would feel comfortable in the role of a professional reference. Not everyone wants to be in this position, so seek permission before listing a person as a reference.

Compile and create a list of references that can be attached to your résumé and job application when requested to do so. At the top of the document, add your name and the phrase *Professional References.*

List each person and his or her contact information, as shown in Figure 5-2.

It is helpful to create a spreadsheet of people you meet and whether or not they are part of your professional network. For those whom you consider to be in your network, note each person's name, contact information, industry, when you met him or her, and any other important information. Also include whether or not this person is a reference. This will make it easy to tailor your résumé and references each time you submit them. Your spreadsheet should be updated regularly to reflect changes in your network. Consider saving your spreadsheet with a cloud-based storage service; that way you can access it from your mobile device whenever you have an Internet connection.

CONNECT TO YOUR CAREER

Complete 5-2 Your Professional Network, pg 85

A professional reference is a person who knows an applicant's skills, talents, or personal traits and is willing to recommend him or her.

Francis Massuro
Professional References
(218) 555–1234
fmassuro@e-mail.com
www.linkedin.com/in/fmassuro

Joan Lawrence, Executive Director
Village Plus Corporation
139 South Broad Street
Madison, WI 53558
(608) 555–8792
joan_lawrence@villageplus.com

Bryon Thornton, Public Relations Specialist
Chem-Rite
2020 Main Street
Bemidji, MN 56601
(218) 555–0784
bthornton@chemrite.org

Jason Akiyama, Research Associate
Vivalab Industries
47 Euclid Avenue
St. Cloud, MN 56301
(320) 555–0516
akiyama@vivalab.com

Cheryl Finley, Copywriter
On-Point Media Specialists
903 Joseph Drive
Duluth, MN 55804
(218) 555–1204
finley@onpoint.com

Summary

Discuss the importance of professional networking.
Networking is talking with people and establishing relationships that can lead to potential career or job opportunities. A professional network consists of people who support an individual in his or her career and other business endeavors. Networking can help a person find jobs that may not be advertised to the public. A person in one's network may not only have information about job openings, but may be able to arrange for an interview, as well.

Describe important etiquette necessary while networking.
Etiquette is the art of using good manners in any situation. A person's professional reputation will be molded by the way he or she treats others, so the rules of etiquette should be followed when networking in person and online. Arrive on time, silence all mobile devices, use good communication and listening skills, make eye contact, and do not dominate conversations when networking in person. When networking online, avoid writing negative posts, do not send unsolicited e-mails or network connection requests, and request permission to join industry-related groups on networking sites.

Define professional reference.
A professional reference is a person who knows an applicant's skills, talents, or personal traits and is willing to recommend him or her. References are members of a person's professional network who can vouch for that person's qualifications, work ethic, and personal qualities, as well as work-related aspects of his or her character.

Glossary Terms

etiquette	professional network
informational interviewing	professional reference

Review

1. Why is it important to have a professional network?

2. How can a personal social contact lead to a professional network connection?

3. What is a benefit of informational interviewing?

4. Describe how acting as a self-centered network does *not* help your career.

5. What type of information should be included on a business card?

6. Why is etiquette important when networking?

7. Describe appropriate networking etiquette when meeting with someone in person.

8. What are some behaviors that are *not* accepted when networking online?

9. Why is it important to have a list of professional references?

10. How can you generate a list of professional references?

Application

1. Professional networking can start with your personal network. What are some precautions to take before including friends as part of your professional network?

2. Sometimes, finding a job is more about who you know than what you know. Create a list of people who can be instrumental in helping you find employment.

3. Informational interviews are often overlooked for their importance. Research one individual with which you would like to have an informational interview. What questions would you ask during this interview?

4. What are some actions that you will take to prepare for face-to-face networking?

5. Why is it important to have a personal business card even if you are not currently employed?

6. Make a list of events that you might attend in the next few weeks that would be beneficial for networking. Why did you select these activities?

7. Explain your strategy for networking online.

8. Recall a situation in which you met someone in your industry who did not follow professional etiquette. What was your impression of this person?

9. What are some reasons why you should consider tailoring your list of professional references, depending on the job for which you are applying?

10. Why might someone not want to serve as a professional reference?

CONNECT TO YOUR CAREER
Workplace Connection

5-1 Business Cards

Conduct an Internet search using your industry and the phrase *business cards*. For example, if you work as a medical transcriptionist, key the phrase *medical transcriptionist business cards*. Review the results. Note any common design elements or specific information.

Record the information you will include on your business card. Include your full name, job title, phone number, e-mail address, LinkedIn URL, and other important information.

Once you have recorded all information to be included on your business card, you must determine how it should be presented. In the space provided, sketch a design concept for your business card.

Describe your plan for having your business cards printed. Will you order them online, visit a printing shop, or use your own printer?

5-2 Your Professional Network

As you identify your network, consider creating a tracking document to keep your contacts organized and updated. One method is to use a spreadsheet program.

1. Open a spreadsheet and create columns with headings for the following information: contact name; phone number; e-mail address; position title; company name, address, and URL; industry; where you met; year you met; and whether he or she is willing to be a reference. Save the spreadsheet as professional network.

2. Complete the professional network spreadsheet with information about people in your network.

3. Transfer this data to your mobile device or cloud-based storage service so you can have each person's contact information available at all times.

4. Save the file as *FirstnameLastname*_Network.xlsx (e.g., JohnSmith_Network.xlsx).

How will this spreadsheet aid you in your job search?

6 Protecting Your Identity

Outcomes

1. **Define** identity theft.
2. **Explain** how to recognize and report employment scams.
3. **Identify** potential risks that can be encountered when using the Internet.
4. **Define** malware and list examples.
5. **Summarize** how to create and maintain a security plan.

CONNECT TO YOUR CAREER

Workplace Connection

6-1   Identity Theft
6-2   Employment Scams
6-3   Malware

OVERVIEW

The job-search process can take place almost exclusively online. As you establish and refine your online presence, it is important to know how to stay safe on the Internet. You must be aware of the ways in which you can prevent your identity from being stolen. In simple terms, do not provide private information to people you do not know.

Limiting the amount of personal information you post online is only half of the battle, however. You should also be wary of employment scams, which may seem harmless at first. Furthermore, understanding the types of malware that exist to jeopardize your computer and the data that is stored on it is increasingly important in today's society. Create, maintain, and, most importantly, use a security plan to protect yourself, your identity, and your computer.

Identity Theft

Identity theft is an illegal act that involves stealing someone's personal information and using that information to commit theft or fraud. Each time you connect to the Internet, there is a risk that your computer or mobile device can be hacked and your identity stolen.

During the job-search process, it is especially important to be diligent in protecting your privacy. Avoid being lulled into a false sense of security when communicating with others, especially with those whom you do not know personally. This includes communication via phone calls, mail, and especially the computer.

Use caution and common sense when posting information to sites with which you have registered an account. Determine which personal details are appropriate and safe to share with strangers, and resist the urge to share too much information that could be stolen. For example, rather than listing a personal address on application forms or e-mail, provide your professional e-mail address as contact information.

While it may seem harmless to post information such as your date of birth to your Facebook, Twitter, or Instagram accounts, you may be potentially setting yourself up for identity theft. If someone manages to bypass the security of these sites, your date of birth can be stolen.

If a job application includes a field for a Social Security number, place all zeros in the spaces provided. You are *not* under obligation to provide this information anywhere when searching or applying for a job.

If you suspect your identity has been stolen, visit the Federal Trade Commission website at www.identity-theft.gov for guidance. Time is of the essence, so if this unfortunate situation happens to you, act immediately.

Complete 6-1 Identity Theft, pg 98

Employment Scams

When you begin to apply for jobs online, you will visit many websites that are unfamiliar. While most of the sites will be legitimate, some might be designed to gain personal information for the purposes of compromising your identity. Those who are trying to commit identity theft have mastered the art of creating fake job ads to lure visitors onto their websites.

If you post your résumé on a website, there is a chance you will receive unsolicited e-mails from companies asking you to apply for a job. To protect your privacy, research the company to make sure the posting is legitimate before responding.

Recognizing Employment Scams

There are multiple signs that indicate an employment scam, starting with the e-mail address listed on a job advertisement. For example, if the ad claims to be from a corporation but the contact e-mail address is a Yahoo address, something is wrong. Companies typically have their own URL that is a part of the e-mail address.

Another way to identify fraudulent employment advertising is to look for misspelled words and grammatical errors in the listings. Reputable companies sometimes make errors, but fraudulent advertisements are known for poorly written content. If a job advertisement contains a high number of spelling or grammatical mistakes, chances are it is not legitimate.

One common type of employment fraud happens when criminals create phony employment ads and contact people using information they find online in résumés. After contact has been made with a potential applicant, the applicant is informed that, in order to proceed with employment, the company needs to set up a direct-deposit account. Unfortunately, many unsuspecting people provide bank or PayPal account numbers, convinced they are dealing with a legitimate company. Criminals use many variations in payment-forwarding scams. Never provide any bank account or payment information in preparation to obtain a job.

The Best App for That

Shapr

The *Shapr* app is a networking app that connects users with others who have similar interests, locations, and professional experiences. Shapr is a swipe-based interface and users are anonymous. You can swipe right on those you are interested in meeting and will be notified when there is a match. An algorithm is used which tags your professional experience and interests to suggest profiles of those with whom you may want to network. This allows you to expand your network by meeting new people in your industry.

Under no circumstances should an applicant pay a potential employer. Legitimate companies do *not* request payment of any kind during the application process. However, a fraudulent company might insist that you pay for a background check or pay fees related to the application process. The request may include asking for a credit card number to cover these fees. An applicant should never pay for an interview or for any portion of employment verification. Beware of anyone who requests a credit card during an application process.

Carefully evaluate job advertisements to determine whether they are legitimate. Job ads that make grandiose claims are usually not genuine. Avoid any job posting that advertises making large amounts of money for little work or over a short period of time. A good rule of thumb to remember is that if the job seems too good to be true, it probably is.

Multi-level marketing companies should be avoided. **Multi-level marketing (MLM)** is a business strategy in which employees are compensated for sales they personally generate and for the sales of the other salespeople they recruit. Another term for MLM is *pyramid scheme.* This term is applied because every person in the company has recruited those below him or her. If you are recruited by a representative to work in MLM, he or she will make money off your efforts. MLM companies often look like legitimate companies, but many are not. They often promise easy money for little work, which is rarely, if ever, true.

It is easy to become distracted when finding the perfect job advertisement on a website. Before you start submitting personal information, slow down and investigate the site. A legitimate website will list a physical address and additional information about the business. If you are unfamiliar with the organization, search for its name online, and evaluate what you find. Sometimes, conducting a search for the name of the business plus the word "scam" can reveal whether the business is legitimate.

Social Media Slipup

A young man recently graduated from a local community college with an associate degree in accounting. He was seeking an entry-level job and was hoping to eventually earn his CPA certification. His résumé was complete and ready to use for the job-search process.

His friends told him to try looking for a job using social media. He quickly found that he had numerous connections that could potentially help him. He logged onto his Facebook account and posted that he was looking for an entry-level accounting job. He received several e-mails from friends of friends saying they were in human resources for accounting firms and wanted more information. He was invited to interview for a position he was interested in, but was told he would have to travel out of state for it.

In anticipation of the interview, he was asked to provide some personal details, such as his Social Security number, birth date, and bank account information for travel reimbursement. He provided the information and was told he would be contacted with a follow-up e-mail regarding instructions for selecting a flight.

goodluz/Shutterstock.com

After days of waiting for an e-mail, he forgot about the job and moved on. Two months later, he received a call from a credit-card company saying that his account was overdue, which was strange because he did not have an account with this company. After some investigation into the matter, he discovered he had been a victim of identity theft.

When applying for jobs through social media or the Internet, it is necessary to research a company to make sure it is legitimate before providing personal details. Many impostors post job advertisements on job boards hoping to trick someone into giving information. No credible company will ever ask for banking information or an application fee, and you are not legally required to provide a Social Security number when applying for a job.

The *Better Business Bureau (BBB)* is a nationwide, nonprofit agency dedicated to providing free business reliability reviews. The BBB gives businesses a rating of A+ through F. If you have suspicions about a company, you can check its rating with the BBB. It is possible that other people have also had negative experiences with the same company in the past. As a result, its rating can reveal whether you should get involved with the company.

Reporting Employment Scams

If you encounter a suspicious business or website when searching for jobs online or are the victim of an employment scam, report the incident immediately. Reporting the incident helps law enforcement track down scammers and thieves. There are several agencies that are dedicated to the protection of job seekers from such scams.

The *Internet Crime Complaint Center (IC3)* is a governmental organization that was established as a means to receive complaints of Internet-based crimes and report them to the appropriate local, state, or federal law enforcement agency. The IC3 is a partnership between the Federal Bureau of Investigation (FBI) and the National White Collar Crime Center (NWC3).

Another federal organization that handles claims of online scams is the Federal Trade Commission. The *Federal Trade Commission (FTC)* is a governmental agency that focuses on consumer protection. The FTC addresses complaints regarding identity theft, business practices, work-at-home cons, job scams, and multi-level marketing schemes, among others.

CONNECT TO YOUR CAREER

Complete 6-2 Employment Scams, pg 99

Websites

Each time you access a search engine or visit a web page, your computer's identity is revealed. Your name might not be visible to the public, but the computer's Internet protocol (IP) address is shown. The **Internet protocol address**, known as an *IP address*, is a number used to identify an electronic device connected to the Internet. While your personal information, such as your name and address, cannot be easily discovered, an IP address can reveal your approximate geographic location based on your Internet service provider. Any e-mails you send

from your computer or mobile devices have that device's respective IP address attached to them, so use caution when doing so.

One way to protect your online identity is to ensure that you are only transmitting data over secure web pages. Before uploading documents to a website, ensure the site is secure by checking that the URL begins with https. The *s* stands for secure. This is not 100 percent foolproof, but generally is a sign of protection. Secure websites may also display an icon somewhere in the browser to indicate the communication is secure. Be wary of uploading applications, résumés, cover letters, or any material that contains personal information to sites that do not display such protection.

In general, it is a good idea to avoid public Wi-Fi hotspots. While convenient, these networks are generally not secure and put your computer devices at risk for being hacked, therefore inadvertently exposing data. Hackers are able to create "fake" hotspots in locations where free or paid public Wi-Fi exists. For example, a hacker could create a local Wi-Fi hotspot from the parking lot of a restaurant and use the name of the restaurant as the name of the network. Patrons then unknowingly connect to the fake network, which allows the hacker access to any data being transmitted over that connection.

The Wi-Fi signal with the best strength may not always be a legitimate hotspot. An easy way to avoid fake hotspots is to check with an employee of the business providing the Wi-Fi to get the name of the network and the access key. If a Wi-Fi authentication screen is asking for credit card information, confirm that the Wi-Fi is legitimate. For example, hotels will generally not ask for a credit card number when guests are logging into Wi-Fi because they already have a card number on file.

Cookies

Cookies are bits of data stored on a computer that record information about the websites a user has visited. Cookies contain information about where you have been on the Internet and the personal information you enter on a website. Some advertisers place them onto your computer without your knowledge or consent. Most cookies are from legitimate websites and will not harm your computer. Marketers use the information for research and selling purposes. However, if a hacker gains access to the cookies stored on your computer, you could be at risk. Cookies are encrypted by the sites that place them on your computer, but if they are decrypted, they can be used to steal personal information you have entered on a website. Cookies also can be used to target you for a scam based on your Internet history.

As a precaution, there are ways to protect your computer from cookie-based attacks. One way is to opt out of accepting them. Some Internet browsers allow you to opt out of cookies by setting a preference that says to *accept* or *never accept* cookies. This is sometimes referred to as *incognito* or *private browsing* mode. Check your browser for specific instructions. Some websites will require a user to allow cookies in order to view the website. In this situation, the browser settings can be configured to temporarily accept cookies or accept cookies only from a list of approved websites.

Another way to protect your computer is to delete cookies on a regular basis. They can be removed by selecting the **Tools** or **Settings** menu from your browser, and then **Options**. Depending on the version of the browser, you can select an option that will automatically delete the cookies on a regular basis or after every time the browser is closed. Still another way to remove them is to run a disk cleanup from the **Start** menu of your PC.

In addition to cookies, websites often place temporary files on your computer that store information about the websites you have recently visited. These files slow down your computer system, and they can potentially put you at risk. To delete temporary files on a PC, open the **Start** menu and key the word *Run* into the search bar. Select the Run program. When prompted, key the phrase *%temp%* into the dialog box and select **OK**. All temporary files associated to your user account will then display. Select all the files and press the [Delete] key on the keyboard. If you are using a Mac, press [Command][Y] on the keyboard to open your browsing history. From there, delete the temporary files using the same method as outlined for a PC.

Session Hijacking

Session hijacking occurs when an unauthorized person takes control of a user's computer to monitor Internet sessions privately. It is sometimes called *cookie hijacking*. If successful, a hacker could gain access to personal information. The user whose computer is being hijacked has no way to detect that a hijacking has occurred. Since one method of hijacking involves the interception of cookies, regularly deleting them from a computer can help prevent it from happening.

Phishing

Phishing is the use of fraudulent e-mails and copies of valid websites to trick people into providing private and confidential personal data. The most common form of phishing is done by sending a fake e-mail to a group of people. The e-mail message looks like it is from a legitimate source, such as an employment agency. The e-mail asks for certain information, such as a Social Security number or bank account information, or it provides a link to a web page. The linked web page looks real, but its sole purpose is to collect private information that is then used to commit fraud. It is important to never open an e-mail attachment that you are not expecting. It is better to send an e-mail asking about the attachment before opening.

Malware

Malware, short for *malicious software*, is a term given to software programs that are intended to damage, destroy, or steal data on a computer. The purpose of malware can be to disrupt your productivity, gain access to your personal data, or to compromise your online identity.

Beware of an invitation to click on a website link for more information about a job advertisement. A large percentage of websites contain malware. One click can activate a code, and your computer could be hacked or infected. An illegitimate website may encourage visitors to download applications or templates that contain malware. Malware comes in many forms, including software viruses, adware, spyware, and ransomware.

Software Viruses

A **software virus** is a computer program designed to negatively impact a computer system. A virus may destroy data on the computer, cause programs on the computer to malfunction, or collect information and transmit it to some other location. Viruses can be introduced onto a computer by downloading virus-infected programs from an e-mail or from a website.

Adware

Adware is a form of software that displays or downloads advertisement material automatically without the user's knowledge. While navigating the Internet, you may often have an unwanted advertisement that pops up on your screen and interrupts your session. Some of these ads are made in the hopes the user will see it and respond by clicking to a website. This type of advertisement itself is usually harmless to your computer and is no different from a television commercial. However, certain types of adware are programmed to collect data with the consent of a user, which is unknowingly given by clicking on the ad. After you have clicked on it, the advertisement will record specific information, such as your computer's IP address, approximate geographic location, when you clicked on the ad, and browsing habits. Some adware even logs keystrokes entered by the user, such as passwords and banking information. This information then goes to the owner of the ad.

The goal of most adware programs is to customize future advertisements to better reach a potential consumer. For example, if you click on a travel advertisement, you will notice more travel, airline, car-rental, and hotel advertisements as you browse the Internet. There is a fine line between adware and computer spying. If an advertiser does not notify you that it is gathering information about clicking habits, it is considered spying.

Spyware

Spyware is software that spies on a computer. Spyware can capture information such as Internet activity, e-mail messages and contacts, usernames, passwords, bank account information, and credit card information. Often, affected users will not be aware that spyware is on their computer.

Ransomware

Ransomware is a software program that takes over a computer system and locks it until the owner pays a sum of money to regain control of his or her computer system. Ransomware can target any computer user, including corporations and governments, as well as personal PC users. Anti-ransomware software protection, similar to other virus-protection software, can be purchased for a computer system to protect users against this threat.

CONNECT TO YOUR CAREER

Complete 6-3 Malware, pg 99

Create and Maintain a Security Plan

Fortunately, there are steps you can take to protect yourself while applying for jobs online. If you have any suspicions about communicating with someone or giving your information via a website, do not proceed. Investigate the person or the company with whom you are dealing. You may be able to avoid a scam before it is too late.

Your online identity is yours alone. When your information becomes public, it becomes vulnerable to identity theft. Hackers hope to gain access to personal bank account or credit card numbers, as well as personal information, such as a Social Security number, birth date, or physical address. In order to protect your identity online, a multi-tiered security plan should be developed. Figure 6-1 shows a security plan checklist that can be used to develop your own security plan.

Antivirus Software

Virus-protection software, also referred to as *antivirus* or *antimalware* software, can be purchased from a reputable company to help protect a computer. New computer viruses are being created every day, and the only way to

FIGURE 6-1

In order to protect your identity online, develop a multi-tiered security plan.

Security Checklist
☐ Secure passwords created for computer
☐ Secure passwords created for mobile device
☐ Password information stored in a safe place
☐ Antivirus protection software installed and running
☐ Data back-up completed
☐ Internet browser updated
☐ Security settings set to high
☐ Windows automatic updates in *on* position
☐ Pop-up blocker turned on
☐ Suspicious e-mails deleted
☐ Unknown links avoided
☐ Cookies deleted
☐ Firewall turned on
☐ Wireless router password set
☐ Flash drives checked for viruses before using
☐ Automatic wireless connections disabled
☐ Free public hotspots avoided
☐ Public hotspots or wireless connections used with caution
☐ Privacy settings on for social networks

Goodheart-Willcox Publisher

ensure your antivirus software will recognize them is to update its database regularly. Once installed, adjust the settings so the software runs on a regular basis, such as once a week or once a month. By selecting this option, the software updates itself with the latest virus programs, scans the computer for viruses, and deletes them from the computer.

Your virus-protection software should also have a firewall. A **firewall** is a program that monitors information coming into a computer and helps ensure only safe information gets through. Firewalls function by following a set of rules that determines what can and cannot pass over a computer network. Think of a firewall as a traffic light; it controls what can safely pass and what gets stopped by the network.

Mobile devices are not entirely safe from hackers. In fact, as mobile devices become more advanced, they become just as susceptible to malware as desktop and laptop computers. Consider downloading and running antivirus software for your mobile device. As a society, we rely heavily on mobile devices, so it is important to guard them against theft and viruses that would otherwise disrupt your primary means of communication.

Mobile Security

It is wise to put a plan in place to protect your mobile devices from theft. You carry them with you almost everywhere you go. However, if you become careless and leave them in an unexpected location, your device can be stolen as well as your identity. You may also be stuck with a large telephone bill.

Some digital devices have thumbprint readers or retina scanners that allow the owner to unlock the phone with *biometric verification*, or verification by biological traits. Other devices can be protected by creating a passcode. A *passcode* is similar to a password but uses numbers instead of words. An example of a passcode is

a banking PIN. This code should be kept in a safe place so that if the unexpected happens, you can contact your service provider. Your provider may be able to track the phone through GPS or remotely delete private information before it is stolen and used maliciously.

Secure Passwords

Recall the strategies discussed in Chapter 4 for creating secure passwords. Implement these strategies when you create a password for an online account. Passwords are grouped into categories: weak, medium, and strong. Figure 6-2 describes these three levels of password strength.

To protect your identity while applying for jobs online, remember to do the following:
- Change your passwords often.
- Use at least 10 characters with an unpredictable capitalization, a number, and a symbol.
- Record your passwords on a dedicated hard-copy document to keep track of them and the accounts for which they are used. Include an abbreviation of the account name, password, and date that you created the password.
- Record security questions that you answered to create an account and how the account system will contact you if you forget your password.

If given the option, selecting two-step authentication can help establish an even more secure password setting. **Two-step authentication** is a process in which a host requires two identity verifications before granting permission to an account. For example, when logging into a professional networking site, you may have to enter a password then retrieve a temporary access code from the linked e-mail account. This ensures that the person attempting to log into the networking site has access to both the account password and e-mail address. Some websites may require you to answer verification questions instead of sending an access code.

FIGURE 6-2

Passwords are grouped into categories: weak, medium, and strong.

Password Strength	
Strength	**Description**
Weak	Contains one easy-to-remember word, uses lowercase letters with no symbols, usually six to eight characters in length
Medium	Contains one uppercase letter in a lowercase word and one number or symbol, usually eight characters in length
Strong	Contains a mixture of uppercase and lowercase random letters, numbers, and symbols and is 10 characters or longer

Goodheart-Willcox Publisher

Career Portfolio

michaeljung/Shutterstock.com

Testimonials. A *testimonial* is a formal statement from a customer, client, or other professional that certifies a person's qualifications or character. Generally briefer than a letter of recommendation, a testimonial focuses on a specific action a person executed that was exceptional in nature. The person writing the testimonial may not know you personally, but is validating the work or service you provided.

For example, if you work at a computer store and help a customer set up a computer, the customer may be very happy with your work. That customer may contact your supervisor through an e-mail with a testimonial that says, "Justin was an outstanding technical support person. He was patient, set up my computer, and helped me get started. I want to convey my appreciation for his help." Similar to letters of recommendation, testimonials validate claims of abilities that you made in your résumé and portfolio. If your employer forwards any positive written customer comments about you, save these for inclusion in your portfolio.

You may also have testimonials from instructors who made complimentary remarks on a paper you wrote or a project in which you participated. Your counselor may have sent you an e-mail with congratulations on a personal accomplishment that you made. These are all testimonials that validate your abilities.

Have you been the subject of a newspaper article that summarizes contributions, services, or accomplishments you have made? This, too, is a testimonial of your skills and talents. Include newspaper articles in which you are the subject.

You can also include employer evaluations in your portfolio. Evaluations serve as a snapshot of your performance as an employee. They reflect your work habits, strengths, and contribution to an employer. If including an evaluation, be selective in the one you choose. Do not use one that is too old or from an employer that might be competitive with the company for which you are applying for a job.

1. Sort through testimonials that you have collected. Include assignments that have an instructor's written comments about your work. Print any e-mails from instructors, community members, or other professionals that complemented your actions on something you did for that person. Attach notes to each document to identify what it is and why it is included in the portfolio. For example, a note on a research paper you wrote might say, "Research paper, Professor Dansby, commenting on my writing skills."
2. Search through recent employer evaluation forms you have kept. If you have evaluations that are appropriate, include them.

Security Settings

Before using the Internet, become acquainted with the security settings and features of your browser. First, look for a menu called **Tools**, **Settings**, or something similar. Within this menu, locate your web browser's security features, sometimes called **Internet options**, **Privacy settings**, or **Security**. Change your settings to protect your computer and your information. Enabling a *pop-up blocker* prevents your web browser from allowing you to see pop-up ads, which often contain malware.

If your computer or mobile device has a built-in web camera, consider keeping it covered or deactivated when not in use. Even if they are not actively being used, these cameras can be accessed remotely by unauthorized users, essentially gaining access to a live stream of your day-to-day life.

Back up Your Computer

An important part of a security plan is backing up the data on your computer. If a virus invades your computer or the hard disk crashes, it may be too late to retrieve your files and computer programs. Having a backup can prevent losing files.

Put a plan in place to perform regular back-ups. Decide on a storage device and method for backing up your files. Place the backup in a fireproof container and store it at a location other than your home, if possible.

Summary

Define identity theft.

Identity theft is an illegal act that involves stealing someone's personal information and using that information to commit theft or fraud. Common sense should always be used when deciding what information is shared online, and a person's personal address or Social Security number should never be included on online employment forms.

Explain how to recognize and report employment scams.

There are multiple signs that indicate an employment scam. These signs include an e-mail address that does not include a company URL, poorly written content with misspelled words and grammatical errors, job ads that request payment, and grandiose claims of payment. A good rule of thumb to remember is that if the job seems too good to be true, it probably is. Employment scams should be reported to *Internet Crime Complaint Center (IC3)* or the *Federal Trade Commission (FTC)*.

Identify potential risks that can be encountered when using the Internet.

Potential risks that can be encountered when using the Internet include transmission of data over unsecure web pages, fake Wi-Fi hotspots, theft of cookies, session hijacking, phishing, and various types of malware.

Define malware and list examples.

Malware is a term given to software programs that are intended to damage, destroy, or steal data on a computer. Malware comes in many forms, including software viruses, adware, spyware, and ransomware.

Describe how to create and maintain a security plan.

The creation of a multi-tiered security plan can help protect a person's identity online. This includes downloading, installing, and running virus-protection and firewall software; setting security parameters on mobile devices; establishing secure passwords; becoming acquainted with security settings of a browser; and regularly backing up a computer.

Glossary Terms

adware	Internet protocol address	ransomware
cookies	malware	software virus
firewall	multi-level marketing (MLM)	spyware
identity theft	phishing	two-step authentication

Review

1. Describe methods of avoiding identity theft.

2. List and explain three ways to recognize an employment scam.

3. What type of information can be revealed by a computer's IP address?

4. Describe two methods of removing cookies from a computer.

5. What is *phishing*?

6. What is the purpose of malware?

7. List and describe four types of malware.

8. Describe the benefits of creating a security plan.

9. How does a firewall help in protecting a computer?

10. Why is it important to back up your computer?

Application

1. What are some reasons a hacker would want to obtain a person's identity online?

2. How could you confirm a company's information before applying for a job?

3. Why might it be an inefficient use of your time to get involved with a multi-level marketing company?

4. Recall a job advertisement you have seen that looked suspicious. What caused you to suspect that it might be a scam? Explain.

5. Make a list of Internet activities that can possibly put your online identity at risk. What can you do to safeguard your identity?

6. How would you know if your computer had a virus?

7. What is the best way to protect your e-mail account from being hacked?

8. What would you do if you received an e-mail from an unknown source with a subject line of, "Hey, check this out!"?

9. Security settings may be found in different locations on different types of Internet browsers. Describe how to find the security settings on the Internet browser you use in your job search.

10. When is the best time to use a security plan to protect your computer? Why?

CONNECT TO YOUR CAREER
Workplace Connection

6-1 Identity Theft

Identity theft can cause serious, ongoing problems affecting your credit and other areas of your life. Visit the Federal Trade Commission website at www.identitytheft.gov. Read the information that pertains to reporting identity theft, and summarize the steps that should be taken if this should happen to you.

Next, on the same website, read about victims' rights. Summarize your findings.

What computer-security steps does the Federal Trade Commission suggest you take if you are a victim of identity theft?

6-2 Employment Scams

Conduct an Internet search using the phrase *avoiding employment scams*. Record three facts you learned.

Fact #1:

Fact #2:

Fact #3:

6-3 Malware

Conduct Internet research on the latest antimalware software. Recommend five software programs you would consider using on your computer. List the name of each program, its cost, and the types of utilities included, for example Internet security, adware protection, etc.

Antimalware Software		
Software Name	**Cost**	**Utilities Includes**

List the make and model of your mobile device(s). Visit your service provider or manufacturer's website, and search the site to find current information about malware that may affect your device.

Make:

Model:

Potential Malware:

How susceptible to viruses is your device?

Conduct Internet research regarding how to protect your mobile device against malware. What did you find?

In the space provided, outline your personal security plan.

Why It Matters

One of the first challenges you will face as a job seeker is persuading a potential employer to believe you are the perfect candidate for a position. In most cases, your résumé will be the key to this process. Once you identify a job opening, you must create a résumé that convinces the reader to invite you for an interview. The résumé should be stellar and perfect in form. Along with the résumé, you will submit a cover letter. If you are required to complete a formal application form, it should be as presentable as your résumé and cover letter.

Company websites, professional networking sites, and job-search websites will be valuable sources for finding advertisements for positions. You can make these resources work for you by adopting a Sunday Evening Plan. The plan includes updating your online presence on a regular basis and managing the application process.

CHAPTER

7

Résumés

Outcomes

1 **Explain** the purpose of a résumé.

2 **Discuss** the importance of keywords.

3 **Identify** sections of a résumé.

4 **List** three types of résumés.

5 **List** three formats that can be used to resave a master résumé.

6 **Discuss** two examples of a nontraditional résumé.

CONNECT TO YOUR CAREER

Workplace Connection

OVERVIEW

When a person is seeking employment, the résumé he or she prepares is an important first step in getting an interview. A job applicant gets one chance to impress the reader, so a résumé must make a strong and positive statement about who he or she is. The candidate must persuade the potential employer that the skills and experience listed on the résumé fits the position he or she is seeking to fill.

A good résumé is a marketing tool that sells an individual as the perfect candidate for a position. What makes a good résumé? First, it must be well-written and presented in an organized manner. Second, it must have searchable keywords. Finally, it must have content that entices the reader to request an interview.

Résumé

A **résumé** is a written document that lists an individual's qualifications for a job, including work experience and education. It is a glimpse into a candidate's professional preparation and pertinent qualifications for work. Its chief purpose is to convince a potential employer that an applicant's experiences and skills match the qualifications of the job. Think of a résumé as a powerful summary of *who* a person is and *why* he or she would be an asset as an employee. It is often the first impression most employers will have about a job applicant prior to a first meeting.

When creating a résumé, consider using a template to get the process started. A *résumé template* is a pre-formatted word-processing document that contains a standard layout with adequate margins of white space. Templates look balanced on a page and include pre-selected fonts, bullet points, headers, footers, and, some-times, separator lines. They are documents designed to give a résumé a professional look and feel. It can be easier to use a template and customize it for personal needs rather than to start from scratch. If you choose to start with a template, remember to customize it so that it looks original and reflects your personality.

When reviewing the many available templates, con-sider the following:

- adequate white space and margins
- font that is black in color
- headings that are larger than the body text
- plain styling without elaborate headings, text boxes, or tables

There is a myriad of free templates available online from Microsoft, Google Docs, and other online resources that can be saved as editable documents.

As you progress in your career, you will take on new responsibilities, and you will experience changes in your jobs, education, and interests. Therefore, you will have to continually update your résumé for subsequent job applications. Keep in mind that a résumé should be well-written, free of errors, and organized in a way that high-lights your skills and qualifications. It is worth spending the time to perfect your résumé. It is the gateway for a potential interview and, ultimately, to a great job.

CONNECT TO YOUR ▶ CAREER

Complete 7-1 Résumé Templates, pg 120

Keywords

As you begin sifting through job ads, you will notice certain words that are used frequently. These repeated words often include specific terms related to the posi-tion, such as *leadership*, *degree*, and *specialist*, to list a few. These are known as *keywords*. As explained in Chapter 1, keywords are words that relate to the func-tions of an open position. Most keywords are nouns or noun phrases, not verbs. Examples of keywords are shown in Figure 7-1.

FIGURE 7-1

Keywords are words that specifically relate to the functions of a position for which an employer is hiring.

Keywords			
accounts payable	customer service	logistics	scheduling
administration	data analysis	manager	social media
advocacy	data entry	marketing	management
banking	debt refinancing	Microsoft Word	Spanish
benefits administration	editing	networking	spreadsheet expertise
bilingual	education	patient services	statistics
billing	engineer	payroll	team building
budget analysis	financial planning	planning	technological literacy
business development	health and safety	product representation	telecommunications
business to business (B2B)	health care	professional	underwriting
certified public accountant (CPA)	high-tech industry	project management	video editing
collections	HTML5	public relations	volunteer
construction	information technology	real estate	web design
credit management	internship	retail	written communication skills
curriculum development	investments	risk management	
	leadership	sales experience	

Goodheart-Willcox Publisher

Employers use keywords in job advertisements to describe the duties associated with requirements for open positions. Employers select keywords that are important to the job and then look for those words in the résumés submitted by candidates. This can help identify potential matches for a job opening. The job advertisement in Figure 7-2 uses the following keywords:

- journal entries
- reports
- monthly reconciliation of bank accounts
- tax schedules
- bank draws
- project reports
- workflow timing
- process and procedure improvements
- honesty
- responsibility
- integrity
- fulfillment of commitments

Reading job advertisements and identifying keywords to use in your résumé can be a helpful exercise. Using the right combination of keywords is the best way to become visible to an employer or recruiter. One way to ensure visibility is to include the same keywords that employers use in the advertisement for the job for which you are applying.

Résumés with the correct keywords trigger responses, while those without matching keywords are ignored. A lack of keywords associated with a specific job decreases the chances of an applicant being flagged during the early stage of the screening process.

Trending

Trending refers to keywords and phrases that have the highest number of online searches on any given day.

Many Internet search engines list what is trending, as do social-media websites. Trending information is saved, and the data are tabulated. These tabulations are ranked and posted on the sites. For example, if you conduct a search for "technology jobs," the search engine will rank your search terms and offer the most popular results for the job posting keyword phrase. If enough employers use consistent wording for job posts, search engines will categorize those posts and record how often they are repeated. In addition, as job seekers enter terms into search engines to find open positions, those terms are also tabulated. For example, if a candidate is looking for an accounting job, a search engine will list keywords associated with accounting jobs that are most popular at the moment.

As the needs of employers change, keywords related to a job will also change. For example, during the hot summer months, employers might be looking for summer lifeguards. The keyword *lifeguard* would be popular, or currently trending. In the colder winter months, this is likely to change. Instead, keyword trends during the winter months would include *seasonal retail help*. Consider the job for which you are applying and determine the appropriate keywords to use on your résumé to match what is trending.

Automatic Data Tracking (ADT) Software

Automatic data tracking (ADT) software is often used to scan résumés for keywords. The software is used by employers and recruiters to sort through résumés and flag the ones that match the keywords for which they are looking. Over the last decade, the job-search process has transitioned from employers reading print résumés to computer software programs that scan

---

FIGURE 7-2

Using an appropriate combination of keywords in a résumé is the best way to become visible to an employer or recruiter.

Essential Duties and Responsibilities
- Assist in the monthly close process by preparing journal entries, reports, analysis, and supporting schedules, as needed, under the directions of management
- Perform monthly reconciliations of bank accounts
- Assist in the preparation of tax schedules
- Assist with bank draws, file uploads, and project reports
- Concurrently perform multiple assignments and self-manage schedule to determine workflow timing and duration
- Perform special projects under the direction of management, and respond appropriately to requests from other company personnel
- Apply principles of accounting and use judgment and professional skills in determining appropriate procedures for preparation and maintenance of accounting records, transaction research, and reporting
- Identify opportunities for process and procedure improvements and work with management to implement
- Demonstrate honesty, responsibility, integrity, and fulfillment of commitments

Goodheart-Willcox Publisher

electronically submitted résumés for keywords. With hundreds of résumés and job postings available online, it may be difficult for a person to read each résumé that is received. For that reason, some larger companies rely on computer programs to scan the content for keywords to expedite the screening process.

In order to know which keywords will result in ADT software finding a résumé quickly, research can be conducted on trending keywords in a given career field. For example, for an entry-level position in a corporation, one might think of the words *clerk* or *receptionist*. However, research may show that the phrase *front desk assistant* is the preferred terminology for the same position.

Complete 7-2 Résumé Keywords, pg 121

Sections of a Résumé

Résumés have standard sections employers expect to see. Some sections, however, are optional and should be included only if they apply to you and the position you are seeking.

As you apply for positions, you will find the need to customize your résumé to fit the job for which you are applying. You may apply for more than one type of job or job title at any given time. For example, a qualified marketing professional might find several positions for which to apply. One position may be for a marketing manager, a second might be for a communications manager, and another may be for a promotions manager. He or she is qualified for all three, so three résumés will need to be created. Each version will have different keywords, objectives, and profiles, but the core material will likely remain the same.

Keep in mind that customizing may simply mean changing a few keywords. On the other hand, it could mean major rewrites to sections of your résumé. It is important to be flexible and cognizant about what an employer wants.

When deciding how to format each section, consider the overall length of the final document. Will it be one page or two? Typically, a recent graduate should have a one-page résumé, while those with several years of experience may have two pages. Regardless of page count, adequate white space should be allowed on the page for readability.

Heading

A **heading** is a person's full name, phone number, e-mail address, and geographic location. This is a standard part of a résumé and is the most prominent feature that identifies a job applicant. At a quick glance, a potential employer can learn the geographic location or proximity to the job location and the personal contact information of the person applying for a job.

The first line of a heading is your legal name. Nicknames and abbreviations are *not* acceptable. However, it *is* acceptable to use only a first name and last name. Middle names or initials are optional.

On a résumé that is printed and physically submitted for a job application, an exact street address should be listed followed by a phone number beginning with the area code. On a résumé that is submitted electronically, the exact street or home address should *not* be added to the heading, as shown in Figure 7-3. It is likely that the résumé will be posted on the Internet, so it is unnecessary, and possibly unsafe, to list an exact street address and city. It is acceptable, and recommended, to use a general geographic area and zip code. For example, you can provide a major city or a general metropolitan area in close proximity to where you reside.

FIGURE 7-3

A heading is a person's full name, phone number, e-mail address, and geographic location.

Sample Résumé Headings	
Submitted in Person	**Submitted Electronically**
Shelley Jones 111 Main Street Baltimore, MD 21202 555-555-1234 sjones@e-mail.com www.linkedin.com/in/shelley-jones	Shelley Jones Greater Baltimore Area 21202 555-555-1234 sjones@e-mail.com www.linkedin.com/in/shelley-jones

Goodheart-Willcox Publisher

Next, list the telephone number at which you can be contacted. There is no need to indicate whether the number is a mobile or land line. It is obvious that it is the preferred phone number.

A professional e-mail address should appear next, followed by links to your professional social media accounts. Links to profiles such as LinkedIn, Twitter, and Instagram make it easy for employers to verify a candidate's digital footprint. Remember that social media searches are sometimes an employer's first choice to screen candidates. If there are more than three sites that you feel necessary to include, consolidate them so the list does not become overwhelming. This can be done by creating an account with a technology-management tool, such as Hootsuite.

Career Objective and Career Profile

After creating the heading for a résumé, the next sections are often the career objective and profile. A **career objective** is a brief statement that explains an individual's career goals to an employer. The objective tells potential employers what value you can bring to their companies. A **career profile** details an individual's accomplishments, skills, and current career level.

The objective and profile can both be customized for each position for which a résumé is being submitted. Keywords play an important role in these two sections to show a person is qualified for the position.

In some instances, it may be preferable to omit these two sections. For example, a person still in school may not have enough professional experience to write a strong career profile. In that situation, it is best to eliminate these two sections rather than try to write irrelevant sentences.

Career Objective

An objective articulates the type of job you want to secure. It should reflect how you can help the employer rather than how you can help yourself. An objective should be user-centered and focused on the company and the position.

Some consider a career objective optional, but people who review résumés often read the objective before the work experience and education sections. If the objective matches a job opening, the person reading will continue reading. A hiring manager wants to find candidates who announce a clear desire to work in a particular position. A general rule to follow when creating an objective is to write one line that summarizes your goal.

Career Portfolio

mimagephotography/Shutterstock.com

Clubs and Organizations. Participating in a club, sport, or organization demonstrates that you have the skill set to work with others and be a team player. Many soft skills, such as appreciation for diversity, leadership, and social responsibility, are learned from participating in a club or group. Networking skills can also be learned from interacting with club members and its leadership. Documenting that you have been a part of an organization shows an employer that you are responsible and a hard worker.

Most postsecondary institutions offer academic fraternities, such as Sigma Tau Delta English Honors Society, and career and technical student organizations, such as Phi Beta Lambda. Participating in these organizations shows you are not only committed to your industry but able to work with others. For example, Phi Beta Lambda, like other CTSOs, hosts competitive events in which you may be involved as part of your university's PBL team. Taking part in these events shows you have a competitive spirit.

You may have an opportunity to join professional organizations, such as the American Nurses Association, which demonstrates your commitment to your profession. Some professions have student chapters that provide opportunity to be a part of a professional group before graduation.

1. Identify clubs, sports, or organizations to which you belong. Create a word-processing document with the names of each organization, its contact information, and the dates that you were active. Use the heading "Academic Clubs," or another appropriate title, and your name. Save the document.
2. Identify any organizations of which you are a member. Create a word-processing document with the names of each organization, its contact information, and the dates that you were active. Use the heading "Organizations" and your name. Save the document.

Objective College graduate seeking concierge position to apply customer service skills to create the ultimate guest experience in the hospitality industry.

Note how, in the objective, the applicant accomplished the following:

- stated the desired job position: "concierge"
- included the preferred industry in which to work: "in the hospitality industry"
- noted a hard or soft skill: "to utilize customer service skills"
- added a goal: "create the ultimate guest experience"

It is important to keep the objective brief and professional. A general rule is to avoid first-person or second-person pronouns, as they can sound unprofessional. For example, "*I am* a college graduate seeking a concierge position in a hotel lobby to utilize *my* customer service skills to create the ultimate guest experience" is not as professional as the former example.

Even if you do not have extensive experience in a desired field, reflect the job you desire in your objective. Applying for multiple positions will require the objective to be adjusted to meet the requirements of the position. Do not feel locked in with the first objective you create.

Career Profile

The profile, also known as a *qualification summary*, tells who a person is. It details a candidate's accomplishments and skills in the present tense. A career profile is lengthier than an objective as it provides the potential employer with a synopsis of the benefits the company will gain from hiring a specific candidate.

The profile is a brief summary of a person's entire résumé written in active voice rather than passive voice. Include work experience that will strengthen your résumé, even if it was on a volunteer basis. Generally, the order of a career profile is as follows:

1. Strongest work experience
2. Hard skills
3. Soft skills
4. Abilities
5. Aptitudes

A profile should be composed using short, powerful sentences. It should not exceed one-third of the space for the total résumé, which is equivalent to five to six lines.

Profile Bilingual, top contributor, and provider of reliable information to guests. Responds to queries, gives directions, and makes detailed reservations and recommendations. Utilizes and shares knowledge of local events and venues in addition to local transportation options. Personable and engaging in casual conversation with guests.

CONNECT TO YOUR ▶ CAREER

Complete 7-3 Résumé Heading, Objective, and Profile, pg 121

Experience

Most often, experience is included as the next section on a résumé immediately followed by education. However, if you are a recent graduate without much work experience, you may consider the reverse and list your education first, followed by experience. This is a personal preference, and there is no right or wrong way to present this information.

Past and current jobs or internships comprise the experience section of a résumé. When listing a job, include the name of the company or organization, followed by the city and state. Additionally, note the start and end dates of employment. If still employed with a company, use the word "present," such as "August 2019 to present."

Under the company information and dates, list the position held with a description of the work experience. Use keywords when possible to trigger a match for job-related search criteria. For example, if a job recruiter is looking for an accountant, scanning software will search for résumés on the Internet that include keywords such as *ledger accounts*, *balance sheets*, *financial audits*, *operational data*, and *reconciling discrepancies*. Keywords that are unrelated to the job description should not be used.

Education

Most often, education is included on a résumé immediately following work experience. However, as noted earlier, if you are a recent graduate without much work experience, you may consider listing your education first, followed by experience.

The label of this section can be changed from "Education" to "Relevant Coursework" or "Relevant Education." If you are still in school, indicate the number of years you have attended and provide your expected graduation date. List the courses you have taken that are most relevant to the position for which you are applying. Include any training, workshops, or seminars you have completed, even if you participated in classes for a previous employer.

If you are no longer a student, your education should be listed beginning with the most recent diploma or degree earned. Include colleges as well as business or technical schools. Graduates should indicate the year a degree or diploma was earned, type of degree received, major subject, and minor subject, if any. Also, any certifications earned, special courses or training programs completed, or any other related educational achievements should be included. If you have earned multiple degrees, such as an associate degree and a bachelor degree, each degree should be listed separately. If you are an outstanding scholar in your college career, or if you have achieved other academic recognition or awards, add them to you résumé.

College students have an implied high school diploma or GED, so adding high school information is optional. High school information should only be added when there are outstanding achievements or honors and awards to highlight.

Special Skills

The *special skills* section of a résumé is an opportunity to focus the reader's attention on the skills gained in school or from previous jobs. These skills may not be noted or highlighted in other sections of a résumé. Job postings will likely include hard skills, which are job-specific skills, and soft skills, which are transferrable skills. Soft skills may include skills related to teamwork, organization, management, or other areas of expertise an employer might look for in a candidate. The goal is to list top skills that will entice the reader to schedule an interview. A bulleted list of points that reflects your leadership, management, communication, and team-building skills should be included here.

Carefully review a job advertisement for the job you are seeking and focus on the required skills. If you have the relevant experience, use the same words to describe it. Only use the keywords that fit your background. Do not stretch the truth.

CONNECT TO YOUR ▶ CAREER

Complete 7-4 Résumé Experience, Education, and Special Skills, pg 122

Résumé Formats

After you finish gathering information for your résumé, you are ready to select a format. Depending on the industry and job for which you are applying, you may find that it is best to use one format over the other. Three types of common résumé formats are timeline, skills, and combination.

Timeline Résumé

A **timeline résumé**, also known as a *chronological résumé*, is a résumé that emphasizes employers and work experience with each. Work experience is listed in reverse chronological order with the most recent information first. If your most recent work experiences are the best qualifications you possess when applying for a job, use this résumé format. An example of a timeline résumé is shown in Figure 7-4.

On a timeline résumé, beginning dates and end dates should be listed for each job under the *experience* section of the résumé. One of the following options should be used to format the dates:
- month and year: September 2019
- month, day, and year: September 1, 2019
- year only: 2019

Remember that a résumé presents a broad overview of your experience to an employer and is the vehicle to gain an interview. The exact duration of your work at a particular job might be of interest in detail to a potential employer later. However, at the résumé stage, your task is to display information accurately without giving an employer an initial negative impression. For example, if you only worked at an organization for two months, you might want to state just the year, such as "2019" as opposed to "November 2019 to December 2019." Using a two-month time period is not necessary if you want to emphasize the skills you gained as an employee, rather than the fact that you were employed as seasonal help.

Skills Résumé

A **skills résumé**, also referred to as a *functional résumé*, is a résumé that lists work experience according to categories of skills or achievements rather than by employer. A skills résumé lists work experiences according to relevant achievements rather than by time. For example, if you have programming skills, but your last job was as a restaurant server, you might want the programming experience to be the first information seen by a potential employer. In that case, you would use a skills résumé to highlight your skills over your most recent work experiences. An example of a skills résumé is shown in Figure 7-5.

Skills résumés typically have the dates of employment omitted. Therefore, if you have significant gaps in your employment history, it is appropriate to create and submit this type of résumé. It also presents an opportunity to focus on the skills and experiences you are capable of utilizing, even if they are not applicable to your current job. List your strongest experience or skills first, followed by the least-developed skills or experience.

FIGURE 7-4

A timeline résumé is a résumé that lists work experiences in reverse chronological order with the most recent information first.

JALIA CORTEZ

111 First Street, Redwood City, CA 94061   (650) 555–1234

jcortez@e-mail.com   www.linkedin.com/in/jalia-cortez

CAREER OBJECTIVE

College graduate seeking concierge position in the hotel lobby to utilize customer service skills and create the ultimate guest experience.

CAREER PROFILE

Bilingual, top contributor, and provider of consistent information to guests. Responds to queries, gives directions, and makes detailed reservations and recommendations. Utilizes and shares knowledge of local events and venues in addition to local transportation options. Personable and engaging in casual conversation with guests.

EXPERIENCE

College of San Mateo, Redwood City, CA
August 2017 to present
Administrative Assistant to the Director of Education
- Screen the director's correspondence and assist with preparation of responses
- Prepare e-mails, memorandums, and letters
- Assist with research, editing, and final preparation of reports
- Manage the calendars of five staff members and the director
- Schedule meetings and make special arrangements, such as catering and A/V equipment
- Maintain up-to-date personnel data for staff members

Jefferson High School, Redwood City, CA
June 2016 to August 2017
Receptionist and Administrative Assistant, Principal's Office
- Scheduled appointments for students, faculty, and parents
- Maintained calendars
- Answered telephones, screened, and directed calls
- Greeted visitors, faculty, and students and provided assistance as needed

EDUCATION

Associate of Arts in Office Administration, 2016
Lincoln Community College, Redwood City, CA

SPECIAL SKILLS

Computer: Microsoft Office Suite
Language: Spanish, intermediate-level speaker
General: Excellent verbal and written communication, superior organizational skills, and multi-tasking talents

FIGURE 7-5

A skills résumé is a résumé that lists work experiences according to relevant achievements rather than by date.

BRANDON BARTA

New York City Area 10002   (212) 555–1356

bbarta@e-mail.com   www.linkedin.com/in/brandonbarta

CAREER OBJECTIVE

Publishing professional seeking a managing editor position to use editorial leadership skills to develop top-selling titles.

CAREER PROFILE

Leader in the development of trade books on scientific topics. Uses knowledge of the market and team-building skills to create profitable collections of book titles.

KEY ACHIEVEMENTS

- Developed impeccable editing skills, including the ability to review content for accuracy, substance, sourcing, and the correct use of grammar.
- Managed the Greenhouse & Thomas lists of scientific and environmental titles, including environmental sciences reference books and collections of historical papers. Representative titles include *Conservation of Inland Wetlands*, *Animals of the Great Lakes Regions*, *Marine Sources of Organic Fuels*, and *The Role of Light in Evolution*.
- Recruited authors from leading faculty of major universities and from technical, research, and engineering staffs in the environmental sciences industry. Signed approximately 100 new titles.
- Delivered presentations to sales staff and to company management describing new books and editorial plans.
- Demonstrated leadership, collaborative nature, and flexible attitude.

SPECIAL SKILLS

- Knowledgeable about editorial development, copyediting, copyright concerns, production, photo research, and artwork preparation for scientific and technical books.
- Successful with promotion methods for scientific and technical books, including direct mail, online advertising, cataloging, and professional publication sales.

EXPERIENCE

Greenhouse & Thomas, New York City, NY, Managing Editor

Moss & Wallace Book Company, New York City, NY, Senior Editor

Eldridge Press, Boston, MA, Special Projects Editor

EDUCATION

Smith College, Northampton, MA, Bachelor of Science in Biology, minor in Journalism, 2000

Goodheart-Willcox Publisher

What Employers Want

Leadership is the process of influencing others or making things better. It is a soft skill that reflects professionalism. Certain traits such as honesty, competence, self-confidence, communication skills, problem-solving skills, and dependability are examples of leadership characteristics. Setting goals, following through on tasks, and being forward-thinking are also important leadership abilities. *Leaders* are those who guide others to a goal.

Combination Résumé

A *combination résumé* is exactly as it sounds—a combination of both the timeline and skills résumés. This format is used when you want to emphasize that your skills are your strengths against the backdrop of more recent work experience. The organization of this type of résumé consists of your career objective and profile, followed by achievements and skills. A brief listing of work experience should appear after. A combination résumé is illustrated in Figure 7-6.

Saving a Résumé

Once a résumé is created, it is a good idea to save it as a master résumé document. The résumé file should be named MasterResume or something similar. This will be the document to return to when customized versions are needed to apply for different positions. The master résumé is not the file to send to a potential employer. It is a working document to use as a basis for future submissions.

When you have finalized your résumé and are preparing to post it or attach it to an e-mail, you will want to resave the file with a new name to keep your master file intact. When saving the master résumé for submission, remember to save it as a secondary file with a professional name. There are many naming conventions that can be used. Select the one you are comfortable with and stick to it. Include your name in the file name so the employer can identify your résumé. For example, Christopher Jeffries may save his master résumé file as ChristopherJeffriesResume before sending it to a potential employer. However, he may save three versions of his résumé for three different positions as:

- JeffriesMktMgrResume
- JeffriesComMgrResume
- JeffriesProMgrResume

When resaving the file, consider using one of three commonly accepted file formats employers request. These formats are Microsoft Word document, PDF, and plain text.

CONNECT TO YOUR CAREER

Complete 7-5 Master Résumé, pg 123

Microsoft Word Document

There will be times when you will attach a résumé to an e-mail when applying for a position. When you created your master file, you more than likely used Microsoft Word. Microsoft Word's default .DOC and .DOCX file extensions are the most common formats for saving a document. To prepare a file for submission, renaming the file as a Word document is one option. Word files are easy to save by the creator and easy to download by the person receiving it as an attachment. However, one drawback to using a Word file is that it can be changed, either accidentally or on purpose, by the person who opens it.

PDF

While it may seem logical to attach the résumé as a Microsoft Word document, consider attaching it as a PDF file. A PDF file will keep the file intact, including the formatting, and protect it from changes. The PDF file can be created in Microsoft Word by resaving the file. Select the **Save As** option in Word to display the Save As dialog box, and then choose **PDF** from the list of options.

Plain Text

There may be times during the job-application process when you are required to copy and paste information from a résumé to an application on an employer's website. In doing this, formatting of a Word document will likely become distorted. Therefore, it will be necessary to prepare a version of your résumé that removes special formatting, such as bulleted lists. This can be accomplished by saving a plain text version of the résumé. When a file in Microsoft Word is saved as plain text, the file name will appear with a .TXT extension. To create a plain text résumé, select the **Save As** option in Word to display a dialog box. Select **Plain Text** from the list of options.

When a plain text document is launched, it will often open in Notepad. An example of a plain text résumé is shown in Figure 7-7. Notice all of the formatting has been removed. This will make it easy to cut and paste information into an online form.

FIGURE 7-6

A combination résumé is a combination of both the timeline and skills résumés.

Peter Jesse Owosu

Greater San Diego Area
Phone: (619) 555–4023 • E-mail: pjowosu@e-mail.com
www.linkedin.com/in/peter-jesse-owosu

CAREER OBJECTIVE

College graduate seeking a project coordinator position to use organizational expertise to manage complex projects for a fast-paced office.

CAREER PROFILE

Detail-oriented professional with strong organizational skills and the ability to manage projects so they are completed on time and within budget. Provides accurate schedule estimation and funding reviews for projects.

EDUCATION

Grandhill College, San Diego, CA, Associate of Arts in Communication, 2017

SKILLS

Project Coordinator Skills
- Utilized knowledge of project coordination software to input project data such as milestones, budget, expenses, internal team members, scope, subject matter experts, and due dates.
- Provided support by designing and producing project milestone charts with due dates and internal newsletter layout.

Team Skills
- Communicated with employees to resolve discrepancies and to bring focus to specific responsibilities, roles in the project, duties necessary to complete the project, and accountability.
- Scheduled meetings with workers and followed up to promote smooth project workflow.
- Handled general questions with professional courtesy and diplomacy.

EXPERIENCE

Grandhill College, San Diego, CA
June 2017 to present
Office Assistant, Recruitment Office
- Manage projects; answer questions concerning recruitment department events and services from students, staff, community agencies, and the general public; and direct students to appropriate college resources concerning recruitment issues.
- Assist in the organization of Recruitment Day, including contacting college representatives, making room reservations, and designing floor plan logistics.
- Provide production support for the Recruitment Office counseling staff by developing flyers, brochures, and letterhead.

Insightful Vision Center, San Diego, CA
May 2015 to June 2017
Customer Service
- Tactfully and professionally handled customer inquiries, complaints, and concerns regarding merchandise.
- Scheduled appointments with clients and followed up to promote continued business.

Goodheart-Willcox Publisher

A plain text résumé does not have special formatting and is helpful when applying for jobs online.

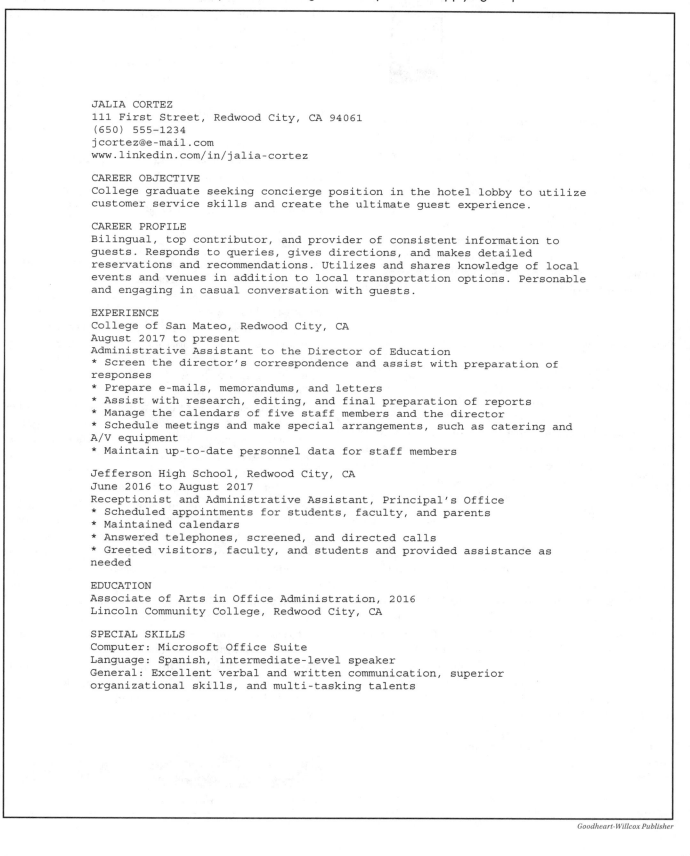

JALIA CORTEZ
111 First Street, Redwood City, CA 94061
(650) 555-1234
jcortez@e-mail.com
www.linkedin.com/in/jalia-cortez

CAREER OBJECTIVE
College graduate seeking concierge position in the hotel lobby to utilize customer service skills and create the ultimate guest experience.

CAREER PROFILE
Bilingual, top contributor, and provider of consistent information to guests. Responds to queries, gives directions, and makes detailed reservations and recommendations. Utilizes and shares knowledge of local events and venues in addition to local transportation options. Personable and engaging in casual conversation with guests.

EXPERIENCE
College of San Mateo, Redwood City, CA
August 2017 to present
Administrative Assistant to the Director of Education
* Screen the director's correspondence and assist with preparation of responses
* Prepare e-mails, memorandums, and letters
* Assist with research, editing, and final preparation of reports
* Manage the calendars of five staff members and the director
* Schedule meetings and make special arrangements, such as catering and A/V equipment
* Maintain up-to-date personnel data for staff members

Jefferson High School, Redwood City, CA
June 2016 to August 2017
Receptionist and Administrative Assistant, Principal's Office
* Scheduled appointments for students, faculty, and parents
* Maintained calendars
* Answered telephones, screened, and directed calls
* Greeted visitors, faculty, and students and provided assistance as needed

EDUCATION
Associate of Arts in Office Administration, 2016
Lincoln Community College, Redwood City, CA

SPECIAL SKILLS
Computer: Microsoft Office Suite
Language: Spanish, intermediate-level speaker
General: Excellent verbal and written communication, superior organizational skills, and multi-tasking talents

Goodheart-Willcox Publisher

The Best App for That

Monster.com Job Search

The *Monster.com Job Search* app allows you to stay connected to the job-search process when you are away from your computer. Easy access to your Monster account enables you to access and update your account as well as apply for jobs directly from the app. You can also receive notifications for jobs that fit your criteria as well as upload your résumé via Dropbox or Google Drive. In addition, you can have discreet communication with recruiters via the Message Center in the app.

Nontraditional Résumé

Not all résumés will follow a traditional résumé format. For example, if a person were applying for a job as a website developer, he or she may choose to create an online résumé to reflect his or her abilities with creating and maintaining online environments. Similarly, if a person were applying for a graphic design position, he or she can create a résumé that highlights his or her strengths in a graphical format. Two common types of nontraditional résumés are web-based and visual.

Web-Based Résumé

When preparing a résumé for your electronic portfolio or personal website, you can save the document as a web page in Microsoft Word. Select the **Save As** option in Word to display the Save As dialog box, and then choose **Web Page** or **Single File Web Page** from the list of options. This creates an HTML version of your résumé document, which will open in a web browser when launched. This type of résumé will look similar to the Word version, as it will retain the formatting that was applied in Word. If you decide to save your résumé as a web page, upload it to your electronic portfolio site so all employment documents are in one convenient place.

Rather than just saving your résumé as a web page, you may choose to create a separate, site-based résumé. This type of résumé serves as its own website

and can be highly designed to include various types of content, such as images, sound clips, and video clips. A job seeker can use a web-based résumé to display his or her design abilities, technical skills, or other talents and experience. For example, a musician can post sound or video clips of past performances directly to his or her résumé website. Similarly, a web developer can include a demo of a program he or she created. There are many free templates available online that can help you get started.

Before you create this type of résumé, conduct research to make sure this format is appropriate for the job you seek. It is a good idea to have both a web-page résumé and résumé website available for potential employers. If you use a web-based résumé, add a link to it in your professional e-mail signature block.

Visual Résumé

A creative way to highlight your résumé is to create a visual résumé. A **visual résumé** is one that presents information in a graphically appealing format. An **infographic résumé** is a visual résumé in which the content is displayed using a combination of words and graphics to present information clearly and quickly. Others can view your information without having to read through many lines of text.

There are many websites that offer templates for visual résumés for free or at a minimal cost. This makes it practical for anyone to create a visually appealing document. No graphic design experience is necessary. Similar to other templates, information can be pulled from a master résumé into a new format using charts, tables, and other graphic elements, as shown in Figure 7-8. By customizing your résumé to be visually appealing, you can gain an edge on the competition. However, it is important to note that most visual résumés look appealing but are not scannable for keywords. Additionally, it may not be appropriate for your industry or desired position. When you post your résumé online, include both the print and visual versions.

Conduct a final check before posting or submitting your résumé to make sure every detail of the résumé is complete. This includes proofreading, running a spell check, and reading each line for sense. Make sure the file is formatted correctly and all other guidelines have been followed. Using the checklist in Figure 7-9 will help you as you finalize the document.

CONNECT TO YOUR ▶ CAREER

Complete 7-6 Nontraditional Résumés, pg 123

FIGURE 7-8

An infographic résumé is a résumé in which the content is displayed using a combination of words and graphics to present information clearly and quickly.

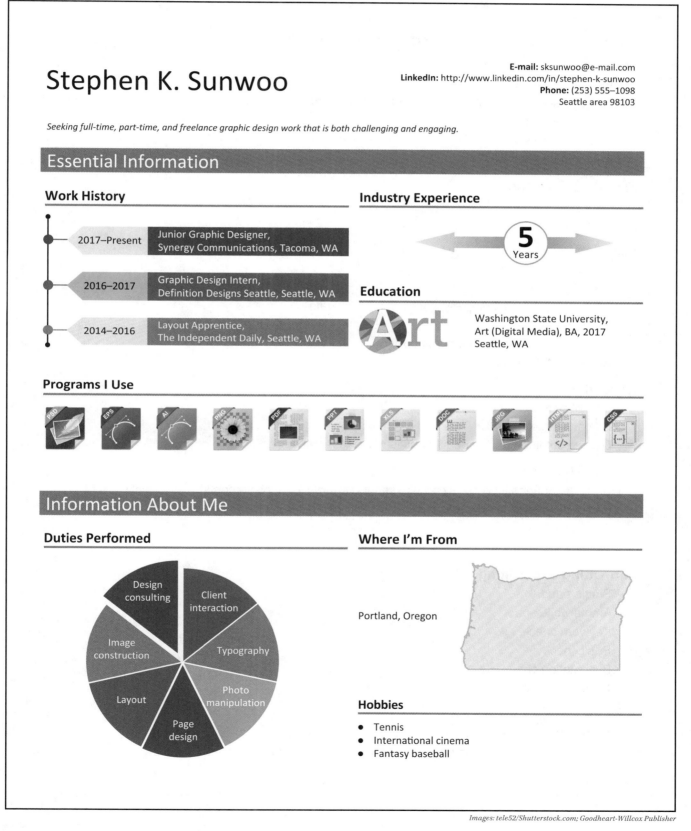

Stephen K. Sunwoo

E-mail: sksunwoo@e-mail.com
LinkedIn: http://www.linkedin.com/in/stephen-k-sunwoo
Phone: (253) 555–1098
Seattle area 98103

Seeking full-time, part-time, and freelance graphic design work that is both challenging and engaging.

Essential Information

Work History

- 2017–Present — Junior Graphic Designer, Synergy Communications, Tacoma, WA
- 2016–2017 — Graphic Design Intern, Definition Designs Seattle, Seattle, WA
- 2014–2016 — Layout Apprentice, The Independent Daily, Seattle, WA

Industry Experience

5 Years

Education

Washington State University, Art (Digital Media), BA, 2017 Seattle, WA

Programs I Use

PSD EPS AI PNG PDF PPT XLS DOC JPG HTML CSS

Information About Me

Duties Performed

Design consulting, Client interaction, Typography, Photo manipulation, Page design, Layout, Image construction

Where I'm From

Portland, Oregon

Hobbies

- Tennis
- International cinema
- Fantasy baseball

Images: tele52/Shutterstock.com; Goodheart-Willcox Publisher

FIGURE 7-9

A checklist of items can be used to confirm the résumé is accurate.

Résumé Checklist

Heading

___ Full, formal name
___ City and state for e-résumés or full address for hard-copy résumés
___ Phone number
___ E-mail address
___ Personal LinkedIn URL

Specific Information

___ Career objective
___ Career profile

Experience

___ Beginning and ending dates of employment
___ Company name
___ General location of company, such as city and state
___ Position held
___ Specific descriptions of work performed
___ Keywords that match the position

Education

___ Official college name
___ City and state
___ Degree obtained or degree title that is in process with expected date of graduation

Optional Information

___ Skills, languages, special accomplishments, awards, or achievements
___ Personal website or blog address
___ E-portfolio link
___ Twitter account name

Formatting and Editing

___ Single page
___ Ample white space
___ Keyword check
___ Spell check
___ Punctuation check
___ Grammar check

Saving

___ Master version of the résumé
___ Customized version of the master résumé for specific job application

Goodheart-Willcox Publisher

Summary

Explain the purpose of a résumé.
The chief purpose of a résumé is to convince a potential employer that a candidate's experiences and skills match the qualifications of the job.

Discuss the importance of keywords.
Keywords are words that specifically relate to the functions of the position for which the employer is hiring. Using keywords in a strategic manner is important, as it can help land an interview. Researching and using keywords that are trending can help better customize a job search.

Identify sections of a résumé.
Résumés have standard sections that employers expect to see. Standard sections include a heading, experience, education, and special skills. A career objective and profile can be included as well.

List three types of résumés.
Three types of résumés include timeline, skills, and combination résumés.

List three formats that can be used to resave a master résumé.
A master copy of a résumé should be saved as a Word document. Using the master document, the file can be saved as a PDF or plain text file, as opposed to a DOC or DOCX file.

Discuss two examples of a nontraditional résumé.
Web-based résumés can be created by saving a master résumé file as a web page instead of a Microsoft Word document or through the use of online templates. Visual résumés can also be created using online templates, or a person can use an original design.

Glossary Terms

career objective	infographic résumé	timeline résumé
career profile	résumé	trending
heading	skills résumé	visual résumé

Review

1. Explain the purpose of a résumé.

2. What is a résumé template? What are the advantages to using one?

3. Discuss the importance of keywords.

4. Describe the relationship between trending topics and keywords.

5. What is the function of ADT software?

6. Identify and describe sections of a résumé.

7. List and describe three types of résumés.

8. List three formats that can be used to resave a master résumé.

9. List and describe two examples of a nontraditional résumé.

10. Explain the benefit of a web-based résumé.

Application

1. What does your résumé suggest about who you are and how you could be an asset as an employee?

2. Locate and read three job advertisements. Imagine you are applying for each job. Highlight the keywords in each advertisement and draft one skills section of a résumé that could be submitted for each job.

3. Explain the relevance or importance of trending searches in your desired industry.

4. How do you plan to customize your résumé for different job applications? Explain how customizing your résumé for each application is impacted by your chosen career field.

5. Which section of your résumé is the most challenging to write? Why?

6. A career objective is a brief statement that explains an individual's career goals to an employer. Write your career objective.

7. A career profile details an individual's accomplishments, skills, and current career level. List information you would include in your career profile.

8. Which résumé format is best suited to your background and qualifications? Describe how you would modify this version of your résumé to use a different format.

9. A plain text résumé is one that is stripped of formatting, such as bullet points or font sizes. This can make a résumé difficult to read. What can you do to your existing plain text résumé to ensure it will be easy to read despite not having formatting options?

10. Explain the relevance nontraditional résumés have in your industry.

Workplace Connection

7-1 Résumé Templates

Which résumé type will you use when applying for a position—timeline, skills, or combination? Explain how you made your decision.

Conduct an Internet search using the phrase *résumé templates*. Record several URLs of templates you would consider using.

URL #1:

URL #2:

URL #3:

URL #4:

Which template do you prefer? Why?

How would you adapt this template to better fit your résumé needs?

7-2 Résumé Keywords

Research keywords that are used in your preferred industry or career field. Review job advertisements, conduct an Internet search, or use any other resources that will help you create a list of the top ten keywords you can use in your résumé.

1.

2.

3.

4.

5.

6.

7.

8.

9.

10.

Consider your top ten keywords. Why do you think these are important to use in your résumé?

7-3 Résumé Heading, Objective, and Profile

Create two headings that you might use for your personal résumé. One heading could be used for print résumés, the other for an electronically submitted résumé. Later, you will transfer this information to your résumé.

Heading for print resume:

Heading for electronic resume:

Write a career objective for your résumé. Use the information provided in the chapter as a guide. You will transfer this information to your résumé.

Create a career profile for your résumé. You will transfer this information to your résumé.

7-4 Résumé Experience, Education, and Special Skills

Create a list of your work experience that you want a potential employer to see. Make sure it is accurate, complete, and follows the guidelines in the chapter.

List your education history to be included on your résumé. Put the most recent information first.

Make a list of special skills you will include on your résumé.

7-5 Master Résumé

Create a master résumé using the drafts from Workplace Connection activities 7-3 and 7-4. Assume this is a resume that will be submitted electronically and will not include a detailed home address. When you are finished, run a spell check and proofread the document. Ensure that the master résumé is saved as a Word document.

1. Save your Word document as *FirstnameLastname*_MasterResume.docx (e.g., JohnSmith_MasterResume.docx)
2. Save the master résumé file as a plain text document.
3. Return to the Word version of the master résumé file and save it as a PDF document.
4. Return to the Word version of the master résumé file and save it as a web-page document.

7-6 Nontraditional Résumés

Conduct an Internet search using the phrases *visual résumés* and *infographic résumés*. Compare the examples you found. Which résumé do you prefer? Why?

Next, create your own visual or infographic résumé. Use the information in your master résumé to create this new version. Save your document as *FirstnameLastname*_InfoResume.docx (e.g., JohnSmith_InfoResume.docx)

Consider the aspect of posting your résumé to sites such as Twitter that limit the number of characters you can use per post. How does this affect the information you plan to include in your résumé?

Create a version of your résumé that contains 140 characters or fewer that would be acceptable to post to your Twitter page. Save your document as *FirstnameLastname*_TwitterResume.docx (e.g., JohnSmith_TwitterResume.docx)

8 Cover Letters

Outcomes

1 **Explain** the purpose of a cover letter.

2 **Identify** sections of a cover letter.

3 **Cite** three methods of cover letter submission.

CONNECT TO YOUR CAREER

Workplace Connection

8-1   Cover Letter Template

8-2   Master Cover Letter

OVERVIEW

Writing a cover letter is an important part of the application process. The goal is to convince an employer that you are the best person for the position. A cover letter highlights your abilities while reinforcing your desire to work for the company. More importantly, it is an opportunity to market yourself and convince the reader to grant you an interview.

A sound cover letter presents your personal qualifications in a way that attests to your ability to be a good employee. It shows that you have a genuine interest in the company as well as the position. Once you have captured the reader's attention with your cover letter, make it count. Create an impression that will ensure an invitation to interview.

Cover Letter

A **cover letter** is formal written communication that accompanies a résumé or a job application to introduce an applicant and express his or her interest in a position. It provides an explanation of why you are the best candidate for the job. It must create an immediate, positive impression of your persuasive communication skills. Effective cover letters are brief, no longer than one page, and written in a way that invites and encourages potential employers to read your résumé. If your letter is ineffective, you will not be considered a viable candidate.

A cover letter is about you and your interest in the company and job for which you are applying. Conduct research about the company and use your findings to support your interest in working there. A compelling cover letter succinctly demonstrates to an employer that you would be an asset to the company.

Consider using a template to get the writing process started. Similar to a résumé template, a cover letter template is a pre-formatted, word-processing document that contains a standard layout with adequate margins of white space. Use of a template will establish a balanced look that can be customized for your personal needs rather than starting from scratch.

You may need to create different types of cover letters during the course of the job-search process. The type of letter you write depends on how you learned about the position for which you are applying. Three basic types of cover letters typically used include application, networking, and inquiry.

An **application cover letter** is a letter used to apply for and provide personal qualifications for a position that has been posted by an employer. The goal of this type of letter is to convince someone in the company to schedule an interview with you. It generally begins with an opening statement in which you introduce yourself and list the specific position for which you are applying. This statement can also include how you learned of the opening. The following is an example of an opening paragraph for an application cover letter:

> My name is Janet Hernandez, and I was excited to learn of the opening of a sales position in your company. I read the job posting on your website and would like to offer my résumé for consideration.

A **networking cover letter** is a letter that introduces an applicant noting that a person in his or her network recommended he or she apply for the position. Ideally, a hiring manager reading this letter would recognize the person referenced in the letter and contact the applicant for more information.

The opening statement for this type of letter is similar to that of an application cover letter, but includes the name of person who recommended you apply for the job. An example of an opening statement for a networking cover letter is as follows:

> My name is Janet Hernandez, and I recently spoke to Ms. Patty Williams who suggested I forward my résumé to you for consideration in the open sales position in your company.

An **inquiry cover letter** is a letter written to learn if any potential positions are available for which the job seeker would like to be considered. Sending this type of letter is also known as *prospecting*. Generally, these letters are written for positions that have not been posted publicly. In this letter, the applicant is asking to be considered for a specific position if an opening becomes available. The hope is that the company will keep the cover letter and résumé on file for future opportunities.

By default, the opening statement for an inquiry cover letter is different from that of an application or networking letter. This is because there is no specific job opening or person referenced. Instead, the goal is to explain the type of position for which you are looking and offer your résumé for consideration in any potential openings. It should also include a brief summary of how you retrieved contact information for the company. The following is an example of an opening paragraph of an inquiry cover letter:

> My name is Janet Hernandez, and I am currently seeking employment in a sales position at a reputable company such as yours. I located your contact information through research of the industry, and I would like to provide you with my résumé for future consideration of openings that may become available.

The Best App for That

Google Drive

Google Drive is a cloud-based file storage service offered by Google to Google account holders. Google Drive allows users to store, synchronize, and share files across devices and platforms. The app enables you to store résumés, cover letters, portfolio materials, and other important employment documentation in your Drive. Each file is available on your mobile device when you are away from your computer and need it. Account holders are given 15 gigabytes of free storage with the option of purchasing additional storage plans.

FIGURE 8-1

A cover letter is formal written communication that accompanies a résumé or a job application to introduce the applicant and express interest in a position.

Best Practices for Writing Cover Letters	
Do...	**Do Not...**
customize each cover letter so that it is unique.	use the same cover letter for each job for which you apply.
include the exact title of the position and job posting number, if included, for which you are applying.	omit the position name and job posting number, if included, of the job for which you are applying.
compose a professional, well-written cover letter that will resonate with the reader.	compose a hastily written letter because you assume that the reader will understand your intent.
use Standard English.	use informal language, slang, jargon, or texting language.
explain why you are a good fit for the company because you are regarded as a team player.	omit skills that represent why people would describe you as a team player.
add job keywords in the cover letter from the job posting.	omit keywords from the job posting.
explain why you are applying for the job.	omit the reason you are applying for the job.
summarize skills and talents you can bring to the company.	omit your skills and talents that demonstrate you are a qualified professional.
add personal contact information.	omit contact information.
run spell check and proofread the letter.	submit before running spell check and proofreading carefully.
add a cursive signature to the cover letter.	print or key your signature.
assume that the employer will read all submitted letters.	assume that the employer will ignore your letter.

Goodheart-Willcox Publisher

Cover letters are dynamic. The information in each version of the letter changes slightly to match specific job requirements. It is a good practice to create one foundational letter and save it as a master document, similar to creating a master résumé. This document can later be modified each time a résumé or a job application is submitted. Figure 8-1 provides examples of best practices to consider when making your cover letter.

CONNECT TO YOUR ▶ CAREER

Complete 8-1 Cover Letter Template, pg 138

Parts of a Cover Letter

A cover letter includes the following sections, as shown in Figure 8-2:
- heading
- date
- inside address
- greeting
- introduction
- body
- complimentary close

Employers expect these sections to be included in every letter that is submitted from a job applicant. Not having the appropriate sections can appear unprofessional and result in a cover letter going unread.

FIGURE 8-2

Cover letters are dynamic and should be changed as needed to match specific job requirements.

Peter Jesse Owosu

1006 Mountain View Parkway, San Diego, CA 91932

(619) 555–4023 • pjowosu@e-mail.com • www.linkedin.com/in/peter-jesse-owosu

September 24, 20--

Susan Taylor
Standard Manufacturing Company
553 Cleveland Street
San Diego, CA 91911

Dear Ms. Taylor:

Marie Franklin at Dynamics Supply Company informed me that you have a position open for a project coordinator. After reviewing the job description and requirements, it was clear that my experience and skills are a perfect match for this open position. My degree and work experience have focused on communication and project management. A position as project coordinator is the ideal job opportunity for which I am seeking. I help companies make the most of their talent by using proven, systematic project coordinator methods.

As a person who is known for organization and problem solving, I am able to set achievable goals and complete projects on schedule. My reputation for following up on unresolved issues and working well with clients has helped me succeed in project management. Being results-oriented leads me to success.

Please find my résumé enclosed with this communication. I would appreciate an interview to discuss this position. Please contact me at your convenience at the phone number or e-mail above. I look forward to the opportunity of meeting with you for an interview for this position.

Sincerely,

Peter Jesse Owosu

Peter Jesse Owosu

Enclosure

Heading

A cover letter includes a heading that states your contact information. The contact information in the heading should match the contact information found in your résumé. The heading should be formatted so that it looks similar to letterhead, but with simpler elements.

Date and Inside Address

Next, the date the letter is being written is keyed followed by the inside address. The *inside address* is the address of the person receiving the letter. It includes the recipient's name, title, company, and mailing address.

Greeting

Every cover letter should open with a formal greeting. A formal greeting begins with "Dear" followed by "Mr." or "Ms." and the last name of your contact. Begin the letter with "Dear Sir or Madam" or "Dear Hiring Team" if you do not have a contact name. Avoid using "To Whom it May Concern," as it is generally perceived as impersonal.

Introduction

Begin a cover letter with a direct opening paragraph that explains exactly why you are sending the communication. For example, "I am applying for the position of hotel concierge." In the next sentence, state how you heard about the available position. Indicate if you learned about the position from an instructor, for example. Next, add a sentence that describes your enthusiasm and desire to hold this position. If you have created a personal brand statement, incorporate it in this paragraph. The following is a sample cover letter introduction with a personal brand statement as the closing line:

> I am applying for the position of hotel concierge at your company. I saw your ad for this position on your corporate website. I am a customer-first people person who interacts with guests successfully and ensures their comfort at all times during their stay. Whether providing recommendations for restaurants, entertainment, or transportation, the key is to create positive interaction. My passion is to guide and serve.

Social Media Slipup

A young woman recently graduated with a teaching degree in history. Social studies positions are hard to find in her rural community, so she sent applications to every school system within a 250-mile radius. Interviews were sparse, so she sought advice from her college advisor for ideas on how to get the attention of hiring managers. Her counselor suggested she join a networking group where she could meet other professionals and learn more about school systems and their hiring processes.

The aspiring educator took the advice and joined the student chapter of a local teachers' association. At her first meeting, she learned a valuable piece of information about networking with other educators. A common thread of advice was to create social media accounts to establish an online presence.

wavebreakmedia/Shutterstock.com

She created a LinkedIn account as well as a Facebook account. Following suggested guidelines for creating professional profiles, she posted information that highlighted her teaching degree and career goals. She polished her résumé and cover letters and started the application process again. This time, she included URLs for her social media accounts on her documents.

Within a matter of days, she received her first invitation to interview at a school system in her county. She thought it went well and was sure she would be called back for a second interview. Days went by, and no calls were received. Finally, her impatience got the best of her, and she wrote on her Facebook page, "Just had a fake job interview with Perry County School District."

That one careless statement likely changed her future. The derogatory comment, mention of the school system, and her display of attitude was a reflection of poor decision making and immaturity. The job-search process can take time. Slow response from an employer does not mean you are out of the running for an opportunity.

Body

The body is the longest part of the letter. Its purpose is to demonstrate that you meet or exceed the qualifications of the job. Do not restate the information in your résumé. Instead, explain why you are qualified for the position. Use pertinent keywords from the job requirements to show the strength of your qualifications. This will help demonstrate why you are a good, long-term fit for the company.

There are two ways the body of a cover letter can be written. You can write it in paragraph form, as shown in Figure 8-2, or you can use a bulleted list of the employer's requirements followed by a list of your matching qualifications, as shown in Figure 8-3. If space permits, it is acceptable to place the bulleted list in two columns rather than one column, as shown in Figure 8-4.

It is expected that you will ask for an interview in the body of your cover letter. In the closing paragraph, request an opportunity to discuss your qualifications with the reader in a sincere and confident statement. State when you are available, and express your eagerness and anticipation to hear from the employer.

Complimentary Close

The **complimentary close** is the sign-off for the letter. Examples include *Sincerely yours*, *Respectfully*, and *Cordially*. Only the first word is capitalized.

The complimentary close is followed by the signature block, which includes your name and title. Add a signature to your cover letter above your keyed name. It is preferable to have a cursive signature rather than one that has been keyed. *Cursive* is a style of handwriting in which each letter of a word is joined to the letters adjacent to it. It is more formal than printing your name.

Examples of ways to add a cursive signature to your cover letter include:

- print and sign the letter then scan the letter into the computer in a PDF file
- sign a blank sheet of paper, scan the signature into the computer, or take a photo of the signature and e-mail it to yourself, open the image, and insert it into the letter's signature area, resizing as needed
- save your cover letter as a PDF file, and add a cursive signature through the Fill & Sign pane
- use a decorative, cursive font in lieu of a hand-signed signature

CONNECT TO YOUR CAREER

Complete 8-2 Master Cover Letter, pg 138

Cover Letter Submission

Before submitting a cover letter, it is important to do one final review for accuracy. Your letter should be perfect without grammar, punctuation, or spelling errors. The body should be keyed in a font that is professional and easy to read. Microsoft Word's default font, Calibri, is recommended. The font size should be kept between 11 and 12 points. A font smaller than 11 points will be difficult to read, and a font larger than 12 points will look too aggressive. Margins should be set to 1 inch on all sides, but if your cover letter is short, consider using 1 1/2-inch margins. The checklist in Figure 8-5 will help you as you finalize the document.

Once perfected, there is a variety of ways to submit a cover letter to apply for a position. The most common methods are submitting by e-mail, uploading to a job board, or submitting a hard copy. A cover letter should be submitted simultaneously with your résumé.

Submit by E-mail

When submitting a cover letter and résumé via e-mail, use your professional e-mail account. Include a brief, professional, and clear subject line. The proper way to state the subject is to use your last name, the words "application for," followed by the title of the position. The following is a sample of a subject line:

| Cortez Application for Front Desk Concierge

When creating a subject line, it is important to avoid these common mistakes:

- omitting the subject line entirely
- using exclamation points
- using all caps
- creating a subject line that is confusing or generic
- using a lengthy subject line that becomes truncated

FIGURE 8-3

The body of a cover letter can include paragraphs as well as bulleted lists.

Jalia Cortez
111 First Street, Redwood City, CA 94061
(650) 555–1234 • jcortez@e-mail.com • www.linkedin.com/in/jalia-cortez

---

November 30, 20--

Human Resources
Great Corporation
12344 Main Street
Redwood City, CA 94061

Dear Sir or Madam:

I am applying for the position of hotel concierge at your company. I saw your ad for this position on your corporate website. As a catalyst for positive interaction, I have a history of engaging people so that they are comfortable. A concierge has the responsibility to make a difference for guests in the hotel. Whether providing recommendations for restaurants, entertainment, or transportation, the key is to create positive interaction. My passion is to guide and to serve.

I have reviewed the qualifications posted for this position. I am certain that my skills and talents match the requirements for which you are looking.

Your Requirements:
- Proven professional with excellent verbal communications skills
- Outgoing personality
- Ability to create and edit written materials
- Self-motivated
- Ability to multi-task

My Qualifications:
- Appointed lead speaker for staff meetings held each month
- Recognized as employee of the month
- Researched and edited professional reports
- Initiated a program that highlights student accomplishments
- Expanded contacts with key people at local businesses by 20 percent

Working with the guests at a well-known hotel is appealing and challenging. I would appreciate an opportunity to discuss this position with you. My résumé is attached for your review. I will follow up with an e-mail to request an appointment. Thank you for your time and consideration.

Sincerely,

Jalia Cortez

Jalia Cortez

Enclosure

The body of a cover letter can be two columns to help illustrate a candidate's qualifications.

Jalia Cortez

111 First Street, Redwood City, CA 94061

(650) 555–1234 • jcortez@e-mail.com • www.linkedin.com/in/jalia-cortez

November 30, 20--

Human Resources
Great Corporation
12344 Main Street
Redwood City, CA 94061

Dear Sir or Madam:

I am applying for the position of hotel concierge at your company. I saw your ad for this position on your corporate website. As a catalyst for positive interaction, I have a history of engaging people so that they are comfortable. A concierge has the responsibility to make a difference for guests in the hotel. Whether providing recommendations for restaurants, entertainment, or transportation, the key is to create positive interaction. My passion is to guide and to serve.

I have reviewed the qualifications posted for this position. I am certain that my skills and talents match the requirements for which you are looking.

Your Requirements:	**My Qualifications:**
Proven professional with excellent verbal communications skills	Appointed lead speaker for staff meetings held each month
Outgoing personality	Recognized as employee of the month
Ability to create and edit written materials	Researched and edited professional reports
Self-motivated	Initiated a program that highlights student accomplishments
Ability to multitask	Expanded contacts with key people at local businesses by 20 percent

Working with the guests at a well-known hotel is appealing and challenging. I would appreciate an opportunity to discuss this position with you. My résumé is attached for your review. I will follow up with an e-mail to request an appointment. Thank you for your time and consideration.

Sincerely,

Jalia Cortez

Jalia Cortez

Enclosure

FIGURE 8-5

A checklist of items can be used to confirm the cover letter is accurate.

Cover Letter Checklist

Heading
____ Included full name
____ Stated mailing address
____ Included phone number
____ Added e-mail address
____ Added applicable URLs

Date and Inside Address
____ Used correct date
____ Included recipient's name, title, company, and mailing address

Greeting
____ Added formal greeting
____ Included name of contact if known

Introduction
____ Stated reason for sending the communication
____ Included how you heard about the position
____ Showed enthusiasm for position
____ Used personal brand statement

Body
____ Demonstrated qualifications for this position
____ Displayed career successes
____ Used job requirement keywords
____ Emphasized accomplishments

Closing Paragraph
____ Requested an interview
____ Stated availability
____ Included contact information

General
____ Customized for this position
____ Limited to one page
____ Formatted attractively and professionally
____ Used professional tone throughout
____ Proofread and spell-checked
____ Reviewed by instructor or peer
____ Printed on high-quality white paper

Goodheart-Willcox Publisher

The formal content in the body of the e-mail is comprised of the body of your print letter. As with other professional correspondence, it is a good idea to include your e-mail signature block after the complimentary close. A well-written and well-formatted cover letter in an e-mail is shown in Figure 8-6.

You may opt to attach a cover letter to your e-mail rather than include it in the body of the message. However, not all employers open attachments due to potential exposure to malware. If you choose to attach it, state the purpose of the attachment and reference it in the body of your e-mail message. Save the letter as a PDF file before attaching it to the e-mail.

Some e-mail software includes the option to mark an e-mail as *priority*. You can use this option if you are sending your résumé and cover letter immediately before the submission process is scheduled to close. A high-priority e-mail also indicates that the sender would like the recipient to open the e-mail shortly after it is received.

Upload to an Online Job Board

You may have an opportunity to apply for a position through an online job board. An **online job board** is a website that hosts job postings for employers and allows applicants to apply for jobs seamlessly.

FIGURE 8-6

A cover letter can be submitted as an e-mail and should be properly formatted.

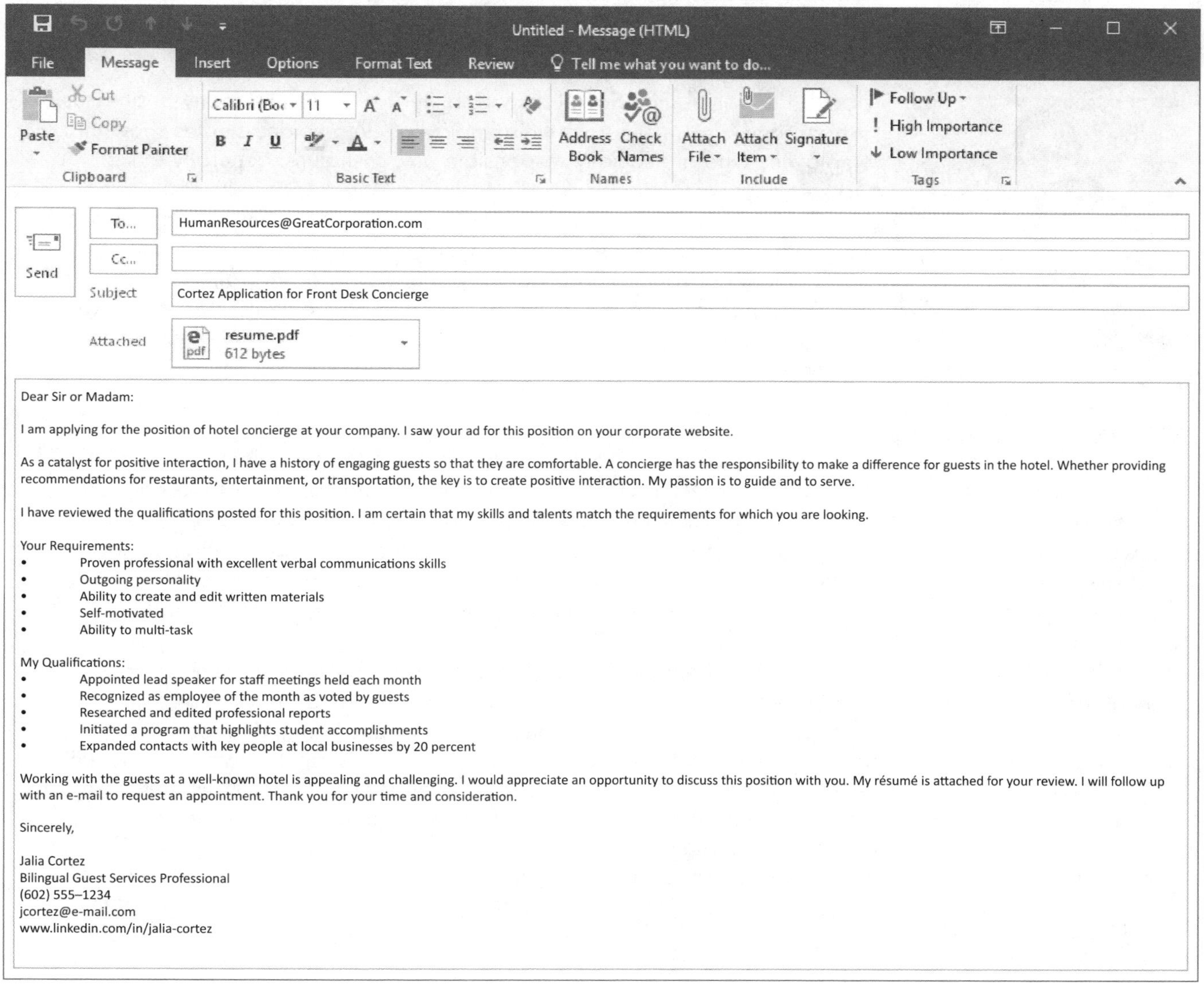

To: HumanResources@GreatCorporation.com

Subject: Cortez Application for Front Desk Concierge

Attached: resume.pdf 612 bytes

Dear Sir or Madam:

I am applying for the position of hotel concierge at your company. I saw your ad for this position on your corporate website.

As a catalyst for positive interaction, I have a history of engaging guests so that they are comfortable. A concierge has the responsibility to make a difference for guests in the hotel. Whether providing recommendations for restaurants, entertainment, or transportation, the key is to create positive interaction. My passion is to guide and to serve.

I have reviewed the qualifications posted for this position. I am certain that my skills and talents match the requirements for which you are looking.

Your Requirements:
- Proven professional with excellent verbal communications skills
- Outgoing personality
- Ability to create and edit written materials
- Self-motivated
- Ability to multi-task

My Qualifications:
- Appointed lead speaker for staff meetings held each month
- Recognized as employee of the month as voted by guests
- Researched and edited professional reports
- Initiated a program that highlights student accomplishments
- Expanded contacts with key people at local businesses by 20 percent

Working with the guests at a well-known hotel is appealing and challenging. I would appreciate an opportunity to discuss this position with you. My résumé is attached for your review. I will follow up with an e-mail to request an appointment. Thank you for your time and consideration.

Sincerely,

Jalia Cortez
Bilingual Guest Services Professional
(602) 555–1234
jcortez@e-mail.com
www.linkedin.com/in/jalia-cortez

Goodheart-Willcox Publisher

If you are applying through a job board, you may be required to upload your résumé and cut and paste your cover letter into a web form. The website will give directions regarding how to complete these tasks. Always follow the directions as specified. It may be necessary to use plain text for your cover letter as the form may omit formatting. In this case, it is better to be safe and use unformatted text.

Submit a Hard Copy

Some employers require submission of a printed cover letter and résumé to be considered for a position. Hard copies should be printed on high-quality white paper. The documents should not be stapled together but may be secured with a paper clip. The documents should be placed, unfolded, into a folder or large manila envelope with the intended recipient's name clearly indicated on the outside. If you are mailing the documents, consider taking the manila envelope containing the documents to the post office to have it weighed so the appropriate amount of postage can be affixed to the package.

Once you secure an interview, take copies of your documents to present to the interviewer. In this case, it is not necessary to put the interviewer's name on the outside of the folder or envelope, though it *is* necessary to include your own. Be prepared with an adequate number of documents for each person who may be part of the interview team. If you are unsure of how many copies to make, it is appropriate to call the company ahead of time and ask how many people with whom you will be meeting.

Career Portfolio

mangostock/Shutterstock.com

Social Responsibility. Social responsibility is a cause that many businesses support and encourage from their employees. Workplace studies show that employees who are socially responsible are, by nature, generally ethical workers, loyal employees, and productive in their responsibilities.

Social responsibility can be demonstrated in many ways, and you can start with activities at your current job. For example, you may have organized a green team at your company to initiate a recycling program. Or you may have participated in a campaign to "turn off the lights" and conserve energy for your employer. Documentation of these activities reflects social responsibility.

Participating in community services is an example of social responsibility. Evidence of community service can sometimes be criteria that employers use when vetting potential job candidates. Serving the community shows that a candidate is well rounded, socially aware, and capable of working with others. For some individuals seeking a job, volunteer work could substitute for actual paid employment. Showing that you spent regular hours supporting a social cause is as valuable, in some situations, as paid work experience. By including evidence of community service or other socially responsible activities, a candidate can attract the attention of a person reviewing job applicants and move up on the list of potential interviewees.

If you have participated in an activity that reflects social responsibility, consider creating a video that informs viewers about it. Suppose you volunteer with a group that helps repair homes for elderly homeowners. The video could show scenes from the worksites and comments from the residents.

1. Create a word-processing document that lists social responsibility projects in which you have taken part as an employee at your company. Use the heading "Employer Service Projects" on the document along with your name. List the name of the programs, date(s) of service, and activities that you performed. If you received an award related to this service, mention it here.
2. Create a word-processing document that lists service projects or volunteer activities in which you have taken part. Use the heading "Community Service" on the document along with your name. List the name of the organization or person you helped, date(s) of service, and activities that you performed.

Summary

 Explain the purpose of a cover letter.
The purpose of a cover letter is to provide an explanation of why a person is the best candidate for a job and create an immediate, positive impression of his or her persuasive communication skills. There are three basic types of cover letters: application, networking, and inquiry cover letters.

 Identify sections of a cover letter.
Cover letters include a heading, date, inside address, greeting, introduction, body, and complimentary close.

Cite three methods of cover letter submission.
When applying for a position, cover letters may be submitted by e-mail, uploaded to a job board, or delivered as a hard copy.

Glossary Terms

application cover letter	cover letter	networking cover letter
complimentary close	inquiry cover letter	online job board

Review

1. What is the purpose of a cover letter?

2. List elements of a compelling cover letter.

3. Identify and describe the goals of each type of cover letter.

4. What is *prospecting*?

5. Identify and describe sections of a cover letter.

6. What type of information should be included in the inside address of a cover letter?

7. Why is the phrase *To Whom it May Concern* not recommended for the greeting of a cover letter?

8. What should be included in the closing paragraph of a cover letter?

9. Describe three methods to submit a cover letter to apply for a position.

10. Some employers will require submission of a hard copy of a cover letter and résumé to be considered for a position. How should these documents be organized when delivering them to an employer?

Application

1. A cover letter describes why you would be an asset to an employer. Write a paragraph that highlights your most important work and personal qualities that would make you an asset to an employer.

2. How do you determine which information is best suited for your cover letter and which information is best suited for your résumé?

3. Your cover letter should sell you as a professional and potential employee but should not be arrogant or conceited. How would you write your cover letter to emphasize your strengths while avoiding arrogance and conceit?

4. When writing the body portion of a cover letter, you can use organize your letter in paragraphs, bulleted lists, or with two columns. Explain which method you think is most effective for your desired industry and why.

5. Review the Cover Letter Best Practices table in Figure 8-1. How would you modify this checklist for your personal job-search process?

6. Read the cover letter in Figure 8-2. If you were a hiring manager, what questions would you have for this person after reading it?

7. Businesses want to hire employees who are excited to come to work. How effective do you think a cover letter is at conveying a person's excitement to work?

8. Each person has his or her own style of closing letters. Examples of complimentary closes include Sincerely yours, Yours truly, and Respectfully. What closing do you anticipate using that represents who you are and your brand?

9. Some younger job seekers print their names rather than using cursive. What is your opinion of printing a signature instead of using cursive when a professional document is being signed?

10. A potential employer will likely formulate his or her first impression of you based on your cover letter. As the adage goes, you will not have a second chance to make a first impression. What steps will you take while writing your cover letter to ensure a positive first impression is made?

CONNECT TO YOUR CAREER
Workplace Connection

8-1 Cover Letter Template

Conduct an Internet search using the phrase *cover letter template*. Record several URLs of templates you would consider using in the future.

URL #1:

URL #2:

URL #3:

URL #4:

Which template do you prefer? Why?

8-2 Master Cover Letter

Using the Internet or other source, search for and select an advertisement for a position that interests you. In the space that follows, record the position title, name of the company, name of the contact person, and mailing address.

Position Title:

Company Name:

Contact Person:

Mailing Address:

In the space that follows, write the first draft of each component of an *application cover letter*. Keep it succinct and to the point. Remember to use keywords as you describe your qualifications. Draft the introduction and the body. In the closing paragraph, remember to request the opportunity for an interview.

Introduction:

Body:

Closing:

Next, revise your draft letter to create a cover letter in final form. Use the template you selected in Activity 8-1. Run a spell check and proofread the document. When you are finished, save your document as *FirstnameLastname*_CoverLetter.docx (e.g., JohnSmith_CoverLetter.docx). Alternatively, you may choose to add an additional identifier to the name such as the company name or month to keep track of where or when you are sending letters. (e.g., JohnSmith_CoverLetter_BatesCo.docx)

1. Save the master cover letter as a plain text document.

2. Return to the Word version of the master cover letter file, and save it as a PDF document.

3. Return to the Word version of the master cover letter file, and save it as a web-page document.

Outcomes

1. **Explain** how to complete a job application.
2. **Describe** the process of applying for a job in person.
3. **Describe** the process of applying for a job online.
4. **Define** Sunday Evening Plan.
5. **Explain** methods for managing the application process.
6. **Define** a job-tracking spreadsheet.

CONNECT TO YOUR CAREER

Workplace Connection

9-1 Job Application
9-2 Job-Search Websites
9-3 Job-Tracking Spreadsheet

OVERVIEW

The job application process does not stop with the résumé and cover letter. You will likely be asked to complete a formal job application form. This form provides information the employer needs during and after the employment process. The application may be a hard copy or online form. Both require the same amount of preparation and care when completing them.

In some cases, you may apply for a job in person. However, you are likely to apply for a job online—one that you might find on a job list or a job board. Both job-search websites and online job boards provide current, up-to-date job advertisements. You can make these job-search resources work for you by adopting a Sunday Evening Plan. This plan involves updating your application documents every week. In addition, managing and organizing the application process will help ease your job search.

Job Applications

A résumé and cover letter are not the only documents a person needs when applying for a job. At some point, most companies require a completed job application. A **job application** is a form used by employers to gain more information about a person applying for a job. A portion of a sample application is shown in Figure 9-1.

A job application requires personal information, names and addresses of the schools you have attended, and degrees earned. Addresses of your previous employers, supervisors' names, and contact information will also be requested. Some applications require additional information beyond your work experience. Be truthful when answering each question, and do not leave any lines blank. If any requested information is not applicable to you, write "N/A" in the space. You may also be asked for the names and contact information for professional references.

The application may contain a line inquiring as to whether previous employers may be contacted. If a former supervisor is no longer employed where you worked, state that the person is no longer with the company and provide contact information for the human resources department.

After the job application is complete, proofread it and compare it with your résumé. If either document contains conflicting information, edit the documents so they match.

CONNECT TO YOUR CAREER

Complete 9-1 Job Application, pg 152

Applying for Jobs in Person

It is not always necessary to wait for a business to advertise employment opportunities. For some businesses, such as retail, it is appropriate to visit and ask for a job application. Some businesses request that applicants take an application with them and return it when it is complete.

If you do not know the employment process of the particular business you plan to target, prepare to stay on-site to complete the application. Bring a quality blue or black pen with you so you will not have to ask to borrow one. Although requesting and completing an application on-site is not a formal interview, dress professionally.

Before your visit, customize a résumé and an inquiry cover letter that best matches the business to which you are applying. Create a separate document that clearly lists professional references and their respective contact information. Print each document and place in a folder or envelope that you can leave with the human-resources manager. If applicable, bring a copy of your portfolio to leave behind.

After you complete the application, sign and date the form. Assemble the application, cover letter, résumé, and list of references in order, and place them in the envelope or folder you brought with you. Make a note in your mobile device that includes the name of the employer and person who took your documents, or to whom you mailed them, along with the date of mailing.

If you have not heard from the company or manager within one week of applying, it is appropriate to call and follow up regarding the application you submitted. From that point, wait for the business to contact you.

While you are waiting, continue applying for as many jobs for which you are qualified. The process of connecting to your career is ongoing. Always apply for jobs and only cease when you are employed.

Searching and Applying for Jobs Online

Many companies prefer candidates complete applications online. The online-application process is similar to the paper-based method. The process of applying for employment online starts with reading and sorting through available job postings. After finding an employment opportunity that fits your skills and desires, submit an electronic application and necessary employment documents.

Searching for Jobs Online

One way to find available openings is by using a job-search website. A **job-search website** is a website on which multiple employers post employment opportunities on a daily basis. These sites allow users to view openings anywhere in the world. LinkedIn, Twitter, and Craigslist are examples of hosted job-search websites. For the most part, using these sites is free, as they are intended for public viewing. In some cases, such as Craigslist, users are not required to register or create a username or password to take advantage of these sites. However, some sites, such as LinkedIn and Twitter, do require people to register for an account. There are two basic types of job-search websites: aggregate job boards and non-aggregate job boards.

FIGURE 9-1

A job application is a form used by employers to gain more information about a person applying for a job.

Job Application

Personal Information

Last Name		First Name	Middle Initial
Address	City	State	Zip

How long at present address?	Phone Number

What date will you be available for work?

Type of employment desired:

_____ Full-time only   _____ Part-time only   _____ Full- or part-time

If hired, can you furnish proof that you are legally entitled to work in the United States?

If hired, can you furnish proof of age?

What position are you applying for?	What are your salary requirements?

Hours you will be available to work:

Have you ever been convicted of a felony?

If yes, please explain:

The XYZ Company is a drug-free employer and you will be required to pass a drug screening as a condition of employment. I understand and agree to participate in testing. (   ) initials

Educational Information

Name and Address of School	Course of Study	Diploma or Degree
High School		
College Education		
Graduate Education		
Other Education/ Training		

The Best App for That

Rake

The job-search process can take a long time. As you submit applications, it will be important to keep track of the details. *Rake* is an app that lets you save job postings from job boards, such as Glassdoor, Indeed, and LinkedIn. In addition, it enables you to prepare job applications and stay current on the jobs for which you apply. You can also set follow-up reminders for tasks that need to be completed and prepare materials you might need for the application process. Currently, the Rake app is only available on Apple devices.

Aggregate Job Board

An *aggregate job board* is a job-search website that collects data from multiple online sources and combines the results. Think of this type of job-search website as a search engine like Google. A search query is entered, and the website searches across the Internet for items matching it. Instead of a user searching through job boards individually, an aggregate job board collects and compiles posted openings onto one site. Examples include Indeed.com and SimplyHired.com.

Often, the job listing will include where the original advertisement for the position was posted. The advertisement may have been a local newspaper, individual job board, or other sources. You can go to the original site of the advertisement and apply there. Alternatively, if you prefer, you may apply for employment directly from the aggregate site. However, you may be required to establish an account in order to do so.

Non-Aggregate Job Board

A *non-aggregate job board* is a website that hosts job postings for employers and allows applicants to apply for them seamlessly. The main difference between aggregate and non-aggregate job boards is that non-aggregate boards list only what was posted to them by employers; they do not search the Internet for additional posts. Examples of online job boards are Monster.com and CareerBuilder.com.

You may be required to register an account and profile. After an account and profile information are completed, it is important to customize the account and privacy settings to reflect your preferences. Be certain that you understand the options before making your decision as this may limit the employers or recruiters who have access to your information. Once an account is created, some online job boards invite users to upload and store cover letters and résumés. These sites offer a one-click method, whereby an applicant's documents are forwarded by the site directly to the employer or hiring agent.

Tips for the Online Job Search

Read online job postings carefully. Keep in mind that the *required* qualifications must be met, but you do not necessarily have to meet all of the *desired* qualifications. A benchmark should be set to help you determine if you have a real chance at the position or if the job is completely out of your league. A *benchmark* is how many of the employment qualifications you believe are necessary to meet before you apply for a position. For example, your benchmark may be to meet 80 percent of the advertised desired qualifications and 100 percent of the required qualifications in a job posting.

If you find multiple postings for which you want to apply but are unable to do so immediately, forward them to your professional e-mail account. This action sends the company name, job title, description, and submission details to your e-mail. Alternatively, you can bookmark the page that contains the postings in your Internet browser. This will allow you to return to the page later.

Most job-search websites encourage applicants to post résumés to their accounts at no cost. It is a good idea to take advantage of this free service. These websites are often good sources of potential job candidates for employers who may search the site. If an employer finds a résumé of a candidate with whom they want to meet, they will contact that person directly.

When posting a résumé to a job-search website, the same customization rules apply as with an electronically submitted résumé. For safety and privacy concerns, provide a general geographic location instead of a physical address. Additionally, remove all contact information aside from an e-mail address.

There are hundreds of new openings posted online each day. This can seem overwhelming. However, the steps to search for available employment opportunities online follow a pattern. The home page of most job-search websites features a text box in which to enter search criteria. The first step is to enter a job title, keywords, or a company name. The next step is to select the desired location for the position. Some sites offer options for an advanced search. In these cases, criteria that are more specific can be selected to narrow your search.

For example, you may be able to set search parameters to find full-time jobs only. To begin searching for jobs, follow the steps of the job-search process:

1. Search for a job title and desired location.
2. Review available job postings and locate the name and e-mail address of a contact person for each job posting. Not every job posting will have a contact person.
3. Research each company name or individual who posts a job advertisement to ascertain whether you are a good fit for that company and position.
4. Determine if each posting is from a legitimate company or individual. Remember, if it seems too good to be true, it probably is.
5. Follow any application-submission instructions listed in the job posting. If no specific or special instructions have been provided, apply directly to the individual listed as a contact person for the job advertisement. If no contact person is included in the post, apply directly to the company by navigating to the company's website and searching the website for a **Careers** or **Employment Opportunities** page. Alternatively, you may be able to apply for the job directly through the job-search website on which you found the listing.

CONNECT TO YOUR ▶ CAREER

Complete 9-2 Job-Search Websites, pg 153

Applying for Jobs Online

As you begin applying for jobs online, you will find that different postings will take you to various websites on the Internet. Some employment advertisements link directly to corporate websites, while others link to recruiting agents who screen résumés. Regardless of where the job posting ultimately leads you, each posting and application should be given equal weight.

Resist the temptation to hurry through an online application form. Spelling, complete sentences, and grammar rules still apply. Everything should be carefully proofread before submission. Once the application is submitted, you will not be able to make revisions or corrections.

After selecting the **Submit** button for an online job post, do not use the **Back** button on your Internet browser. This returns the browser to the previous window and might cancel your online submission.

Career Portfolio

michaeljung/Shutterstock.com

Transcripts. A *transcript* is an official school record of the courses a student has completed, grades received, when the courses were taken, and a cumulative grade point average (GPA). Transcripts may also include standardized test scores, behavioral records, and academic awards received.

Including a transcript as part of your portfolio provides evidence to your scholastic achievements. Transcripts reflect academic successes and confirm the candidate's statements that courses of study have indeed been completed as indicated on a résumé. Most employers will ask for a transcript at some point in the interviewing process. By including one in your portfolio, it shows organization and anticipation on the part of the candidate which are signs of leadership.

When you contact your college or university for a copy of your transcript, you will likely be asked if you want an official or unofficial copy. An unofficial copy can generally be received by a student at no cost. For an official transcript, there may be a small fee requested. However, some institutions may not release official transcripts to students. Each school has different guidelines regarding transcripts, so check with your institution for their policies.

1. Determine if you should request an official or unofficial transcript.
2. Contact and obtain transcripts from your college or university. This may require a wait time, so plan accordingly. If you have attended more than one institution, obtain your transcript from each.

Sunday Evening Plan

Monday morning is a critical day in the job-search process for potential employees. This is when recruiters use advanced search criteria to find new and updated résumés of potential job candidates. Recruiters begin each week by sorting through résumés with keywords that match the criteria they seek.

In order to get your résumé viewed by recruiters on Monday morning, your information should be updated on Sunday night. This can be easily accomplished with a *Sunday Evening Plan*. Every Sunday evening during a job search, update, edit, and proofread all employment documents. After revising your employment information, post these updated documents to active job boards. The timestamp is important. Even if you find that no edits are necessary, delete the existing documents and re-upload them so they are flagged as new. Recruiters are only notified of new and updated documents.

The same strategy holds true as a method of getting noticed on professional networking sites. Every Monday morning, LinkedIn and Twitter feeds shape the entire week. Get in on the Monday morning action by commenting in a group on Sunday evening. When others log in and read their news feeds on Monday morning, your post will be near the top. In addition, Tweet and post about your industry or career on Sunday night, asking if anyone knows of any open positions or reiterating your availability to fill an open position.

A Sunday Evening Plan should take up to 30 minutes each week. Plan to spend, at a maximum, 10 minutes to review and re-upload employment documents, 10 minutes to post on LinkedIn, and 10 minutes to Tweet.

Be consistent. Using just 10 minutes for each online account will yield exponential results by keeping your name near the top of search results.

Managing the Application Process

Managing the application process is a job in itself. Writing a résumé and cover letter are just two of the many tasks that are necessary to find a position. The workplace is more competitive than ever. It will be necessary to put effort into finding employment that fits your needs and interests. Methods for managing the application process include time management, maintaining up-to-date employment documents, staying in touch with one's professional network, setting job alerts, and downloading appropriate applications.

Time Management

Time management is an essential soft skill when looking for a job. Time slips away quickly. The process must be managed so the right position can be found in an amount of time that works for you. Typically, it is helpful to create a schedule that includes an end goal of when you need to be employed. After your goal has been established, fill in the days with the activities that are needed to reach the goal.

Calendar software works well as a time-management tool. It will allow you to set notifications that remind you of various responsibilities you have on certain days. You may prefer a paper calendar. Use what works best for you.

Some of your application-management responsibilities will include the tasks you have learned in this text. You will add others as you progress. Examples of tasks to schedule include:
- draft a career plan
- develop a personal brand statement
- create professional networking accounts
- manage your online presence
- create a résumé
- draft a cover letter
- develop a portfolio
- complete an application
- prepare for an interview

Without a schedule, it can be challenging to accomplish all the activities needed to become employed.

Stay Current

It is important to keep your résumé, portfolio, and other employment documents up to date to reflect your current situation and abilities. This information will be constantly revised and customized to be appropriate and current for job applications. Be proactive and look for reasons to revisit your employment documents. Add an alert to your calendar to review items on a regular basis, and continue performing your Sunday evening updates.

Keep in Touch with Your Network

Maintain regular contact with the people in your network. Note when you contact each person and if you should follow up in the future. If you need to follow up, add an alert in your calendar.

Record each person's name, contact information, and any important notes or tips you receive. For example, "Katie works at Procter & Gamble and knows the human resources director." Save a copy of your networking information to your mobile device or in cloud-based storage so you can access it whenever necessary. A spreadsheet stored only on your computer at home will not be useful if you need to refer to someone in your network and are not at home.

Set Job Alerts

Some websites offer the service of electronic job alerts. After registering for an account and making career preferences, you may be able to set alerts that will help you stay on top of new opportunities. These websites will notify you via text or e-mail of employment opportunities that meet specified criteria. After you receive an alert, you can, in many cases, use a mobile device to apply for jobs. If a position you previously applied for is reposted, some websites will notify you of the repost and indicate you have already applied for this job, saving you valuable time.

Download Apps

Using technology to manage the application process is convenient, but you will not always be in front of a computer when a job opportunity presents itself. It is important to be able to update an account or submit a résumé while on the go. Download apps for websites and social media accounts you use regularly in your employment search. Loading the app on your mobile device will save you time when you want to visit the site on the go.

Tracking Applications

The job-search process can continue for some time. As you submit applications and start interviewing, it will be important to keep track of the details. Mixing details like the names of companies or contact people, job descriptions, or dates and times of scheduled interviews could cost you an opportunity. Organization is essential. Create a job-tracking spreadsheet to help you stay organized. A *job-tracking spreadsheet* is a spreadsheet with individual sheets for applications, leads, and interviews to record and track the jobs for which you apply. An example of a job-tracking spreadsheet with customized sheet tabs is shown in Figure 9-2.

Applications

Tracking applications can be difficult. This is where having a job-tracking spreadsheet can save time and confusion. When you submit an application, create columns in the applications sheet that detail the following information:

- title of the position
- name, address, and URL of company
- name, title, phone number, and e-mail address of the contact person
- source of the job posting
- date of application

If you are responding to an advertisement, keep a copy of the job posting. If it is a printed advertisement, use a folder or envelope to store it. If the advertisement is online, copy it into a folder on your computer.

In many cases after applying online, applicants receive an e-mail response to the submission. Some online job boards monitor application activities and automatically send an e-mail response when an application has been received. Some businesses also send automatic e-mail responses to candidates acknowledging the receipt of their application. Create a folder in your e-mail and label it "Job Responses" or something similar. Move these e-mails into that folder as you receive them.

If you do not get a response to an application for a position for which you applied, do not take it personally. It does not mean you are not qualified. There are many people who apply for posted jobs. Most recruiters and employers select a predetermined number of responses, such as 10 or 20 that stand out. As you will recall, most of the applications are screened through automatic data tracking (ADT) software. A human may not even see the applications until they have been sorted and selected. Ensure your employment documents are up to date and include relevant keywords.

FIGURE 9-2

A job-tracking spreadsheet is a spreadsheet with individual sheets for applications, leads, and interviews to record and track the jobs for which you apply.

	A	B	C	D	E	F	G	H	I	J
	Title of Position	Company Name	Company Address	Company URL	Contact Name	Contact Title	Contact Phone Number	Contact E-mail Address	Source of Job Posting	Date of Application
	Personal Banker	Bottom Line Bank	87 Madison Ave. Augusta, ME 04333	www.blbank.com	Amanda Aulett	Hiring Manager	207-555-2886	aaulett@e-mail.com	Indeed.com	3/9/2018
	Teller	Onyx Bank	176 College Ave. Waterville, ME 04903	www.onyxbank.com	Kevin Johns	Human Resources Manager	207-555-6699	kevin.johns@e-mail.com	Monster.com	4/30/2018
	Junior Loan Officer	Hoover Bank	1029 Main St. Palermo, ME 04353	www.hooverbank.com	Andrew Guerin	Senior Loan Officer	207-555-4668	aguerin@e-mail.com	Company website	6/11/2018
	Apprentice	Johnson & Wheeler Financial	518 South Broad St. Chesterville, ME 04360	www.johnsonwheeler.com	Jessica Downs	Account Executive	207-555-5937	downsj@e-mail.com	CareerBuilder.com	9/3/2018
	Administrative Assistant	Eldertree Financial Services	905 Eastern Ave. Skowhegan, ME 04976	www.eldertree.com	Melissa Foster	Human Resources Director	207-555-3537	melissafoster@e-mail.com	LinkedIn.com	11/23/2018
	Account Assistant	Simmonds and Associates	826 Spruce St. Palmyra, ME 04965	www.simmondsco.com	Joan McFarland	Recruiter	207-555-7467	mcfarland_joan@e-mail.com	Company website	12/4/2018

Applications | Interviews | Leads

Goodheart-Willcox Publisher

What Employers Want

Hearing is a physical process. *Listening* is an intellectual process that combines hearing with evaluating. When an employee listens, he or she makes an effort to process what was heard. The inability to listen carefully usually results in misunderstood instructions and missed opportunities, which can hinder a company's productivity.

Leads

Once you begin receiving responses to applications, these become *job leads*. When a representative from a company to which you have applied contacts you for more information, create columns in the leads sheet of your job-tracking spreadsheet that detail the following information:

- title of the position
- name, title, phone number, and e-mail address of the person who contacted you
- date of the communication
- other pertinent information

A representative from the company making contact with you provides an opportunity to follow up with that person at a later date. Persistence is important. If someone has recognized you as a qualified applicant and you are still interested in the position, it is important to keep the communication open and ongoing.

Interviews

Tracking interviews is an important step in the job-search process. When a potential employer makes contact with you for an interview, he or she will call or e-mail you directly. Therefore, you should closely monitor calls and e-mail messages. All incoming phone calls, e-mails,

and voice-mail messages should be attended to promptly and professionally during the application process.

As you begin to schedule interviews, continue using your job-tracking spreadsheet. Your spreadsheet will grow as interview opportunities arise. In addition to the information you initially recorded about the job lead, include pertinent facts about the interview. Create columns in the interviews sheet of your job-tracking spreadsheet that detail the following information:

- name and contact information of the person who scheduled the interview
- interview date
- interview location
- name and title of the person(s) conducting the interview
- title of the position
- any other pertinent information for the interview

Ensure this information is stored on, or accessible from, your mobile device so you will have it on the day of the interview.

CONNECT TO YOUR ▶ CAREER

Complete 9-3 Job-Tracking Spreadsheet, pg 153

Summary

 Explain how to complete a job application.

A job application must be completed neatly, comprehensively, and in ink. It includes personal information, names and addresses of schools attended, degrees and certifications earned, addresses of previous employers, supervisors' names, and contact information. It may also ask for references. Job applications can be submitted either as a hard copy or electronic file.

 Describe the process of applying for a job in person.

Ask for an application and stay on-site to complete it. After completing the application, assemble it, a cover letter and résumé tailored to the company, and a list of references in an envelope or folder. Deliver the folder to a company employee, and record his or her name in a mobile device for addition to a job-tracking spreadsheet. It is acceptable to follow up with the company after one week.

 Describe the process of applying for a job online.

The online application process consists of searching for a job title and desired location, reviewing available postings and taking note of the contact person for each, researching each company to decide if it is a good fit, determining if each posting is from a legitimate company, and applying directly to the company or contact person.

 Define Sunday Evening Plan.

A *Sunday Evening Plan* involves updating employment documents and posting or reposting on professional networking sites on Sunday evening so they are flagged as new on Monday. Recruiters often begin each week by sorting through résumés with keywords that match the criteria they seek, so updating employment documents on Sunday night can help get an applicant noticed.

 Explain methods for managing the application process.

Methods for managing the application process involve time management, staying current on employment documents, keeping in touch with your network, setting job alerts, and downloading mobile apps to your mobile device. Successful management of the application process will keep you in control of your job search.

 Define a job-tracking spreadsheet.

A *job-tracking spreadsheet* is a spreadsheet with individual sheets for applications, leads, and interviews to record and track the jobs for which you apply.

Glossary Terms

job application   job-search website

Review

1. Explain the steps involved in completing a job application.

2. Describe the steps to apply for a job in person.

3. Compare and contrast aggregate and non-aggregate job boards.

4. Explain how the use of a benchmark for employment qualifications can aid your job search.

5. Summarize the online application process.

6. Why is it important to resist the temptation to hurry through an online application?

7. What is a *Sunday Evening Plan?*

8. What does managing the application process involve?

9. Summarize the importance of good time management during the job-search process.

10. Describe a *job-tracking spreadsheet.*

Application

1. What does an illegible job application form convey to an employer about the job seeker?

2. In what ways is an applicant advantaged or disadvantaged when applying for a position in person rather than online?

3. Types of job-search websites that you can use for your job search include aggregate and non-aggregate job boards. Explain which type you plan on using in your personal job search and why.

4. It is important to set a benchmark of how many advertised job requirements you meet before you apply for a job. Review several job advertisements for open positions in your field. What is your benchmark for each?

5. Applying for jobs online involves a keyword search. List keywords you will use to search for jobs online.

6. Searching for jobs online allows you to set search parameters that include location, salary range, and full- or part-time status, among others. What search parameters will you use when searching for desirable jobs?

7. Describe how you will implement a Sunday Evening Plan in your personal job search.

8. There are many facets to managing the application process, such as time management, keeping in touch with your network, and setting job alerts. How do you plan to manage these tasks?

9. It is important to keep in touch with your network. Explain how you will keep in contact with your professional network during your job search.

10. Staying organized is one of the most important aspects of the application process. Describe how you will use technology to stay organized.

CONNECT TO YOUR CAREER
Workplace Connection

9-1 Job Application

Conduct an Internet search using the phrase *sample job application*. Select one that looks similar to one you might be required to complete for a job opportunity and print it.

1. Complete the application. Refer to your résumé, list of references, or other documents if necessary. Use blue or black ink and your best handwriting. The application must be neat, clean, and free of errors.

2. Proofread your application. Compare it to your résumé and cover letter. If there is any conflicting information, revise your documents appropriately. If you need to correct the job application, print a new copy and start again. Sign and date the form.

3. Next, practice completing the job application electronically by keying your responses directly into the form.

4. Print the completed application. Sign and date the form. Submit it to your instructor along with your handwritten application.

Describe what you learned while completing this job application. What information was requested for which you were not prepared to answer?

9-2 Job-Search Websites

Conduct an Internet search using the phrase *job-search websites*. Record the URLs for several websites you would consider using.

URL #1:

URL #2:

URL #3:

URL #4:

Of the four URLs you listed, which website(s) do you plan to use in your job search, and why?

Create an account on the job-search website you plan to use by following the instructions on the website. Upload your master résumé and cover letter as directed.

9-3 Job-Tracking Spreadsheet

As you apply for jobs, a tracking document can help you manage the process. One method is to create an electronic spreadsheet and organize it to record activities for each phase of the process. Using spreadsheet software on your computer, create a new file.

1. Rename Sheet 1 to *Applications* and create columns for the following data:

   - title of the position
   - name, address, and URL of company
   - name, title, phone number, and e-mail address of the contact person
   - source of the job posting
   - date of application

2. Rename Sheet 2 to *Leads* and create columns for the following data:

   - title of the position
   - name, title, phone number, and e-mail address of the person who contacted you
   - date of the communication
   - other pertinent information

3. Rename Sheet 3 to *Interviews* and create columns for the following data:

- name and contact information of the person who scheduled the interview
- interview date
- interview location
- name and title of the person(s) with whom you will interview
- title of the position
- any other pertinent information for the interview

4. Save the file as *FirstnameLastname*_JobTracker.xlsx (e.g., JohnSmith_JobTracker.xlsx).

How do you think this spreadsheet will aid your job search?

Landing a Job

Chapter 10 Preparing for the Interview

Chapter 11 The Interview

Chapter 12 Evaluating the Interview

Why It Matters

It finally happened—you have been offered an interview. Now, you must prepare for a meeting with an interviewer that may be formal or informal, in-person or virtual. Preparation should include your research about the company, job responsibilities, and a list of questions you would like to ask the employer. Planning is essential, and it is the key to a successful experience that hopefully will generate a job offer.

After the interview process is complete, take time to reflect on your experience. Use post-interview techniques at the conclusion of each interview to help put things in perspective. What went well? How can you improve for the next interview opportunity? If you are offered a position, take your time and evaluate the compensation package. It is your choice to accept or reject the offer. If you are not offered the position, keep moving forward with the job-search process until you find the right job for you.

10 Preparing for the Interview

Outcomes

1 **Identify** three types of job interviews to which a candidate may be invited.

2 **Identify** sources of information for conducting research about a potential employer.

3 **Contrast** in-person interviews with virtual interviews.

4 **List** types of questions that an interviewer might ask.

5 **List** examples of questions that a candidate might ask.

6 **Identify** ways to prepare for an interview.

CONNECT TO YOUR CAREER

Workplace Connection

OVERVIEW

A job interview is the employer's opportunity to ask questions to determine if you are qualified for the position as well as an opportunity to sell yourself as a potential employee. Keep in mind that your answers to interview questions are important in the employer's decision-making process. In addition, your ability to ask the interviewer insightful questions is also important.

The interview may be formal or informal. It may be an in-person interview or a virtual interview. All interview opportunities require preparation and careful planning in order to make a positive impression. The first step in preparing for a job interview is to learn as much as you can about the job and the company.

Invitation to Interview

At some point in your application process, you will be invited to a job interview. A *job interview* is the employer's opportunity to inquire about details included in your résumé and assess you as a potential employee. An invitation to interview will likely come either as a phone call or e-mail. When you receive a personal phone call from a company representative requesting an interview, ask for necessary details to ensure you arrive at the right place and time. Confirm the location of the interview and the name of the person with whom you will be meeting. Ask if there are any specific documents you should bring in addition to your most up-to-date résumé and portfolio. Be polite and reiterate your interest in the opportunity. If you receive an interview invitation via e-mail, netiquette dictates that you respond immediately. Request confirmation of the interview details in your response.

The first interview may be a screening interview. A **screening interview** is a preliminary, informal interview designed to determine if a candidate's skills qualify him or her for a formal interview. Screening interviews are brief and involve questions about your skills, experience, and availability. These interviews are typically conducted by a recruiter or hiring manager via phone, e-mail, or video conference. This type of interview helps employers narrow the list of potential candidates who will be scheduled for formal interviews.

If all goes well, the next step in the process is a structured interview. A **structured interview**, also known as a *directive interview*, is a formal interview in which a predetermined list of questions is posed to each candidate interviewing for a position. All job candidates are asked the same questions so responses can be compared objectively to evaluate each candidate. These questions range from general to specific.

Rather than a structured interview, an employer may opt to conduct an unstructured interview. An **unstructured interview** is an interview that is less formal and may not necessarily consist of a specific list of questions. The questions asked will typically change from one candidate to the next. Unstructured interviews are typically used to get to know a candidate's personality in a relaxed situation, such as over lunch or dinner.

CONNECT TO YOUR CAREER

Complete 10-1 Informal Interviews, pg 169

Company Research

After you have scheduled a formal interview and confirmed the date and time, familiarize yourself with the company, its products, services, size, and potential for growth and expansion. Your first source of information is the company's website. Navigate to the company's official website, and search for a section titled About Us, or something similar. Read the contents carefully, and review details about the products and services the company offers. Take notes on the information found here so that you may study them before the interview. If the website includes employees' names, search for your interviewer by name to learn more about him or her. Additionally, if the company has a page on LinkedIn, it can be useful in your research.

After learning about the company from its website, enter its name in a search engine. Locate news articles, press releases, and comments from customers. Note how the company promotes its brand on social media. If possible, research its competitors; this information will help you to determine how it compares to the rest of its industry. Your research will help you prepare talking points about the company and its mission.

CONNECT TO YOUR CAREER

Complete 10-2 Company Research, pg 170

Job Interview

A job interview is one of the most important steps in the job-application process. At the interview stage, you have captured the interest of an employer or hiring manager, and you will have a chance to convince that person to hire you. It is also an opportunity for you to learn if the company and position are the right fit for you.

What Employers Want

Humility means being modest. A person who possesses humility does not judge other people as less important or less competent. Possessing humility does not mean to be meek or have diminished self-esteem or self-image. Instead, it means treating people respectfully, being confident in one's abilities, and behaving as a professional. When soft skills are mastered, some aspects of humility naturally happen. For example, simply saying "thank you" to someone demonstrates humility.

During an interview, you are the focus. The interviewer will ask questions to uncover information about you as a job candidate. At the same time, it is your opportunity to exhibit your personality while discussing your skills and abilities as a potential employee.

Companies are no longer confined to face-to-face interviews. It is important to remain flexible as the actual meeting may be an in-person or virtual interview.

In-Person Interview

An *in-person interview* is one that is conducted with all of the participants at the same location. Usually, a job candidate is invited to the company office to meet with the hiring manager. In-person interviews can also take place away from company property, such as a restaurant. *Remote-location interviews* are in-person interviews held at an off-site location, such as a college campus or job fair. For some remote-location interviews, it is common to prearrange an interview time, just as you would if you were visiting the company office, and meet the interviewer at the determined location.

You may be interviewed by one person or multiple people. A **panel interview** is an interview in which a candidate talks with multiple interviewers in one room. Each member of the panel might present different angles or questions related to the candidate's ability and the job for which he or she is being interviewed. If you know you will be interviewed by a panel, ask questions about the details before you arrive, such as how many members there will be and the names of each. Some candidates are required to deliver a brief demonstration or presentation for panel interviews. If so, you will have advance notice and time to prepare.

Plan to arrive 15 minutes before the appointment time, but no earlier than that. Allow plenty of time for traveling and wait in your vehicle if you arrive too early. Take into consideration weather, traffic, or other factors that might delay your arrival. It is unprofessional and unacceptable to arrive late to a job interview.

It is important to know exactly where the interview is being conducted. Some companies have several locations, and you must be sure that you arrive on time at the correct place on the day of your interview. This information is usually provided by the person with whom you arranged the interview date and time.

If possible, visit the interview location before the day of your interview to gain a sense of the time it takes to get there, including any necessary walking time. If you are unable to visit the company in person, use an online map program, such as Google Maps, that allows you to see the building, parking locations, and other surrounding areas online. Use these programs to plot a route to the building and estimate the amount of time needed for arrival.

Some companies have strict visitor protocol. Call the main number for the company, and ask about its protocol for visitors. Is there visitor parking? Will a visitor pass be required? Some companies require identification to proceed past the lobby for an interview. Other companies need only the name of the person with whom you have an appointment. Knowing and understanding these policies prior to your arrival can save time and potentially avoid embarrassment and confusion.

Virtual Interview

One advantage of a virtual interview is that the candidate is not required to commute to the employer's location. However, the potential for technical difficulties can be a disadvantage. Be certain to have a strong phone or Internet connection before the interview. It can be difficult to create a strong first impression when troubleshooting technical problems.

It is a good idea to verify that your employment documents are up to date prior to your virtual interview. This can include updating your LinkedIn profile, blog, or electronic portfolio website. A day or two before the interview, send an e-mail to the interviewer asking if there is any additional material that you will need to submit for the meeting. Attach the most current version of your résumé, portfolio, or other materials with a note explaining that these are the most recent versions of the files. If you want the interviewer to use a website to view your employment documents, provide the URL in your e-mail. Otherwise, the web address you provided in your initial correspondence with the company, which may not have the most recent files, will likely be used. Two types of commonly conducted virtual interviews are telephone interviews and video interviews.

Telephone Interview

For an interview conducted over the phone, the interviewer will arrange to call you, or you will be asked to place the call. If the interviewer is calling you, be at your desk and by the phone at least five minutes early. You should answer the call yourself and identify yourself when the phone rings. If you are placing the call, you will be calling the interviewer's direct line or calling into a conference-call number. Place the call no earlier than five minutes before the scheduled appointment time. For conference calls, call in and hold for the moderator.

Even though you cannot be seen, it can be helpful if you are sitting up straight at a desk for the phone call. Treat the phone interview as though it were a face-to-face interview. This will help you maintain your professionalism for the duration of the conversation.

It will be necessary to have all the materials you would take with you to an in-person interview, such as your résumé and research notes about the company. These materials should be easily accessible during the interview. Avoid the sound of shuffling papers or the clicking of keys on a keyboard, and silence the interview area to eliminate background noise. The interview dialogue should not compete with television, radio, or barking dogs, for example.

Video Interview

Real-time video conferencing using Skype, FaceTime, or other technologies requires the use of a web camera, microphone, and an Internet connection for both parties to make visual and audio contact. If you are not familiar with the video-conferencing software being used, take time before the day of the interview to get acquainted with it. Some video-conferencing software requires users to download and install a program, which can be time consuming. To be safe, ensure you have downloaded the necessary program before the day of the interview. On the day of the interview, log on at least five minutes early. It is considered unprofessional to log on at the start time of the interview, and logging in early eliminates the risk of a last-minute connection loss. In all cases, be the first party to access the virtual interview so when your interviewer arrives, you are in position and ready to greet him or her.

A video interview requires the same amount of care and preparation as an in-person interview in terms of attire and personal details. Find a quiet place away from traffic noise, the radio, or other distractions. Direct the web-camera view so that the interviewer's view reflects a work environment. For example, if your laptop is in your kitchen and the web camera gives a view of dirty dishes, the interviewer will receive the wrong impression. Virtual work environments from a web camera's point of view can be as simple as a plain wall or a wall with framed pictures and a bookcase.

The lighting in the room should be flattering. The interviewer should be able to clearly see you, but you should not appear washed out due to too much light. Overhead or natural lighting tends to work well for use with a web camera. Consider the time of day of your interview, and practice using different light sources.

Social Media Slipup

A recent college graduate concluded an internship with a successful law firm in the town in which she lived. She was well liked during her time with the company and was confident she would be offered a full-time position. The internship provided an opportunity for her to demonstrate her skills to management at the company, giving her an advantage over other recent graduates.

F8 studio/Shutterstock.com

To her surprise, she was not offered a full-time job so she chose to instead apply for an open legal assistant position. She submitted an application and had hopes she would have an opportunity to discuss the position with the hiring manager. Soon after submitting her application, she was contacted to schedule an interview.

The night before the scheduled interview, a friend called her to make plans to go to the beach the next day, unaware of the pending job interview. She agreed to the beach plans and, in the morning, called the HR representative and lied, saying she was feeling ill and was not anticipating being able to keep the appointment. She was permitted to reschedule her interview, largely due to her history with the company.

When the legal firm's human resources department conducted its customary background search, a representative saw a post on the applicant's Instagram page that showed the candidate at the beach. The caption read, "Interview? Beach with bestie? I say beach." The timestamp for the post was dated the same day as her cancelled interview.

Needless to say, the applicant never received a call back from HR. The hiring team agreed that she had abused and taken for granted the reputation she had built during her internship in addition to violating workplace ethics. The power of social media can be your best friend or your worst enemy. A reputation for hard work and success can easily be derailed by one simple Instagram post.

When participating in a video interview, remember to look into the lens of your camera. This simulates eye contact. Looking at your computer screen to see the interviewer or a mirrored image of yourself leaves an impression similar to looking at the floor during a face-to-face interview.

A virtual interview follows the same pattern as an in-person interview. The conversation might begin with a brief, pleasant question about the Internet connection before starting. The interviewer will then most likely take the lead. At the end of the conversation, he or she will offer you an opportunity to ask questions. You will have a chance to ask your questions, respond to any further comments, close the interview, and thank him or her.

CONNECT TO YOUR ▶ CAREER

Complete 10-3 Virtual Interviews, pg 171

Interviewer Questions

Interview questions are intended to assess your qualifications for a position. By asking questions, the interviewer can evaluate your qualifications for the job, as well as your personality and fit with other employees in the company. Many commonly asked questions are posed so the hiring manager can learn more about the experience, education, and skills presented in your résumé.

Not knowing how to answer a question can lead to embarrassment and missed opportunities. To avoid such a scenario during an interview, plan, prepare, and practice potential interview questions. Prior to your interview, read the details of the job posting regarding any specific duties or other requirements so you are prepared to answer questions about those topics. Make a list of the required experience, qualifications, and skills. Next to each requirement, list the ways in which you fulfill it.

The types of interview questions asked can vary depending on the type of interview you attend. However, there are common types of interview questions for which you can prepare answers ahead of time. These question types include general information questions, behavioral questions, and stress questions.

General Information Questions

General information questions are aimed at gathering facts about you, such as your education and work experience.

Some examples of general information questions and answering strategies include the following:

| What can you tell me about yourself?

Suggested strategy: Succinctly summarize your abilities as they relate to the job qualifications. Do not provide a general life history. Begin with your degree and any related courses. Walk through your pertinent duties at each previous job.

| What jobs have you held?

Suggested strategy: Provide your job title, the name of the company, and a brief summary of the duties involved for each job you intend to discuss. This may or may not be every job listed on your résumé. Focus on jobs with skills that relate to the position you are seeking. Use keywords from the job posting if possible.

| What interested you most about this position?

Suggested strategy: Focus on the duties that interested you in the job and how they align with your previous experience and career goals. If the position is higher in your career path than your current occupation, describe your desire to grow as a professional in your industry. Then explain how this position can help you achieve that goal.

| Why do you want to work for this company?

Suggested strategy: This is a good opportunity to share some information you learned about the company during your research. Relate what you know about the company and why you think you would fit in there. Describe how the company's mission relates to your career goals.

| What is your major strength?

Suggested strategy: Select one of your strengths that relates to the requirements of the position, and explain why you consider yourself strong in that particular area. Provide an example of an occasion where you used it in a previous job. Describe the outcome of this occasion and anything you learned as a result.

| Are you comfortable using the technology required by this position?

Suggested strategy: Share any experience you have with the technology required, including the number of years you have used it and whether you consider yourself a novice, intermediate, or expert user. You can also provide some examples of how and when you used the technology. If you are unfamiliar with the technology in question, be honest but explain that you would be willing, able, and excited to learn new technological skills associated with the position.

Not all general information questions are appropriate for an interviewer to ask. For example, federal and state laws prohibit employers from asking questions related to a candidate's

- age;
- disability;
- ethnicity or national origin;
- gender;
- marital or family status; or
- religion.

If an interviewer asks you a question that does not relate to your ability to perform a job, it is acceptable to politely decline to answer the question. For example, "I apologize, but I am not comfortable discussing this matter."

Behavioral Questions

Interviewers may ask questions that relate to your behavior or how you might typically conduct yourself. A **behavioral question** is a question that draws on an individual's previous experiences and decisions. An interview that focuses on behavior-based questions is known as a *behavioral interview*. Your answers to these types of questions indicate past behavior, which can be used to predict future behavioral patterns. These questions are typically more focused than general information questions. They require job seekers to provide a specific example of when they used a skill to successfully complete a task. When answering these questions, include what the task was, the action that was taken, and the results of the action. While you cannot prepare specific answers to these questions, remain poised, answer honestly, and keep your answers focused on the question. Some examples of behavioral questions include the following:

- Tell me about a situation in which you needed to persuade your supervisor to make a change in a process or procedure.
- Tell me about a time when you needed to assume a leadership position in a group. What were the challenges, and how did you help the group meet its goals?
- Describe a time when you missed the opportunity to provide the best possible service to a customer. How would you have changed your approach for a more successful outcome?
- Describe a situation in which you needed to be creative in order to help a customer with a problem. What was the problem and how did you solve it?
- Describe a situation when you made a mistake. Tell me how you corrected the mistake and what measures you put in place to ensure it did not happen again.

The Best App for That

Interview Buzz

Interview Buzz LITE is a free app that contains over 50 frequently asked interview questions with possible answers, as well as a catalog of commonly asked practice questions. The app also provides users with step-by-step instructions for tying a tie, what to do and not to do at the interview, and dining etiquette. This app can be especially helpful when practicing for an upcoming interview. For a larger catalog of questions, consider paying to download the Interview Buzz Pro app. Currently, the Interview Buzz apps are only available on Apple devices.

Stress Questions

Stress questions are posed to candidates to see how they react to pressure. This type of question might shake a candidate's confidence and can indicate whether candidates can "think on their feet." Stress questions are often subjective, and it is difficult to predict the interviewer's preferred response. Most times, employers ask these in order to see how well a candidate can use reason and logic to come to an answer. Some people become defensive when they do not have an answer. Others become embarrassed or tongue-tied. It is critical to remain cheerful and professional. These questions may be uncomfortable or difficult to answer, but answers can be generated through careful thought.

When presented with a stress question, take time to process it and formulate a coherent answer to respond articulately. To gain more time to answer a challenging question, consider using reflective techniques that acknowledge the question while giving you time to think of an answer. Some reflective technique responses are:

- "That is a great question."
- "I had not considered that angle."
- "Exactly. That happens sometimes."

When presented with stress questions, it is your responsibility to transform an awkward moment into a positive one. Answer such questions in a positive manner, and do not panic or lose your composure. Some examples of stress questions and answering strategies include the following:

| What is your biggest weakness?

Suggested strategy: Choose something you are honestly challenged by but will not jeopardize being considered for the position. For example, someone interviewing for a bank teller job would not offer counting money as his or her biggest weakness. After you have provided a response, explain what you are doing to improve your weakness.

| Why are you looking to leave your current job?

Suggested strategy: Avoid saying anything negative about your current employer. This seems unprofessional and can persuade an employer not to hire you. Instead, direct your responses toward your own growth and career goals you have set and how leaving your current job can help you achieve those goals.

| Can you explain why there is a gap in your employment?

Suggested strategy: Provide an honest answer, focusing on the positive aspects of your employment gap. For example, you could discuss classes you have been able to take as a result of your employment gap or any travelling you have done that exposed you to new cultures. If your employment gap is due to a negative reason, such as involuntary termination, be honest and explain what measures you have put in place to better yourself as an employee.

It is important to anticipate difficult questions. Focus on your professional weaknesses and expect them to be exposed throughout the course of the interview. This will allow you to have an answer prepared in case you are asked. For example, if your college major and your work experience are not consistent, recognize these inconsistencies and organize a sound explanation for any disconnect between your education and profession.

Career Portfolio

Africa Studio/Shutterstock.com

Work Samples. One of the most important sections of your portfolio is your work samples. You have explained the *why* in your cover letter. Your work samples will provide the *how*. Work samples are not confined to paid employment. This is your opportunity to provide an interviewer with evidence of what you are capable of accomplishing in the workplace.

For example, if you are applying for a fashion design job, include samples of your work from a class you have taken. If you are applying for a job that requires use of computer-aided drafting software, include printouts of CAD models you created for a class project.

If you have paid employment experience, include samples of work you performed in those jobs. Be selective in work samples that you attach as any work performed for an employer is the property of that employer.

If you have unpaid employment experience, such as volunteer work or an internship, include those samples also. You may have been the editor on a neighborhood newspaper that you could include as a sample of your editorial skills. You may have tutored children after school and have a lesson plan that shows your ability to teach.

For work samples that can only be documented by performing the task, a video can be created. This is appropriate for someone who performs a service, such as a mechanic, hair dresser, or singer. For a photographer or baker, photos could serve as samples. Each profession has its own criteria for what consists of a sample.

When sorting through work samples you have collected, be selective. A few high-quality samples are better than multiple mediocre samples.

1. Create a strategy for the type of samples you will include. The samples may be photographs, a video, or printed evidence.
2. Include documentation that supports each work sample. Attach notes to the documents to identify each item and state why it is included in your portfolio. For example, a note on a newsletter you wrote might say, "Certificate that illustrates computer-networking skills."

If you have gaps in your employment, prepare an explanation as to why those gaps exist.

One type of stress question is a hypothetical question. A **hypothetical question** is a question that requires a person to imagine a situation and describe how he or she would act. Frequent topics of hypothetical questions relate to working and getting along with coworkers. For example, "What would you do if you were waiting on a customer and a coworker was constantly interrupting you?"

Specific answers to this type of question cannot be prepared in advance, so you need to rely on your ability to think on your feet. Bear in mind the interviewer is aware that you are being put on the spot. In addition to what you say, he or she will likely consider other aspects of your answer, as well. Body language is first and foremost. Avoid fidgeting and looking at the ceiling while thinking of an answer. Instead, make eye contact with the interviewer and calmly take a moment to compose your thoughts. Responses to these questions should be brief. If your answer runs too long, you risk losing your train of thought. Try to relate the question to something that is familiar to you and answer honestly. Maintain a professional and calm demeanor. Showing poise and projecting confidence carries a lot of weight, even if the answer is not ideal.

Another type of stress question is a blue-sky question. A **blue-sky question** is one where the interviewer describes a scenario that may or may not be related to the job duties and requires a response from the candidate. This is posed to test the candidate's life values and priorities. For example, "If you had $10 million, what would you do with it?" Answers to these types of questions reveal personal character. Since these are designed to learn about you, it is best to answer them with honesty and brevity.

CONNECT TO YOUR ▶ CAREER

Complete 10-4 Interview Questions, pg 173

Questions to Ask

During the interview, the hiring manager will most likely provide you with an opportunity to ask questions. Be prepared with a list of intelligent questions to pose if given the chance. Study the job description and the company to formulate your list. Understand that this portion of the interview is a moment to demonstrate leadership potential. It is important to remember the interviewer is in charge. Do not be aggressive or overbearing. Avoid redundant inquiries, such as previously addressed topics, and keep in mind that questions you ask reveal your personality. The following are some questions you may want to ask if the interviewer has not already addressed the topic:

- What are the specific duties of this position?
- To whom does this position report?
- What is company policy or criteria for employee promotions?
- Do you have a policy for providing on-the-job training?
- What are the working hours?
- When do you expect to make your hiring decision?
- When is the anticipated start date for this position?

Preface your questions with a signal phrase. A **signal phrase** is a preplanned beginning phrase that enhances a question. These phrases add professional polish to the question and show that you have been listening closely to the information the interviewer has shared. Some examples of signal phrases include:

- You mentioned that...
- You referred to...
- I noted that you said...
- I appreciate the way you addressed...
- You were clear in the expectations, but I have one additional question...

Questions about salary should not be asked during the first interview. It is inappropriate to ask about money as doing so can give the impression that you are more concerned about compensation than the position. Attend the first interview on good faith that the salary offer will be acceptable. In addition to questions about salary, the following questions should be *avoided* in an interview:

- How many other candidates will you interview?
- May I come back so that we can talk about this position again?
- What did you think about your interview with me?
- Are you going to hire me?

If the interview was exhaustive, all potential questions were answered, and there are no further questions about the position or the company, a candidate may ask a question about the hiring process. An example might be, "What is the next step in this process?" Another closing question could be, "When might I expect to hear from you regarding your decision?" If all questions have been addressed, offer a phrase such as, "I have no additional questions to ask at this time. Thank you."

The offer from an interviewer to the candidate to ask questions becomes the best time for the candidate to thank the interviewer as well. This demonstrates professionalism, leadership potential, and recognition of the interviewer's time.

Complete 10-5 Questions to Ask, pg 174

Practice for the Interview

All successful interviews begin with preparation. You are more likely to have a successful interview if you take time to rehearse prior to the appointment. Preparing answers to expected questions is only half of the preparation. The other half involves rehearsing your delivery of those answers.

Answering practice questions in front of a mirror can be beneficial. This activity allows you to see what the interviewer will see. Dress professionally while practicing to become comfortable with the selected clothing. As you rehearse responses, pay special attention to facial expressions and posture. Decide how you will introduce yourself to the interviewer. If possible, record your voice so that you can monitor tone and inflection. It is natural to be nervous during an interview, but learn to sound as relaxed as possible.

Conducting a mock interview is another preparation method for a formal interview. A *mock interview* is a practice interview conducted with another person in which one person role-plays as the interviewer and the other as the job candidate. Participating in a mock interview provides an opportunity to uncover potential mistakes and to determine how prepared you are for the interview process.

When conducting a mock interview, it is best to select a quiet place in which to work. Prepare a table or desk and chairs to simulate an office environment. If possible, record a video of the mock interview. If available, a camera on a tripod works well for this purpose. You will gain insight into how others perceive you when reviewing the video.

After conducting one mock interview as the interviewee, switch roles. This experience will allow you to see the job candidate from the interviewer's position. Observe how another person responds to your questions. Try to gain an understanding of what to do and what not to do during your interview. Regardless of the role you are assuming, be sure to stay in character for the entire mock interview. Mock interviews should be taken seriously. This practice strategy provides training necessary to polish your performance in front of another person, such as a friend, family member, or career-services representative.

CONNECT TO YOUR CAREER

Complete 10-6 Mock Interview, pg 176

Summary

 Identify three types of job interviews to which a candidate may be invited.
Three types of interviews include a screening interview, a structured interview, and an unstructured interview.

 Identify sources of information for conducting research about a potential employer.
A good place to find information about a potential employer, its products, services, size, and potential for growth and expansion is the *About Us* section of the company's website. It is also a good idea to search the Internet for news articles, press releases, and comments from customers. This research will provide you with talking points for the interview.

 Contrast in-person interviews with virtual interviews.
In-person interviews require candidates to research how long it will take to travel to the location and company visitation policies. Virtual interviews differ from in-person interviews because the candidate has to consider elements of his or her home, such as noise, Internet connection, and lighting. However, both in-person and virtual interviews require careful planning and preparation, as well as professional dress.

 List types of questions that an interviewer might ask.
Three types of interview questions commonly used are general information questions, which are designed to gather facts about the candidate; behavioral questions, which draw on an individual's previous experiences and decisions; and stress questions, which are asked to see how candidates react to pressure.

 List examples of questions that a candidate might ask.
Examples of questions that a candidate might ask include questions about the specific duties of the job, to whom the position reports, company policies or criteria regarding promotions, policies regarding on-the-job training, the hours of work, when a decision will be made, and the anticipated start date for the position.

 Identify ways to prepare for an interview.
The best way to prepare for an interview is to practice interviewing. Answering practice questions in front of a mirror can be beneficial because it allows a person to see what the interviewer will see. Conducting mock interviews can also help a job candidate prepare. This provides an opportunity to uncover and resolve potential mistakes.

Glossary Terms

behavioral question	panel interview	structured interview
blue-sky question	screening interview	unstructured interview
hypothetical question	signal phrase	

Review

1. Describe the purpose of a screening interview.

2. Differentiate between a structured interview and an unstructured interview.

3. Identify sources of information for conducting research about a potential employer.

4. Explain how an interview is an opportunity for both the interviewer and the candidate.

5. Compare and contrast in-person and virtual interviews.

6. What is a *panel interview*?

7. What types of questions are commonly asked during a job interview? Describe the purpose of each.

8. Explain how a person can prepare responses to potential questions that may be asked during an interview.

9. List examples of appropriate questions for an applicant to ask during an interview.

10. Describe two ways to practice for an interview.

Application

1. What can you do during a screening interview to increase your chances of being offered a structured interview?

2. Imagine you are invited to interview for a position in the corporate office of a restaurant chain. What type of information would be important for you to have before the interview?

3. A panel interview is an interview in which a candidate talks with multiple interviewers in a room. Describe how you would prepare for a panel interview.

4. How would your preparation for an interview for a sales position at a local sporting goods store differ from an interview for an administrative assistant position at a local law firm?

5. There are different types of questions that a hiring manager might ask. One type of question is general information. Select one general information question that was presented in this chapter, and read its suggested strategy. How would you answer this question?

6. Provide an answer to the following stress question: How can you make this company better?

7. Imagine you are being interviewed for a job in your desired line of work. How would you respond to the following blue-sky question: If you had $10 million, what would you do with it?

8. What questions are most important for you to ask during an interview based on your career goals and your chosen career field?

9. Provide an example of an inappropriate question you asked during a job interview you wish you could take back. In what ways was the question inappropriate, and what did you learn from the experience?

10. Consider a time when you went on a job interview without rehearsing or practicing first. How could your interviewing experience have been improved by practicing your answers ahead of time?

CONNECT TO YOUR CAREER
Workplace Connection

10-1 Informal Interviews

The first step in the interview process may be a screening interview. Conduct an Internet search using the phrase *screening interview tips*. List several tips you find most helpful.

Screening Interview Tip 1:

Screening Interview Tip 2:

Screening Interview Tip 3:

Screening Interview Tip 4:

Screening Interview Tip 5:

You may be invited to interview at a restaurant while having a meal with the interviewer. Many unstructured interviews are at mealtime, held during lunch or dinner. Conduct an Internet search using the phrase *mealtime interview tips*. List five tips you find most helpful.

Mealtime Interview Tip 1:

Mealtime Interview Tip 2:

Mealtime Interview Tip 3:

Mealtime Interview Tip 4:

Mealtime Interview Tip 5:

10-2 Company Research

Conduct an Internet search for a job that interests you. List the position and company name.

Position Title:

Company Name:

Conduct research on the company you selected by visiting the company's official website. Read the *About Us* or equivalent section carefully. Continue reviewing the site to learn about the products and services the company offers. List any important information that you find.

Next, key the name of the company in a search engine. Avoid returning to the company's official website. Look for press releases, articles, comments from customers, and social media posts in your search results. Record the URLs of several sites, as well as any important information you found, that you could use to prepare for an interview.

URL #1:

URL #2:

URL #3:

URL #4:

10-3 Virtual Interviews

One type of virtual interview is interviewing via the telephone. Conduct an Internet search using the phrase *how to interview over the telephone*. List 10 details that should be considered when interviewing via the telephone.

1.

2.

3.

4.

5.

6.

7.

8.

9.

10.

Many employers who conduct virtual real-time video interviews use software such as Skype. Visit the Skype website to learn more about this technology. Make a list of 10 items you will need if an employer suggests a Skype virtual interview.

1.

2.

3.

4.

5.

6.

7.

8.

9.

10.

10-4 Interview Questions

Write a response to each of the following general information questions often asked during job interviews.

1. What can you tell me about yourself?

2. What other jobs have you held?

3. Why do you want to work for this company?

Write a response to each of the following behavioral questions often asked during job interviews.

1. Describe a situation in which you made a mistake. How did you correct it, and what measures did you put in place to avoid making the same mistake in the future?

2. Tell me about a time in which you were faced with adversity. How did you overcome it, and what did you learn as a result?

3. Describe a time when you had to work with an upset customer. What was the customer's complaint, and how did you solve the problem? What was the level of satisfaction with your solution?

Write a response to each of the following stress questions often asked during job interviews.

1. What is your biggest weakness?

2. Why are you looking to leave your current job?

3. How do you handle rejection?

10-5 Questions to Ask

There are standard questions you will ask about any job for which you are interviewing. Those questions will be about items such as on-the-job training and hours worked. Make a list of five common questions that you would ask about working for an employer.

1.

2.

3.

4.

5.

Conduct an Internet search for questions to ask during a job interview. List five questions that resources suggest you ask specific to the job.

1.

2.

3.

4.

5.

Conduct an Internet search for questions *not* to ask. List five questions that resources recommend you avoid asking.

1.

2.

3.

4.

5.

10-6 Mock Interview

Prepare for a mock interview. List ten questions to be used for the mock interview. You can refer to the chapter content for questions an interviewer might ask, or create your own list of questions. After each question, write your response.

1.

2.

3.

4.

5.

6.

7.

8.

9.

10.

Practice your answers in front of a mirror. Record your thoughts on the experience.

Ask a friend to assume the role of interviewer and conduct a mock interview. This person should use the questions you prepared. Remember to introduce yourself and shake hands with the interviewer. If possible, ask another friend to record the interview. If this had been a real interview, how impressed do you think the interviewer would have been with your answers?

What did you learn from this experience?

11 The Interview

Outcomes

1 **Discuss** how to make a positive first impression at an interview.

2 **Describe** a typical job interview.

3 **Explain** the purpose of a second interview.

CONNECT TO YOUR CAREER
Workplace Connection

OVERVIEW

There are many factors at play on the day of a job interview. While many of these factors are out of your control, such as traffic and weather, you are in complete control of your own actions. Understanding how to present yourself on a first interview can mean success or failure. Being on time and making a good first impression are basic behaviors that can influence the employer's ultimate decision.

At the interview, be prepared for introductions, questions, and the closing segment. Dress appropriately and come with the necessary documents. Have your questions prepared for the interviewer and allow time, if needed, for pre-employment tests. If you are successful, the opportunity for a second interview might be extended at a later date.

First Impressions

During an interview, subjective elements can influence the perception of a hiring manager. A **subjective element** is a factor that contains bias and is more emotional than logical. Subjective elements are psychological nuances that occur when people meet for the first time.

Often unintentionally, an interviewer will make split-second judgments about an interviewee. While subjective elements may not be a fair assessment of a candidate's skills and qualities for the job, the first visual impression makes a powerful impact on potential employers.

From within the first few seconds of meeting an interviewer, that person will decide a great deal about you based on the way you look. This judgment is a first impression of you, which usually comes from outward appearances, such as eye contact; the way you dress, smile, and walk; and even your handshake. It is important to make these first moments count in your favor.

The way in which a candidate dresses will make an immediate impression with the interviewer. While each company will likely have different expectations for employee attire, there are interview clothing choices that are acceptable across many types of professional environments. An appropriate way to dress for an interview is to wear conservative, neutral clothes. A business suit is appropriate for both men and women. If the weather is inclement, plan for outer garments as well. A single outer garment that you can easily remove, such as an overcoat or raincoat, is an asset to a professional wardrobe. Suggestions for appropriate interview attire for men and women are shown in Figure 11-1.

Clothing should be neat, clean, and in good condition. Shoes should be clean and free of scuff marks or obvious wear. A nice wristwatch can complete a professional look and promote your punctuality. For all jewelry choices, choose conservative items over flashy or gaudy accessories. Do not wear anything to the interview that will disrupt or distract a potential interviewer from focusing on your skills. The goal is to help the interviewer focus on your strengths as an employee, not on your clothes.

Pay close attention to personal grooming, hygiene, and cleanliness. Refrain from wearing cologne, and style your hair in a conservative manner. Your hands are important aspects of the impression you make at an interview as well. Make certain that your fingernails are clean and not broken or uneven. In addition, downplay piercings and cover all tattoos. Your smile should be inviting. One of the single, most-effective personal details is a genuine, warm smile.

FIGURE 11-1

Appropriate attire for an interview is an example of a subjective element.

Appropriate Attire for a Job Interview

Women

- Wear a suit or dress with a conservative length.
- Choose solid colors over prints or flowers.
- Wear pumps with a moderate heel or flats.
- Keep any jewelry small.
- Have a well-groomed hairstyle.
- Use little makeup.
- Avoid perfume or apply it very lightly.
- Nails should be manicured and of moderate length without decals.
- Cover all tattoos.

Men

- Wear a conservative suit of a solid color.
- Wear a long-sleeved shirt, either white or a light color.
- Tie should be conservative.
- Wear loafers or lace-up shoes with dark socks.
- Avoid wearing jewelry.
- Have a well-groomed haircut.
- Avoid cologne.
- Nails should be neatly trimmed.
- Cover all tattoos.

Daxiao Productions/Shutterstock.com; Hugo Felix/Shutterstock.com; Goodheart-Willcox Publisher

In addition to proper attire, you can make a positive first impression by showing the interviewer how much time and effort you put into preparing for the interview. This will demonstrate your professionalism and initiative. On the day of the interview, carry a bag that complements your professional attire, such as a briefcase or satchel. The following items should be included in your interview bag:

- appointment calendar
- bottle of water
- business cards
- hard copies of your résumé printed on high-quality white paper
- list of references
- multiple pens with which to write
- notes from your company research
- pad of paper for taking notes
- prepared questions for the interviewer
- the list you created of job requirements compared to your experience, qualifications, and skills

Employment documents can be secured with a paper clip but should not be stapled or folded. Consider keeping those documents in a separate envelope, folder, or binder with organizational dividers to give to the employer. If you have created a print portfolio, bring a copy to leave with the interviewer. For electronic portfolios, include the URL on your business card to leave behind.

CONNECT TO YOUR CAREER

Complete 11-1 Interview Checklists, pg 186

The Interview

Upon arrival, you will likely have to check in at a reception desk. The front-desk attendant will need to know your name, reason for visit, and whom you have come to see. He or she will then alert the interviewer of your arrival. A company representative will greet you and escort you to the room where the interview will take place. The greeter may be the interviewer or an employee from the human resources department.

Introduction

The initial introduction is your opportunity to make a positive first impression with the interviewer. It is appropriate to extend your hand to deliver a firm handshake when the interviewer approaches you. Make eye contact and offer a pleasant greeting.

Introductions often begin with preliminary comments and a greeting that might include brief questions such as, "Did you have any difficulty finding our offices?" These preliminary questions are meant to break the ice and allow the interviewer to gain an impression of how the candidate handles new challenges. Avoid complaining about traffic, commute time, unclear directions, or other obstacles that you negotiated in order to arrive successfully. A good example of a response is, "I made a trial run yesterday based on the directions from your assistant, which made the drive today very easy." This shows that you listen, follow directions well, and take initiative.

After introductions have been made, wait to be seated. The interviewer might say, "Please, have a seat," or something similar. Most interviewers use a hand gesture to indicate the appropriate seat for the interview candidate. At that time, it is advisable to sit in a formal seated position. A **formal seated position** entails sitting upright, with both feet on the floor and both hands comfortably resting either on chair armrests or in the lap. This is the opposite of slouching and projects professionalism. Your body positioning may change slightly during the interview process as the conversation begins to unfold; however, try not to fidget during the conversation.

It is likely your interviewer will not remember your credentials from your application. Before he or she begins asking questions, offer a hard copy of your résumé. If applicable, also offer a copy of your portfolio. This will help refresh the interviewer's memory as to who you are and why you are qualified for the position.

Interview Questions

Your interview preparation will pay dividends as you answer questions posed by the interviewer and ask questions that you might have. In all interview situations, be aware of your body language. **Body language** is communication sent through gestures, facial expressions, and posture. These nonverbal cues should reinforce your professionalism, qualifications, and enthusiasm for the job opening.

Employer Questions

Do not be distracted by the interviewer's outward appearance. Focus on the keywords of the available position when articulating personal qualifications. Language choices should be respectful and formal as well. For example, if the interviewer elicits a response where a "yes" is expected, do not offer "yeah" as a substitute. Your primary focus as an employment candidate is to answer interview questions to the best of your ability and sell yourself as the best candidate for the job.

Candidate Questions

After the interviewer has finished with his or her questions, you will likely be asked if you have any questions of your own. This is the time to ask questions you have prepared. Be respectful of the interviewer's time. If you believe the interview is complete, do not extend time by asking additional, unnecessary questions.

However, make certain that you have asked for any important information that was not already covered.

Interview Closing

When the interview concludes, wait for a signal from the interviewer to offer your closing remarks. Take the opportunity to reiterate your brand statement or elevator speech while briefly summarizing your skills. If during the interview you did not highlight a skill or some experience that fits the position, use this time to highlight these positive qualities. Reinforce your interest in the position to the interviewer, and express the belief that you would make many positive contributions in the organization. Ask for any follow-up activities that must be completed. It is also appropriate to ask when a decision will be made to fill the position.

Thank the interviewer for his or her time. A firm handshake is as appropriate to conclude a meeting as it is to begin one. If convenient, extend your hand to initiate this interaction. Remember, your closing remarks and thank-you should be brief but positive. Ask for a business card from each interviewer and offer one of your own.

Career Portfolio

michaeljung/Shutterstock.com

Foreign Language Skills. Individuals who are fluent in a foreign language may, in some situations, have an advantage over other candidates in the job-search process. As part of an interview with an organization, you may be asked about your ability to speak multiple languages or experience with people who speak a language other than your own. Many organizations are interested in this information for good reasons. They often serve people from a variety of geographic locations, cultures, and languages.

People who speak more than one language and have traveled, studied, or worked in other countries can be valuable assets to an organization. While the employer may or may not have referenced an international aspect of the position in the job advertisement, some companies have offices or factories in more than one region or country. A candidate who notes multilingual skills may be considered to have a competitive edge over other candidates with similar experience.

If the job for which you are applying notes international travel, it is important to be specific and accurate when you list the language skills you posses. By being proactive and noting any experiences you have in working with people in other cultures, you may catch the eye of the interviewer even before the interviewing process begins.

1. If you are fluent in another language, create a document that describes the language in which you are proficient, where you received your training, and your level of fluency. Use the heading "Languages Spoken" and your name.

2. If you have limited language proficiency, create a document that says "Limited Language Proficiency" and list each language and your ability to communicate using it. For example, you may have only a limited proficiency in German that could be helpful in a business situation.

The Best App for That

Dropbox

Dropbox is an app that enables you to take your job-search documents wherever you go. Once the app is downloaded, you can drag and drop files, such as your résumé, portfolio documentation, and cover letters, into Dropbox. The app also allows creation of a shared folder in which each document will have a corresponding URL that links directly to the respective file in read-only format. You can send the URL to allow potential employers access to your shared folder. Or, you can print the URL on your résumé or business card so those you network with will have immediate access to it.

Pre-Employment Tests

Often, employers screen potential job candidates by giving them pre-employment tests. These tests consist of questions to measure basic skills necessary for employment. Employers that give pre-employment tests do not always share the results with job candidates.

Some employers give simple mathematical or grammatical tests, while others administer personality tests. Governmental agencies use their own tests to measure a variety of skills, such as writing ability and reading comprehension. Businesses such as retailers, banks, utility companies, and staffing agencies are likely to administer a test that measures the integrity of a candidate when interviewing for a position related to money, public safety, or merchandise.

If you know you will be taking a test, be certain to get plenty of rest the night before, and eat a healthy breakfast. If possible, conduct a search on the Internet for practice tests common to your industry and complete multiple examples. This will help make you comfortable with the test-tasking process.

CONNECT TO YOUR CAREER

Complete 11-2 Pre-Employment Tests, pg 187

Second Interview

Occasionally, some employers request a second interview. A *second interview* is a second formal interview that occurs after it has been determined that the candidate is qualified and more information is needed about him or her.

If you are contacted for a second interview, prepare for the event as diligently as you did for the first one. The same protocol is in order. Maintain a clear mindset that you are a top candidate, and arriving unprepared could leave the employer with a poor impression. Again, pay attention to your wardrobe and which documents to bring with you. If possible, do not wear the identical outfit worn at the first interview. Vary your attire, even if you only wear something slightly different, such as a different color or type of shirt.

During a second interview, you will have the chance to ask additional questions and to discuss specific working expectations and benefits that were not asked in the first interview. Additional questions might include travel expectations, telecommuting, flextime, job sharing, overtime expectations, and work attire. Make a list of questions prior to the interview, and rank the questions according to priority. Time may be limited, so asking the most important questions first is a must.

Summary

Discuss how to make a positive first impression at an interview.
First impressions usually come from outward appearances, such as the way a person dresses, smiles, and walks. To facilitate a good first impression, professional attire that matches the working environment should always be worn to an interview. Additionally, it is helpful to carry a professional bag, briefcase, or satchel that complements the attire worn so documents such as business cards and printed copies of résumés can be easily carried and produced during an interview.

Describe a typical job interview.
On the day of the interview, a job candidate will likely have to stop at the front desk to check in. From there, a company representative will greet and escort the candidate to the room in which the interview will take place. The interviewer will then make introductions and begin the interview by asking questions. Once the interviewer's questions have been exhausted, the interviewee can take some time to ask questions. The interview should close with pleasantries and a handshake, and the candidate should follow up by taking any necessary pre-employment tests.

Explain the purpose of a second interview.
A second interview is another formal interview that occurs after it has been determined that the candidate is qualified and more information is needed. If called for a second interview, preparation for the event should be as diligent as the first one.

Glossary Terms

body language	formal seated position	subjective element

Review

1. Discuss how to make a positive first impression at an interview.

2. Define *subjective element*. List examples.

3. Identify a safe choice for interview attire.

4. List necessary materials to take to the interview.

5. Describe a typical job interview.

6. What is the purpose of preliminary questions asked by an interviewer?

7. What is a formal seated position? Why is it important during an interview?

8. What should your body language reinforce about you?

9. How can you prepare for a pre-employment test?

10. Explain the purpose of a second interview.

Application

1. Recall a situation in which a person with whom you spoke did not create a positive first impression with you. How can this experience help you in your interview preparation?

2. Describe the type of attire you would wear to a first interview at a company to which you have applied. Why is this attire appropriate for that employer?

3. Explain why a person would wear something other than a business-professional or business-casual outfit to an interview.

4. Aside from the materials list in this chapter, what would you bring with you to an interview and why?

5. Recall a situation in which you had a conversation with someone whose body language did not reflect his or her interest in the discussion. How successful was that conversation?

6. In the previous chapter, you created a standard list of questions to ask during interviews. How would you reorder these questions to ensure you get the most important information first?

7. Write a closing statement that you will present at the conclusion of an interview.

8. What kinds of pre-employment tests would you expect to see in your desired line of work or industry?

9. How would you prepare for a pre-employment test?

10. Describe the differences in your preparation for a first interview compared to that of a second interview.

CONNECT TO YOUR CAREER
Workplace Connection

11-1 Interview Checklists

In the space below, or in a Microsoft Word document, create a checklist that you will use for your interview attire. This will help you prepare for the interview and remember important details.

Attire	Specific Item
1. Suit	_____
2. Shirt/blouse	_____
3. Shoes	_____
4. Jewelry	_____
5. Watch	_____
6. Coat	_____
7. Umbrella	_____
8. Other	_____
9. Other	_____
10. Other	_____

Interview Materials	Specific Item
1. Professional bag	_____
2. Hard copies of résumé	_____
3. Pad of paper	_____
4. Pen	_____
5. Notes from your company research	_____
6. List of job requirements	_____
7. Prepared questions for the interviewer	_____
8. List of references	_____
9. Appointment calendar	_____
10. Business cards	_____
11. Personal portfolio	_____
12. Other	_____
13. Other	_____
14. Other	_____

11-2 Pre-Employment Tests

Conduct an Internet search using the phrase *pre-employment tests*. List five of the most common pre-employment tests used to evaluate job candidates. Describe what each test evaluates.

Pre-Employment Tests	
Name of Tests	**Qualities it Evaluates**

Conduct an Internet search using the phrase *pre-employment test preparation*. Select several of the most helpful tips and techniques suggested for preparing for these tests.

Test Preparation Tip #1:

Test Preparation Tip #2:

Test Preparation Tip #3:

Test Preparation Tip #4:

Summarize what you learned.

12 Evaluating the Interview

Outcomes

1 **Identify** post-interview techniques.

2 **Describe** the employment process after a job offer has been extended.

CONNECT TO YOUR CAREER

Workplace Connection

12-1 Interview Evaluation

12-2 Thank-You Message

12-3 Job Offer Evaluation

12-4 Salary Negotiation

12-5 Job Offer Responses

OVERVIEW

An important part of the interviewing process is to evaluate the interview once it has transpired. If you are successful and get the job, take time to reflect on the experience. If you do not get the job, do not feel defeated. You will not get every position for which you apply. Look at each interview opportunity as an experience to prepare you for the next one. Utilizing the post-interview techniques at the conclusion of each interview will help put things in perspective.

If you are offered a position, take time to evaluate all aspects of the job and compensation package before you accept or reject the offer. Negotiation may be necessary to get the salary that you desire. If you do accept the offer, be prepared for the employment processes that follow.

Post-Interview Techniques

Post-interview techniques consist of a series of steps you will need to complete after an interview. Immediately after an interview has ended, evaluate your experience. This will enable you to learn from the interview and move forward with confidence. Next, follow up in a professional way with a formal thank-you message. Finally, you should think positively and continue your job search. Common post-interview techniques are illustrated in Figure 12-1.

Evaluate the Interview

An effective evaluation technique is to identify how you felt immediately after the interview. It is common to feel doubt and anxiety, but it is important to accept that the interview has ended, and you cannot go back to alter your performance. Instead of dwelling on what is out of your control, evaluate your experience; make notes about your overall impression of the company, interviewers, and process; measure your desire to work for that company based on what you learned; and develop a plan to move forward.

Even if you think the interview was successful, assess your performance and design a plan addressing how you can improve for your next interview. Look at each interview as an opportunity to learn and grow as a professional. You can assess your performance by asking yourself the following questions:

- Did I articulate my prepared responses as planned?
- Did I answer the questions with thoughtful intelligence?
- Did I have all of the documents requested?
- Did I dress appropriately?
- Did my voice project confidence but not arrogance?
- Did I smile pleasantly and naturally?
- Did I talk too much?
- Did I not talk enough?
- Did I remember to shake the interviewer's hand when I arrived and when I left the interview?
- Did I prepare as thoroughly as I should have for the interviewer's questions?

Expand this list with your own set of questions to evaluate your interview skills. Each job interview is an opportunity to practice, learn, and improve.

CONNECT TO YOUR CAREER

Complete 12-1 Interview Evaluation, pg 200

Send a Thank-You Message

After an interview, follow up with the interviewer in the form of a written thank-you message. A *thank-you message* is unsolicited communication demonstrating professional courtesy from you to the interviewer. This communication reaffirms your interest in the position and exhibits your professionalism. Etiquette dictates a thank-you message be sent within 24–48 hours of the interview to each person with whom you met. For example, if you met with the head of your potential department and the head of human resources, then each person should receive a separate thank-you message. Thank-you messages can be sent as a letter, card, or an e-mail. If you discussed any follow-up actions on your part during the interview, such as providing references or work samples, include these materials with your thank-you message.

If you are sending your thank-you message as a letter, write it using a standard letter format similar to a cover letter. Thank the interviewer for his or her time, express your continued interest in the position, and close with the desire to hear back concerning the hiring decision. If any follow-up material was promised, add an enclosure notation to your message and enclose the material with the letter in the envelope. Insert one of your business cards into the envelope before mailing. Figure 12-2 shows an example of a thank-you message as a keyed letter.

FIGURE 12-1

Post-interview techniques consist of a series of steps you will need to complete after an interview.

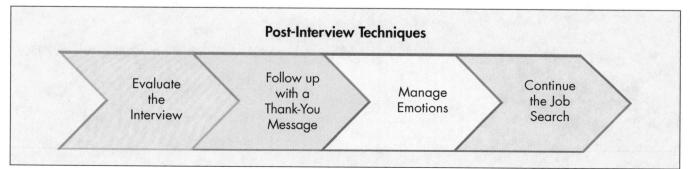

Goodheart-Willcox Publisher

FIGURE 12-2

A thank-you message is unsolicited communication demonstrating professional courtesy from you to the interviewer.

Jalia Cortez

111 First Street, Redwood City, CA 94061

(650) 555–1234 • jcortez@e-mail.com • www.linkedin.com/in/jalia-cortez

---

November 30, 20--

Mr. Joshua Mitchell
Great Corporation
12344 Main Street
Redwood City, CA 94061

Dear Mr. Mitchell:

Thank you for the opportunity to interview for the position of hotel concierge with Great Corporation on Wednesday, December 2. The interview process provided me with a clear synopsis of the role and responsibilities for the position.

My enthusiasum for the position has grown after talking with you and members of your team. My desire to work in the hotel business and serve customers is my passion. I would enjoy being a part of the company and having the opportunity to contribute to its success.

Thank you, again, for your time and consideration. As requested, I am enclosing a copy of professional references. I look forward to hearing from you soon.

Best regards,

Jalia Cortez

Jalia Cortez

Enclosure

Goodheart-Willcox Publisher

Thank-you letters can also be handwritten. Some candidates purchase thank-you cards to handwrite and send in the mail. Interviewers often appreciate hand-written cards, as they are more personal and take more time. If you decide to handwrite a thank-you note, select a high-quality card or stationery, and be sure your handwriting is legible. Again, include one of your business cards in the card or letter before mailing.

A thank-you message sent via e-mail is also acceptable, as shown in Figure 12-3. If you decide to e-mail your thank-you message, attach any follow-up material to the e-mail.

Complete 12-2 Thank-You Message, pg 202

Manage Emotions

Finding a job is far from a relaxing experience. Waiting for the results after an interview can be stressful, and not knowing how an interviewer perceived your performance might be unnerving. It is important to

FIGURE 12-3

A thank-you message can be sent as an e-mail for a timelier response.

To... jmitchell@e-mail.com

Cc...

Subject: Cortez Interview Thank You

Attached: Cortez Personal References.pdf 116 KB

Dear Mr. Mitchell:

Thank you for the opportunity to interview for the position of hotel concierge with Great Corporation on Wednesday, December 2. The interview process provided me with a clear synopsis of the role and responsibilities for the position.

My enthusiasum for the position has grown after talking with you and members of your team. My desire to work in the hotel business and serve customers is my passion. I would enjoy being a part of the company and having the opportunity to contribute to its success.

Thank you, again, for your time and consideration. As requested, I am attaching a copy of professional references. I look forward to hearing from you soon.

Best regards,

Jalia Cortez
Bilingual Guest Services Professional
(602) 555–1234
jcortez@e-mail.com
www.linkedin.com/in/jalia-cortez

Goodheart-Willcox Publisher

recognize there are parts of the job-search process that you *can* control, such as positive or negative thoughts, what you include on your résumé, and how you perform at a job interview. One of the things you *cannot* control is who the company chooses to select for a position. Focus on the items you can control, and try not to concern yourself with what you cannot. This will help you control your stress. Keep in mind that interviewing multiple times for various companies helps you gain confidence and much-needed experience in the job-search process.

Some companies communicate to candidates that they were not chosen for the position. However, many companies do not contact candidates at all if they are not selected. If you do not hear from a representative of the company after a period of time, it often means another person was selected for the position. Nearly every person has had the experience of interviewing for a job and not being selected for the position. This is part of the job-search process. Not every job for which you interview is the best match for you. In fact, you may find that you are not offered a position for a majority of the jobs for which you apply.

Continue the Job Search

Some job-seekers become confident after one interview, ending their search while waiting to hear from the interviewer. However, the best course of action is to continue to look for a position until you have a job. While you wait to hear the results from an interview, continue to seek additional employment opportunities. You can always decline an offer of employment if need be. Be persistent in searching for the job that you want.

The Employment Process

There is excitement and personal gratification that comes from being selected for a position for which you interviewed. However, the process is not complete once you receive a job offer. First, you will evaluate the offer. Next, if necessary, you will negotiate the compensation. Then, you must respond to the job offer. If you accept the position, employment verification will conclude the process.

Evaluate the Job Offer

At some point during this process, you will be offered a position. If the interview process was successful, an employer will contact you by telephone or e-mail with a job offer. A **job offer** is a formal invitation to work under mutually agreed terms and conditions.

The job offer typically includes the title of the position, description of duties, expected hours, location of work, and the compensation package you will receive.

Career Portfolio

makistock/Shutterstock.com

Introduction. The portfolio should open with an introduction that gives an overall snapshot of who you are. This will serve as one of the first pages of the portfolio and set the tone for your presentation, so you want to make a good impression. Tell the reader who you are, your goals, and any relevant biographical information. You may want to highlight information by making references to sections or page numbers of items in the portfolio.

This document should also include links regarding your online presence. For a print portfolio, include URLs to your LinkedIn, Twitter, and Instagram accounts in your introduction document. If you are creating an electronic portfolio, provide live links to your professional networking pages as well as any page containing documents of importance.

The introduction is the last document that you will create. You have collected various items for your portfolio; now it is time to organize the contents. Review the items and select the ones you want to include in your final portfolio. There may be documents that you decide not to use. Opt for quality over quantity. Remember to remove any working documents that you have inserted, such as your objective description.

Next, create a flowchart to determine the organization for your portfolio. The table of contents will come first, followed by the introduction. Organize the sections in a sequential order that makes sense for your needs. This flowchart should serve as a blueprint or map of your portfolio. You can also use this document as a guide when completing the table of contents later.

The **compensation package** is everything an employee receives in return for his or her work. Part of the compensation is *salary*, which is the amount of money an employer agrees to pay an employee. A compensation package may include paid time off, such as vacation days and sick days, and retirement benefits, such as a 401(k) plan. Other types of compensation include the following:

- annual bonuses tied to personal or company performance
- employer-paid medical, dental, and life insurance
- overtime pay
- reimbursement for job-related travel
- salary increases per performance reviews
- tuition reimbursement for continuing education

When you are offered a job, it is your responsibility to evaluate the offer. Consider whether it is the job you want. While it is flattering to be offered a position, you must make sure the job, benefits, responsibilities, and compensation fit your expectations. Examine the position and the expectations of the job. Remember, the decision to accept or reject a job offer is entirely yours.

Determine if the company and job meet your career expectations. To evaluate a job offer, first carefully read all of the details. Then ask yourself important questions, such as the following:

- Does the job offer meet the expectations I had at the interview?
- How does this position fit within my career plan?
- Is the job interesting?
- Does the salary offered represent a fair value for the skills I offer?
- Do I want to work for this company?
- Am I comfortable with the required duties?
- Will I need training or additional education right away?
- Does the growth potential for this position fit within my career plan?

Weigh the financial benefits offered with what it costs you to work each day. Calculate the amount of money you will take home after commuting expenses and taxes are paid. To determine this, consider the following questions:

- Will I be entitled to, or expected to, work overtime?
- If overtime work is expected, what is the rate of any hourly overtime pay?
- Does the employer offer health insurance?
- If the employer offers health insurance, how much will be deducted from my pay to cover the premium?
- If the employer does *not* offer health insurance, how much will I have to pay to get health insurance?
- Will there be costs for clothing or uniforms?
- What will it cost to commute to the job location?
- What is the cost of gas and parking?

The Best App for That

Switch

Switch is a job-search app that uses a match algorithm to help employers find the right talent for an open position. Unlike other job-search apps, Switch uses swipe-based viewing. As a job-seeker, while viewing job postings, you can use your finger to swipe right on opportunities in which you are interested. This action will send your profile directly to the person looking to fill the job. If the hiring manager also swipes right after viewing your résumé, you will be able to chat with the manager directly using the app's message feature.

You may be offered a benefits package and salary. Discuss the details of the benefits with the employer, and make sure you understand what is being offered. Carefully consider the job offer, and do not rush through your decision. It is important that you are comfortable with the offer and all details before you accept a position. Once you accept the offer, you agree to all of the terms of employment.

CONNECT TO YOUR ▶ CAREER

Complete 12-3 Job Offer Evaluation, pg 202

Negotiate

If the job meets your expectations, but the salary or compensation is not sufficient, consider negotiating. If you have been offered a salary and benefits package that does not meet your expectations, inquire about the opportunity to discuss a more appropriate package with the employer. Some items are negotiable, while others are not. Generally, the salary for minimum-wage jobs and entry-level jobs is not negotiable.

When you negotiate for salary, you are taking a risk. If your negotiation is baseless, the employer can withdraw the offer of employment. Remember that the employer may have multiple candidates willing to take the position at the salary offered.

If you decide to negotiate, establish a strong position by compiling the research to support your stance. For example, if you believe the job warrants a higher salary, research trends in your field for the same job title at various companies. Conduct research on the Internet using phrases such as "salary comparisons" or "median annual pay" to locate comparative information about the salaries of people with similar job titles and responsibilities. Free online salary calculators can also help you project what salary you can expect based on the job title and your location, years of experience, and education.

Next, prepare a brief presentation with a script so that you can create a logical argument. Your presentation should include an introduction, the research you found noting the discrepancy in salary offerings, and a closing with a request for a moderate increase in your compensation package. Have a firm number in your mind and suggest it. Rehearse your presentation in front of family members or friends. Ask someone to role-play an employer in the situation to help you think about your request. Solicit feedback before you present it to an employer.

Finally, contact the employer. Always begin with gratitude and acknowledgement of the position offered. Explain how you feel about the prospect of the new position and that you want to be compensated fairly. Ask if the salary is negotiable. If the response is a flat "no," thank him or her and say that you will consider the matter further. If the response indicates the salary or benefits package is negotiable, present your information. Close with your counter offer. Wait for the response, and proceed from there. Do not ask the employer to come up with a better number.

Avoid giving the company an ultimatum. An *ultimatum* is a proposition in which one party issues a final demand or set of conditions that, if unmet, can result in severance of the relationship. Sometimes, especially in highly competitive fields, ultimatums can be effective. However, most times issuing one will backfire on the candidate, and the job offer will be rescinded.

CONNECT TO YOUR CAREER

Complete 12-4 Salary Negotiation, pg 204

Respond to the Job Offer

Regardless of whether you will be accepting or rejecting the offer, a timely response is required. Notifying the employer of your decision is an important professional courtesy. Failure to do so will reflect poorly on you.

Accept a Job Offer

Once you are offered a job and you have agreed to the terms of employment and salary, formally acknowledge that you accept the position. The individual who contacts you with the job offer is the person with whom you will communicate regarding the acceptance of your position. A personal phone call is preferable. However, an e-mail may be necessary in order to submit a timely response. An example of an acceptance e-mail is shown in Figure 12-4.

FIGURE 12-4

Acceptance of a job offer should be sent to the employer as soon as possible.

Dear Ms. Boswell:

I am delighted to accept the position of Research Assistant for Becker Labs. I am excited about the opportunity of working with you and your team.

As soon as I receive the formal offer letter and additional forms you mentioned, I will complete and return them immediately. As we discussed, I will wait to hear from Mark Evans for further instructions about the medical exam and background check. I understand that there are required forms and processes that must be completed before I can start work.

Thank you again for the opportunity.

Sincerely,

Goodheart-Willcox Publisher

What Employers Want

To be a *team player* means to work cooperatively with others to achieve one goal. The ability to work productively with others is an important skill that employers desire for their employees. In many work situations, employees are assigned to work as teams. Recognizing that a group's goals outweigh those of the individual team players, establishing good working relationships with coworkers, and performing individual roles with efficiency are characteristics of a team player.

If you accept the position, you will receive a *formal offer letter*. This document will include the salary and compensation package that was agreed upon after the job offer was made. It is important that you take your time to read the documents carefully. If there are any passages that you do not understand, ask for clarification. You will be required to sign the document, which affirms that you understand, agree, and accept the terms and conditions of employment.

Decline a Job Offer

If you must decline an offer of employment, contact the person who extended the job offer as soon as possible. Communicate that you are appreciative of the opportunity, but it is necessary for you to decline the position. It is not necessary to state a reason for declining the offer, but be sure your communication is respectful and professional. If the potential employer telephones you, express your decision on the phone, but follow up the conversation with a written notice. You may use e-mail for this message. An example of a rejection e-mail is shown in Figure 12-5.

Handling the rejection of a job offer in a professional manner is important. You never know when, during the course of your career, you will cross paths with the company or its representatives in the future. Therefore, leave a positive, professional impression if you must decline a job offer from a company.

CONNECT TO YOUR CAREER

Complete 12-5 Job Offer Responses, pg 204

Employment Verification Process

There are processes that must be completed before you are officially hired. The employer will complete employment verification using the information on your application or résumé. **Employment verification** is a process in which a job candidate's employment history is checked to confirm the accuracy of the information he or she submitted. Employers typically verify only the dates of employment, position title, and other objective data. Most past employers will not provide subjective information about their employees, such as whether you were considered a good worker.

FIGURE 12-5

It is important to be timely, professional, and respectful when declining a job offer.

Dear Ms. Boswell:

Thank you for offering me the position as Research Assistant for Becker Labs. I considered your offer, but I have decided that I must decline.

I am grateful for the opportunity you extended. I appreciate your confidence in my abilities to perform the tasks required for the position.

Thank you again for the opportunity.

Sincerely,

Goodheart-Willcox Publisher

Social Media Slipup

A young software engineer was offered his first job out of college at a well-known information technology company. This was a high-profile company that most IT professionals would love to have on their résumés. The inexperienced engineer was extremely excited to have such an opportunity and posted to Twitter about the fantastic offer he just received. Unfortunately, he lost track of his thoughts and what he was posting. He thought he was only Tweeting to friends and family. However, during his job search, he used Twitter to reach out to potential employers and network with professionals in his industry. At this very moment, there were people other than family following his Tweets.

barang/Shutterstock.com

Before he knew it, his Tweets of excitement turned to complaints. The company was offering a great salary, but the long commute in traffic was making him think twice. He could not possibly make such a long drive. If they really wanted him on staff, they would have to give him a relocation package.

Shortly after publishing a Tweet regarding his commute and potential relocation, he received a response from the hiring manager, who happened to be on Twitter. The hiring manager responded to his Tweet, writing, "Discussing a confidential job offer on Twitter is an indication of future potential to break confidentiality of our company. We are rescinding the offer."

Confidentiality is an important soft skill that employers seek from employees. Breaking confidentiality is grounds for dismissal or, in this case, losing an employment opportunity. Sharing success on social media about a new job offer can be rewarding. Forgetting that social media is social, and there are many people reading your Tweets, is a serious error.

Another important aspect of the employment process is a background check. A **background check** is an evaluation of personal data that is publicly available. This information is generated from governmental records and other sources, including public information on the Internet. An employer must ask for written permission before obtaining a background check. While you are not legally obligated to give permission, a company can reject you as a candidate based on unknown or unverified background information.

For positions that require interaction with company finances, employers often will request a candidate's credit history. They must demonstrate a viable business need in order to access this information. Similarly to a background check, employers are legally required to obtain your permission before conducting a credit check. If you believe your credit score might impact a job offer, obtain a copy of your credit report first and try to resolve any negative entries.

If an employer decides not to offer employment to a job candidate based on a credit report, the employer should provide a copy of the report to the individual. In addition, a summary of rights should be provided.

Some employers require drug screenings for new employees. The employer pays for the test as part of the hiring process. You are required to use the lab facility designated by the employer. Most times, an offer of employment is contingent on your ability to pass this screening. If you pass it, the hiring process will continue. If not, you will no longer be eligible for employment with the company.

Summary

 Identify post-interview techniques.
Post-interview techniques consist of a series of tasks to complete after the interview. These steps include evaluating the interview, following up with a thank-you message, managing emotions, and continuing the job search.

 Describe the employment process after a job offer has been extended.
After a job offer has been extended, a candidate must complete several steps before the employment process is complete. The job offer must be evaluated and negotiated, if desired. Then, the applicant must respond to the job offer and complete employment verification. Employment verification might include a background check and a drug test.

Glossary Terms

background check	**employment verification**	**job offer**
compensation package		

Review

1. Identify post-interview techniques.

2. What are some ways you can evaluate an interview?

3. Why is it important to send a thank-you message to the person or persons who interviewed you?

4. How can you manage the emotions that come with not being offered a job for which you interviewed?

5. List the steps of the employment process that occur after a job offer has been made.

6. Explain what typically is included in a compensation package.

7. When should you consider negotiating a job offer? What risks are associated with negotiating with a potential employer?

8. Describe how to accept or reject a job offer.

9. What is a *background check*? How do employers access information when conducting one?

10. Why might some employers conduct credit checks on potential employees?

Application

1. What can you expect to learn by evaluating your performance in an interview?

2. Thank-you messages can be a formal letter, a handwritten note, or an e-mail message. Give your opinion as to when each of these formats is appropriate.

3. Managing emotions during the job-search process can be a challenge. How will you put the interviewing process in perspective and manage the emotions and stress of the experience?

4. Not every employer will let you know if a final hiring decision has been made. How will you determine whether you have been eliminated as a candidate or if you are still in consideration?

5. Describe how you plan to continue your job search even after you begin interviewing.

6. Salary is often only part of employee compensation. What other forms of compensation are you hoping to acquire? Are any of them "must-haves"?

7. List criteria you will use to evaluate a job offer.

8. Recall a time when you participated in a negotiation, such as when buying a car. What did you learn from this experience? What can you apply from this experience to negotiating compensation with a potential employer?

9. List reasons why you might reject a job offer.

10. An important part of the employment process is a background check. What steps should you take prior to your interview to ensure your background check will be well received by an employer?

Workplace Connection

12-1 Interview Evaluation

Post-interview techniques help prepare you for the next opportunity to interview for a position. The first step is to evaluate the interview. Answer the following questions that were discussed in the chapter.

1. Did I articulate my prepared responses as planned?

2. Did I answer the questions with thoughtful intelligence?

3. Did I have all of the documents requested?

4. Did I dress appropriately?

5. Did my voice project confidence but not arrogance?

6. Did I smile pleasantly and naturally?

7. Did I talk too much?

8. Did I not talk enough?

9. Did I remember to shake the interviewer's hand when I arrived and when I left the interview?

10. Did I prepare as thoroughly as I should have for the interviewer's questions?

Use the Internet to research additional questions that will help you evaluate your interview experience in an objective manner. List any questions that you think will be important to you.

1.

2.

3.

4.

5.

12-2 Thank-You Message

Writing a thank-you message after an interview is expected, and it demonstrates professionalism. In the space that follows, write the first draft of a thank-you message by composing each message element individually. Your introduction should thank the interviewer for the opportunity to discuss a position; your body should reiterate the interview experience; and your closing should thank the interviewer for his or her time and confirm any necessary follow-up actions. Keep your message succinct and to the point. Remember to use keywords as you describe your qualifications. Follow the example for writing a thank-you message as shown in Figure 12-2 of this chapter.

Introduction:

Body:

Closing:

12-3 Job Offer Evaluation

Conduct research on the Internet for salary calculators, salary-comparison calculators, cost-of-living calculators, and other resources that will help you evaluate the salary offered to you. These calculators will help you determine if the salary meets your requirements. Record the URLs of the resources that are most helpful to you.

URL #1:

URL #2:

URL #3:

URL #4:

After you have evaluated your salary requirements, there will be other questions to ask about the compensation package. In the space that follows, or in a separate document, create a list of questions to ask the hiring manager. Your questions should pertain to the salary, benefits, and other aspects of the compensation package.

Question #1:

Question #2:

Question #3:

Question #4:

Question #5:

The compensation package is obviously an important part of a job offer. However, there are personal factors that you will consider. One subject of importance is that of expenses involved in working for the employer. Make a list of questions you might ask yourself or the employer to help determine if the job is a good financial fit for you.

Question #1:

Question #2:

Question #3:

Question #4:

Question #5:

12-4 Salary Negotiation

There will be job offers in which the salary is lower than you would like to accept. You may consider negotiating a more appropriate salary. Conduct Internet research on *how to negotiate a salary*. The hiring manager may ask you the salary you require. Compile a list of facts and data that you will use as negotiation points.

Negotiation Point #1:

Negotiation Point #2:

Negotiation Point #3:

Negotiation Point #4:

Negotiation Point #5:

12-5 Job Offer Responses

Suppose you are ready to *accept an offer* for a position. However, the person who made the offer is in meetings all day and can only be reached via e-mail. Write a response you would include in an e-mail accepting the job offer for the position.

Consider a situation in which, after careful consideration, you have decided the job offer presented does not fit your career plans. Write a response you would include in an e-mail *declining* the job offer for the position.

Your Career

Why It Matters

Congratulations—you have a job! Your diligence and preparation in the job-search process has paid off. Out of all the candidates considered, you were selected for a position you worked hard to earn. You have put in a lot of time, effort, and energy to make this a reality. Embrace the fact that you were the best candidate for the position, and be proud of your accomplishment. This event ushers in a new chapter of your life.

The first days in a new place of employment can be overwhelming. There will be forms to complete, people to meet, and processes to learn. Professionalism will be a key to your future success. Demonstrate the ability to act responsibly, learn from others, and work hard. Be positive, punctual, and respectful. Stay current in your profession, continue networking, and plan for your financial future. Your career begins now.

13 Your First Day on the Job

Outcomes

1 **Describe** a typical first day of a new job.

2 **Describe** performance evaluations in the workplace.

3 **Identify** ways to be safe in the workplace.

4 **Update** your professional network.

CONNECT TO YOUR CAREER

Workplace Connection

13-1 Employment Forms

13-2 Employee Performance Self-Evaluation

13-3 Workplace Safety

13-4 Update Your Professional Network

OVERVIEW

Your first day on the job is an important step in beginning your career and should be taken seriously. Arrive on time, with a positive demeanor, and ready to work. Be confident in yourself and your abilities. This first impression can have great influence on your success with this company.

As you begin your new position, your employer will require that you complete a variety of employment forms and processes. Once you officially start your job, be the best employee you can be. Performance evaluations will be conducted to make sure you are performing your job well.

Day One

The first day on the job will be both overwhelming and exciting. You will probably spend the first day meeting coworkers and getting to know the facility. It is important to your career to make a positive first impression with those you meet.

Learn all you can about the company *before* your first day of work. During the interview process, you should have acquired information about the company's culture, mission, customers, and other valuable details. Use this information to aid your transition as a new employee. Contact the human resources department to inquire as to whether you need a badge or a security code to enter the premises. Ask which building entrance you should use and whom you should call when you arrive. If you are driving, find out where employees are expected to park and whether you need a parking pass.

Confirm the expected attire so you dress appropriately. The company will likely have a dress code that must be followed. A *dress code* is a set of rules or guidelines that defines acceptable attire in a certain place. In the workplace, dress codes can be used for safety reasons or to ensure a professional atmosphere. Even if there is no official dress code, dress professionally to match the culture of the workplace.

Be on time for your first day of work. Your first impression sets the stage for your working career. Greet each new coworker with an enthusiastic smile and pleasant conversation. Exhibit a positive attitude and your excitement to be part of the team. When you meet with your new supervisor, convey your enthusiasm to be an asset to the company. Ask for guidance on your activities, people you should meet, and other information to make your first few days productive.

Career Portfolio

racorn/Shutterstock.com

Presenting the Print Portfolio. It is suggested that you have a print version of your portfolio. This gives flexibility in the event that the job-application process requires print evidence of your qualifications. It also provides the basis for your electronic version that you will also create.

Start with the flowchart to recall the order of your documents. After you have sorted through the documents and determined the order, create a title page for each section to organize the material. For example, a title page that says *Work Samples* helps give order to your documents.

Conclude your portfolio with an updated résumé, list of references, and letters of recommendation. Consider adding a photo in this section. Some advisors may suggest against this; however, your photo is probably on your LinkedIn or social media pages, so it is not confidential. By including it in your portfolio, it will help the interviewer connect name and face when the evaluation process is underway.

Next, prepare a table of contents for the items. This will help the person reviewing the portfolio locate each item and give a professional appearance to your portfolio.

Select the folder, binder, or other carrier that will be used to house the print portfolio. You will need multiples because, in most instances, you will leave the portfolio with the employer. It is suggested that you initially create two or three at the beginning of the process. As you progress in the job-seeking process, there will be inevitable changes that you will want to make. If you have created too many initial versions, you may find yourself discarding them. Remember, a portfolio is a living document and will be updated regularly.

1. Review the documents you have collected. Select the items you want to include in your portfolio. Make copies of certificates, diplomas, and other important documents. Keep the originals in a safe place.
2. Place the items in a binder, folder, or other container.
3. Give the portfolio to an instructor, counselor, or other person who can give constructive feedback. Review the feedback you received. Make necessary adjustments and revisions.

FIGURE 13-1

The Form I-9 is used to verify an employee's identity and that he or she is authorized to work in the United States.

Employment Eligibility Verification

Department of Homeland Security

U.S. Citizenship and Immigration Services

USCIS
Form I-9
OMB No. 1615-0047
Expires 08/31/20XX

▶ **START HERE:** Read instructions carefully before completing this form. The instructions must be available, either in paper or electronically, during completion of this form. Employers are liable for errors in the completion of this form.

ANTI-DISCRIMINATION NOTICE: It is illegal to discriminate against work-authorized individuals. Employers **CANNOT** specify which document(s) an employee may present to establish employment authorization and identity. The refusal to hire or continue to employ an individual because the documentation presented has a future expiration date may also constitute illegal discrimination.

Section 1. Employee Information and Attestation *(Employees must complete and sign Section 1 of Form I-9 no later than the **first day of employment**, but not before accepting a job offer.)*

Last Name *(Family Name)*	First Name *(Given Name)*	Middle Initial	Other Last Names Used *(if any)*

Address *(Street Number and Name)*	Apt. Number	City or Town	State	ZIP Code

Date of Birth *(mm/dd/yyyy)*	U.S. Social Security Number	Employee's E-mail Address	Employee's Telephone Number

I am aware that federal law provides for imprisonment and/or fines for false statements or use of false documents in connection with the completion of this form.

I attest, under penalty of perjury, that I am (check one of the following boxes):

☐ 1. A citizen of the United States

☐ 2. A noncitizen national of the United States *(See instructions)*

☐ 3. A lawful permanent resident   (Alien Registration Number/USCIS Number): _____

☐ 4. An alien authorized to work   until (expiration date, if applicable, mm/dd/yyyy): _____
    Some aliens may write "N/A" in the expiration date field. *(See instructions)*

Aliens authorized to work must provide only one of the following document numbers to complete Form I-9:
An Alien Registration Number/USCIS Number OR Form I-94 Admission Number OR Foreign Passport Number.

1. Alien Registration Number/USCIS Number: _____
        OR

2. Form I-94 Admission Number: _____
        OR

3. Foreign Passport Number: _____

    Country of Issuance: _____

QR Code - Section 1
Do Not Write In This Space

Signature of Employee	Today's Date *(mm/dd/yyyy)*

Preparer and/or Translator Certification (check one):

☐ I did not use a preparer or translator.   ☐ A preparer(s) and/or translator(s) assisted the employee in completing Section 1.
(Fields below must be completed and signed when preparers and/or translators assist an employee in completing Section 1.)

I attest, under penalty of perjury, that I have assisted in the completion of Section 1 of this form and that to the best of my knowledge the information is true and correct.

Signature of Preparer or Translator	Today's Date *(mm/dd/yyyy)*

Last Name *(Family Name)*	First Name *(Given Name)*

Address *(Street Number and Name)*	City or Town	State	ZIP Code

STOP   *Employer Completes Next Page*   STOP

Form I-9 11/14/20XX N   Page 1 of 3

US Department of Homeland Security; Goodheart-Willcox Publisher

Employment Forms

You will spend a considerable amount of time in the human resources department completing necessary forms for your employment. Come prepared with the personal information or documentation that will be required for a multitude of forms. You will need your Social Security number, emergency contact information, and other personal information. Examples of employment forms you will need to complete include Form I-9, Form W-4, and benefits forms.

Form I-9

Be prepared to complete a *Form I-9 Employment Eligibility Verification.* The Form I-9 is used to verify an employee's identity and that he or she is authorized to work in the United States. This form is from the US Department of Homeland Security. Figure 13-1 illustrates the portion of the form that shows citizenship status. Both citizens and noncitizens are required to complete this form.

You must complete and sign the Form I-9 in the presence of an authorized representative of the human resources department. Documentation of your identity must be presented at the time the form is signed. Acceptable documentation commonly used includes a valid driver's license, state-issued photo ID, or passport. A list of other acceptable documents is listed on the form. The human resources department will explain this form and answer any questions you may have.

Form W-4

You will also complete a *Form W-4 Employee's Withholding Allowance Certificate.* A Form W-4 is used by the employer for the information necessary to withhold the appropriate amount of taxes from your paycheck. Deductions are based on your marital status and the number of dependents you claim, including yourself. Based on your elections, the amounts withheld from your paycheck are forwarded to the appropriate government agency. Figure 13-2 shows a completed Form W-4.

By the end of January, an employer must send each employee a *Form W-2 Wage and Tax Statement* to use when filing income tax returns. This form summarizes all wages and deductions for the previous year for an individual employee. For example, an employee will receive a Form W-2 in January of 2019 that summarizes all wages and deductions received in 2018.

FIGURE 13-2

A Form W-4 is used by the employer for the information necessary to withhold the appropriate amount of taxes from your paycheck.

Separate here and give Form W-4 to your employer. Keep the top part for your records.

Form **W-4**
Department of the Treasury
Internal Revenue Service

Employee's Withholding Allowance Certificate

▶ Whether you are entitled to claim a certain number of allowances or exemption from withholding is subject to review by the IRS. Your employer may be required to send a copy of this form to the IRS.

OMB No. 1545-0074
20--

1 Your first name and middle initial: Kristy A. | Last name: James | 2 **Your social security number**: 000 00 0000

Home address (number and street or rural route): 1027 Cedar Street

3 ☒ Single ☐ Married ☐ Married, but withhold at higher Single rate.
Note: If married, but legally separated, or spouse is a nonresident alien, check the "Single" box.

City or town, state, and ZIP code: Franklin, IL 65432

4 **If your last name differs from that shown on your social security card, check here. You must call 1-800-772-1213 for a replacement card.** ▶ ☐

5 Total number of allowances you are claiming (from line **H** above **or** from the applicable worksheet on page 2) | 5 | 0
6 Additional amount, if any, you want withheld from each paycheck . . . . | 6 | $
7 I claim exemption from withholding for 20--, and I certify that I meet **both** of the following conditions for exemption.
- Last year I had a right to a refund of **all** federal income tax withheld because I had **no** tax liability, **and**
- This year I expect a refund of **all** federal income tax withheld because I expect to have **no** tax liability.

If you meet both conditions, write "Exempt" here . . . . ▶ | 7 |

Under penalties of perjury, I declare that I have examined this certificate and, to the best of my knowledge and belief, it is true, correct, and complete.

Employee's signature
(This form is not valid unless you sign it.) ▶ Kristy A James **Date ▶** 01/02/--

8 Employer's name and address (Employer: Complete lines 8 and 10 only if sending to the IRS.) | 9 Office code (optional) | 10 Employer identification number (EIN)

For Privacy Act and Paperwork Reduction Act Notice, see page 2. Cat. No. 10220Q Form **W-4** (20--)

United States Department of the Treasury, Internal Revenue Service; Goodheart-Willcox Publisher

What Employers Want

Cultural competency is the acknowledgement of cultural differences and the ability to adapt one's communication style to successfully send and receive messages despite those differences. The first step in becoming culturally competent involves recognizing cultural barriers. Being aware of potential disruptions is the best way to prevent or avoid them. The second step of cultural competency involves the willingness to adapt to those barriers.

Benefits Forms

The human resources department will provide you with a variety of forms that are specific to the compensation package offered by the employer. You will complete forms to confirm whether you elect to participate or decline participation in the various programs. A number of these forms will need to be completed on your first day.

One benefit of working full time is that many employers offer insurance coverage for employees. The insurance coverage might include medical, dental, vision, or life insurance. Conditions and terms apply for employees who accept insurance from an employer. For example, premium payments for insurance might be deducted from each paycheck.

Compensation packages are different for every employer, so plan to spend time learning what benefits your new company offers. Inquire about 401(k) plans, tuition assistance, retirement benefits, and day care assistance for dependents. Additionally, ask about your eligibility for these benefits. Some companies require employees to work for 90 days before they are eligible for benefits.

CONNECT TO YOUR CAREER

Complete 13-1 Employment Forms, pg 219

New-Hire Training

As a new employee, you will be a part of an orientation for new hires. If you are one of several people hired at the same time, you may participate in group training. If you are the only individual hired at that time, your training may be one-on-one.

Onboarding is a new employee's introduction to a company's brand, mission statement, values, and practices. Many companies conduct onboarding via PowerPoint presentations conducted by a human resources representative. These presentations will likely include information such as organizational charts, company history, emergency evacuation procedures, and other details that will help you fit in and be successful with your new employer. Most companies have an employee handbook that will be part of the training materials. Topics such as the history of the company, its mission, and company policies will likely be introduced. Certain topics, such as education about harassment in the workplace, will be addressed as mandated by the government. Other topics, such as employee safety and security, compensation, attendance policies, and benefits, will also be covered.

Take notes during the onboarding presentation. Although you may not need all of the information presented on the first day of your new job, you will likely need to refer to your onboarding information throughout the course of your employment.

After the company policies have been presented, your supervisor or someone on your team will train you on the processes and procedures for your specific job. Each team generally has specific guidelines for accomplishing tasks that you will need to learn. This is an opportunity to start learning the expectations for your new position.

As part of your training, you may be taken on a tour of the facilities so that you may become familiar with the layout of the building in which you work. During this tour, you will probably be introduced to the people with whom you will work or have contact during your first few days at work. You may also be invited to sit in on meetings from other departments to learn more about the company and its values, culture, and workflow.

As a new employee, there is much to learn, and you will likely have many questions during the first few days. Your supervisor, coworkers, and human resources department are there to help you, so call on them when you need assistance. Figure 13-3 lists suggested topics for which you might be proactive and ask for answers during your training period.

FIGURE 13-3

Asking questions and taking notes during new-employee training can provide information that will be important for the duration of your employment.

Information to Obtain During Employee Training	
	Ask About
☐	Employee parking or assigned parking spot
☐	Employee entrance to use
☐	Badge or code for entering building
☐	Who to call in an emergency
☐	Hours building is open
☐	What to do if building is locked
☐	Personal workspace location
☐	Who to call for computer assistance
☐	Phone extensions and how to use telephone system
☐	Break room location and policies
☐	Photocopying equipment location and policies
☐	How to request office supplies
☐	Supervisor name, phone extension, and location
☐	Human resources contact person, phone extension, and location
☐	Deadline for completing employment forms
☐	Daily expected working hours
☐	Lunch and break policies
☐	Who to call if time off is needed
☐	Clocking in and clocking out, if it is needed, and how to do so
☐	Time cards

Goodheart-Willcox Publisher

Workspace

On your first day of employment, you will be assigned a workspace. A *workspace* is the specific area within a company's location where an employee works. It is an individual's personal space while at work. *Workspace etiquette* is applying the rules of good manners while you are in your own space and the space of others. Proper respect helps to maintain positive relationships with those with whom you work.

In some businesses, all employees are assigned a cubicle regardless of title or position. Cubicles offer some privacy, but they are not protected from noises or distractions. If this is your assigned area, remember to respect those in the cubicles around you. When in conversations on the phone or with those who are visiting you, remember to keep your voice low so as not to disturb others. If listening to music as you work, use headphones. Digital devices should be turned off or silenced.

Depending on your career and position, you may have your own office as a workspace. Having an office provides a quiet, private space to complete tasks. If you have an office, treat it as a privilege. Close the door when you are in conversations with visitors or on the phone.

Respect should be shown to your employer by keeping your workspace clean, organized, and free from clutter. Over-decorating with photographs and personal items can be distracting in a business situation, so discretion should be used. Personal items, such as briefcases and lunch containers, should be placed in a drawer or closet to maintain discretion and safety, as well as to keep the space presentable and orderly.

Some businesses permit employees to drink coffee and water and eat snacks or lunch at their desks. If you choose to do so, avoid bringing foods to your workspace that have strong odors that might offend coworkers. Remember to maintain a clean work environment and dispose leftovers and packaging in the employee break room or cafeteria rather than in the waste paper can at your desk.

Performance Evaluations

During your career, your performance on the job will be evaluated. A **performance evaluation** is a formal process designed to evaluate an employee's work with productive outcomes. The evaluation will take into account not only your actual job performance and how you execute your duties, but also how well you interact with your coworkers as a team player.

Performance evaluations are generally formal meetings with a manager or supervisor. He or she will review the evaluation with you and discuss the results. These meetings are an opportunity for you to conduct self-evaluations about what you want from your job and where you will advance yourself.

A *performance evaluation form* will be used in an evaluation. Ask for a copy of the form early in your employment. Review the criteria often and execute each category to the best of your ability. If at any time you feel that you are not meeting the minimum criteria as detailed on the performance evaluation form, ask your immediate supervisor for guidance. He or she should be able to provide feedback that you can use to help overcome obstacles that stand in the way of your success.

Remember, you created a two- to four-year career plan. During a performance evaluation, it is up to you to decide if the outcome of your meeting is what you want for your career. Use each evaluation as a chance to revisit your plan.

CONNECT TO YOUR ▶ CAREER

Complete 13-2 Employee Performance Self-Evaluation, pg 220

Workplace Safety

As a new employee, it is necessary to become acquainted with workplace safety guidelines for the organization. Workplace safety in the United States has continuously improved since the beginning of the 20th century. Injury, death, and illness related to working conditions have gradually declined. This is due to a change in the type of work done today and in the safety precautions that have been put in place.

Accident Prevention

Falling hazards, lifting hazards, and material-storage hazards account for most of the workplace accidents that occur in offices. Falls are the most common workplace accidents in an office setting. To prevent falling injuries, take the following precautions:

- close drawers completely
- do not stand on a chair or box to reach an object
- secure cords, rugs, and mats

Lifting hazards are sources of potential injury from improperly lifting or carrying items. Most back injuries are caused by improper lifting. To prevent lifting injuries, take the following precautions:

- make several small trips with items rather than one trip with an overly heavy load
- use dollies or handcarts whenever possible
- lift with the legs, not the back
- never carry an item that blocks vision

Material-storage hazards are sources of potential injury that come from the improper storage of files, books, office equipment, or other items. A cluttered workplace is an unsafe workplace. Material stacked too high can fall on employees. Paper and files stored on the floor or in a hall are a fire risk. To prevent material-storage injuries, take the following precautions:

- do not stack boxes or papers on top of tall cabinets
- store heavier objects on lower shelves
- keep aisles and hallways clear

Maintaining a safe workplace is the joint responsibility of the employer and employee. The employer makes sure the facility and working conditions are such that accidents are unlikely to occur, and the employee uses common sense and care while at the office. Keys to maintaining a safe working environment include reading and understanding equipment safety manuals, following safety instructions, and abiding by safety requirements.

CONNECT TO YOUR ▸ CAREER

Complete 13-3 Workplace Safety, pg 222

Workplace Ergonomics

Ergonomics is the science concerned with designing and arranging things a person uses so they can be used efficiently and safely. In the workplace, it can include designing workstations to fit the unique needs of the worker and the equipment used. Effective application of ergonomic principles results in a comfortable, efficient, and safe working environment.

There are many types of ergonomic accessories that may improve a workstation, including wrist rests for keyboards, specially designed chairs, and back supports. In addition, Figure 13-4 identifies actions and accessories that can be taken to create a comfortable environment and help prevent injury or strain to the worker's body.

FIGURE 13-4

Ergonomics is the science concerned with designing and arranging things people use so they can interact both efficiently and safely.

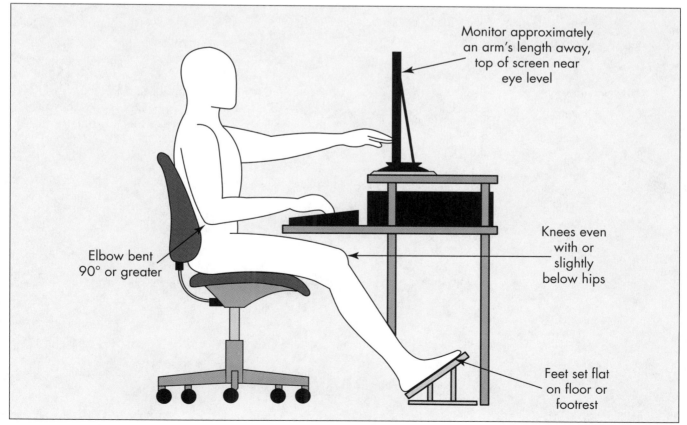

Goodheart-Willcox Publisher

The Best App for That

ZipRecruiter Job Search

The *ZipRecruiter Job Search* app is an aggregate job board that provides links to posted jobs from hundreds of job sites. You can apply instantly for jobs or save those that interest you and apply for them at a later time. ZipRecruiter simplifies the application process by enabling you to upload your résumé in one click. Once you apply, constant notifications are pushed to you to inform you of application views, messages form hiring managers, and much more.

Update Your Professional Network

When you begin your new job, update your LinkedIn, Twitter, Instagram, and other professional networking accounts to reflect your employment status. Enter your new title, the month and year that you begin your job, and the name of the company at which you are employed. After you add your new company to your profile, search for and join the company's groups or social networking pages, if applicable.

It is important to stay up to date with those in your network who agreed to be personal references for you during the employment process. Place a phone call or send an e-mail to each person with the news that you have accepted a position. Provide each person with your new company's name and your job title, and let them know that you appreciate the reference they provided for you. Offer to return the favor and provide them with a professional reference when needed.

Visit the employment websites and job boards where your résumé is posted. Change your job-seeking status from "searching" to "not searching." Otherwise, you will continue to get new job postings in your e-mail. Refer to your tracking documents if you do not remember all of the places where your résumé is posted.

CONNECT TO YOUR ▸ CAREER

Complete 13-4 Update Your Professional Network, pg 223

Summary

Describe a typical first day of a new job.
On the first day with a company, human resources will require certain forms be completed by new hires. This includes a Form I-9, Form W-4, and other documents related to the compensation package. New-hire training and onboarding will also be conducted on the first day.

Describe performance evaluations in the workplace.
Performance evaluations are generally formal meetings with a manager or supervisor. These evaluations take into account job performance and how well a person interacts with coworkers. In addition, they are an opportunity for an employee to conduct self-evaluations about what he or she wants from the job. A copy of the performance evaluation form should be requested when starting a new job and reviewed often.

Identify ways to be safe in the workplace.
Follow simple safety guidelines to avoid workplace accidents and keep everyone safe. Avoid falling, lifting, and material-storage hazards, and use ergonomics to ensure comfort and functionality in a workstation.

Update your professional network.
An individual's professional network should be updated to reflect new employment. Follow up with professional references to thank them for serving as references. Employment status on job-search websites should also be updated to avoid having advertisements delivered to a professional e-mail account.

Glossary Terms

ergonomics	onboarding	performance evaluation

Review

1. How can a person prepare for his or her first day on the job?

2. What is the purpose of the Form I-9?

3. What is the purpose of the Form W-4?

4. What information is included in a Form W-2?

5. Provide an example of an onboarding experience.

6. Describe the performance-evaluation process.

7. Identify how to be safe in the workplace.

8. List three keys to maintaining a safe working environment.

9. List examples of ergonomic accessories.

10. Why is it important to update your professional networks?

Application

1. What information will you inquire about before the first day on the job?

2. What types of benefits do you hope to be offered by your future employer?

3. Why is it important to start saving for retirement early?

4. Describe typical new-hire training in your industry.

5. What types of onboarding would you expect to experience in your chosen career field?

6. How have onboarding experiences helped you in your past work experience?

7. By what criteria do you expect to be evaluated in your desired career?

8. Describe what you think is the most common cause for workplace injury in your chosen career field.

9. What type of safety training have you completed in your industry?

10. Why is it beneficial to stay in touch with your network even while employed on a full-time basis?

CONNECT TO YOUR ▶ CAREER
Workplace Connection

13-1 Employment Forms

Download the Form I-9 Employment Eligibility Verification from the US Citizen and Immigration Services website at www.uscis.gov. Print a copy of this form.

1. Complete the form as a practice exercise. Use blue or black ink and your best handwriting. The form must be neat, clean, and error free. However, *do not* fill in the Social Security information. This should only be completed when you are ready to submit the form to an employer.

2. Review the acceptable forms of identification. Record which documents you have in your possession that you will provide to your new employer. Does your eligibility come from List A, List B, List C, or a combination of the lists?

3. Download the Form W-4 Employee's Withholding Allowance Certificate from the US Internal Revenue Service website at www.irs.gov. Print and complete the form as a practice exercise.

13-2 Employee Performance Self-Evaluation

Self-evaluation is an important part of the performance evaluation process. Often, an employer will request that employees complete a self-evaluation prior to being evaluated by a supervisor. This provides the supervisor with an opportunity to learn more about the employee's professional goals and help guide the employee toward continuous improvement throughout a career. The evaluation form that follows is typical of one that you might receive as an employee. Study the form and review each section.

Employee Self-Evaluation			
Name:		**Title:**	
Department:		**Date:**	
Time in Position:		**Supervisor:**	
Goals or achievements completed over the past year			
1.			
2.			
3.			
Goals that were not completed			
1.			
2.			
3.			
New skills acquired and important experience gained:			
Professional development I completed:			
New tasks for which I'd like to be responsible and assignment preferences:			
Professional development I'd like to pursue:			

Where I see myself in the next 12–24 months:
What I ultimately aspire to be doing:
Additional comments:

What did you learn from reviewing this self-evaluation form?

What type of information or questions would you add to the self-evaluation form and why?

Why would a supervisor want to know an employee's aspirations?

How important do you think a self-evaluation is in terms of an employee's overall performance evaluation?

How can a self-evaluation help prepare an employee for a formal evaluation that a supervisor will conduct?

13-3 Workplace Safety

Workplace safety is different in every industry. Conduct an Internet search for safety concerns in your career field. Summarize your findings.

What are the ergonomic concerns for the equipment commonly used in your career field? Examples of equipment include computers, desks and chairs, machinery, and automobiles. Using the following table, describe these ergonomic concerns and how equipment is designed to be more comfortable and efficient for employees.

Ergonomic Issues for Workplace	
Items	**Concerns**

13-4 Update Your Professional Network

Describe the steps you will take to update your professional networking profiles on social media, follow up with your professional references, and update your job-seeking status on employment websites and job boards.

Step #1:

Step #2:

Step #3:

Step #4:

Step #5:

Step #6:

What does "be the best employee you can be" mean to you? Explain how you plan to carry this out in your career.

14 Starting Your Career

Outcomes

1. **Define** professionalism.
2. **Identify** various generations that make up a multigenerational workplace.
3. **Cite** actions that ensure a successful career.

CONNECT TO YOUR CAREER

Workplace Connection

14-1 Multigenerational Workplace
14-2 Take Charge of Your Career

OVERVIEW

Landing the job you want is just a beginning. You should do all you can to succeed and advance in your chosen field. Exhibiting professional behavior means taking responsibility for your behavior and your work. Certain work habits and traits demonstrate professionalism in almost any job in business and industry, from stock clerk to top executive. These habits and traits include promptness, reliable attendance, dependability, positivity, and eagerness to do the work as best you can.

As your career progresses, remember to put your best foot forward. Embody traits that demonstrate professionalism, and treat coworkers with respect and as valuable contributors to the workplace. This will result in a pleasant working experience and ensure you are able to continually connect to your career.

Professionalism

As a new employee, your primary responsibility is to help the business operate and make a profit. You will be expected to perform assigned job duties to the best of your ability. While performing those duties, your employer will insist that you behave in a professional manner. **Professionalism** is a soft skill that includes the judgment, character, and behavior expected of a person who is trained for a given job. You will be required to exhibit professionalism while at work or when representing the company.

In addition to the workplace skills introduced in Chapter 2, professionalism includes self-management skills. **Self-management skills** are the skills that enable an individual to control personal habits and make the best use of his or her time and abilities. Examples are punctuality, dependability, time management, and emotional regulation.

Punctuality

Punctuality means being on time. It is important to show up ready for work on time every day. Being late or unexpectedly absent is inconsiderate and not tolerated in the working world. If you arrive late or are unexpectedly absent, your coworkers may have to take on your work. In addition to being rude and unprofessional, these actions can lead to resentment or animosity in the workplace. If you know you will be late or have to miss work entirely, it is expected that you will notify your employer with enough time for alternative plans to be established.

Dependability

Punctuality is a sign of dependability. **Dependability** is a person's ability to be reliable and trustworthy. Being dependable means others can count on you to do what needs to be done, keep your word, be honest, and carry your share of the workload. Dependable employees tend to be given the important jobs in a company.

Time Management

Professionals understand how to manage their time and priorities. "Work smarter, not harder" is a phrase frequently quoted in business and industry. **Time management** is the practice of organizing time and work assignments to increase personal efficiency. It is an important soft skill in the workplace because work assignments may include a variety of tasks. Often, you will need to work on several tasks at the same time. You will be expected to prioritize those tasks by determining which ones should be completed before others. When uncertain as to which tasks

are the most important, always ask your direct supervisor. The difference between average and excellent workers is often not how hard they work, but how well they prioritize assignments.

Emotional Regulation

Learning how to control your emotions is a skill that, if you lack, can cost you your job. Your emotional state of being is complicated, and it takes work and determination to keep it under control. Coworkers who annoy you, situations that do not go your way, and other daily work incidents can cause you to be irritable and show how you are feeling. As a professional, this is behavior that can make or break your career. If you think this may be an issue for you, be proactive and get professional help before a situation gets out of hand.

Multigenerational Workplace

As you begin your career, you will find yourself a part of a *multigenerational workplace*. A **generation** is a group of people who were born during the same time period. This means that each generation witnessed the same technological advances and global events at approximately the same age. These events will have impacted each generation differently. For example, Neil Armstrong walking on the moon in 1969 may have affected an adult watching it differently than it did a child watching it.

The Best App for That

CareerBuilder

The *CareerBuilder* app provides continuous and consistent connection to your job search through easy access to your CareerBuilder account. Through the app, you can update your account information as needed. You can also synchronize your résumé and other application documents, as well as review jobs that you have applied for from your account. Applying to jobs is quick and easy, as is reviewing your application history. You can also save jobs and apply later if you choose not to apply immediately after finding the opportunity.

You will probably be most comfortable interacting with those from your own generation. As an effective employee, it will be necessary to learn to work with individuals from all generations. The five generations most common in the workforce today are the Silent Generation, Baby Boomers, Generation X, Generation Y (Millennials), and Generation Z, as shown in Figure 14-1.

Understanding how to communicate with members of a different generation than your own begins with understanding the traits common to each generation. While individuals in a given generation will not share the exact traits, some characteristics are common for people within each group.

Silent Generation

The Silent Generation is comprised of people born between the years 1920 and 1939. This generation accounts for approximately two percent of the workforce. Most of these workers have retired, though some still work in part-time roles. This generation values traditions and history, and they believe in hard work and experience. While sometimes perceived as unwilling to change to accept new ideas, they serve a valuable role in carrying on the traditions of companies while acting as role models up to which younger generations can look.

Baby Boomers

The Baby Boomer generation consists of people born between the years 1940 and 1959. This generation accounts for approximately 29 percent of the workforce. Most "Boomers" are approaching retirement age, though many will likely continue working. This generation values individual goals and achievement, and they believe in starting from the bottom and working up. They are ambitious and loyal to their careers, and they are willing to sacrifice for the success of the team.

Generation X

People who belong to Generation X were born between the years 1960 and 1979. This generation accounts for nearly 32 percent of the workforce. This generation will be the next one to take over once all the Baby Boomers have retired. People in this generation have a tendency to be less loyal to one career than their predecessors and are comfortable moving from one job to another in an industry. They are more independent than Boomers, and they insist on a positive work-life balance.

Generation Y (Millennials)

Generation Y, or the Millennial Generation, consists of people born between 1980 and 1999. Millennials account for nearly 34 percent of the workforce,

FIGURE 14-1

A generation is a group of people who were born during the same time period.

Generations in the Workplace		
Generation	**Born Between**	**Famous Examples**
Silent Generation	1920–1939	Dick Van Dyke, Yoko Ono
Baby Boomers	1940–1959	Carlos Santana, Oprah Winfrey
Generation X	1960–1979	John Cho, Viola Davis
Generation Y (Millennials)	1980–1999	LeBron James, Taylor Swift
Generation Z	2000 and beyond	Finn Wolfhard, Dafne Keen

Goodheart-Willcox Publisher

making them the largest generation in the workforce. This generation has grown up with technology and applies their technological skills in the workplace better than their counterparts. They are efficient multi-taskers who, like the generation before them, value a positive work-life balance, often choosing to work from home.

Generation Z

Generation Z members were born after 2000. They account for only one percent of the population, as a large number of them are just entering the workforce. This generation looks to seamlessly integrate technology into their everyday lives—so much so they are often referred to as the iGeneration. Like the Millennials, they thrive on recognition for their work. They are less motivated by money than their predecessors, but through their reliance on technology, have become more aware of their surroundings.

CONNECT TO YOUR ▷ CAREER

Complete 14-1 Multigenerational Workplace, pg 231

Your Career

You will spend many hours of your life at work, so you must take charge of your career. Start planning for your future as soon as possible. There are many actions that will help to ensure a long, productive, and happy career.

The easiest way to ensure a long, successful career is to be a good employee. Take your work seriously, and maintain your professionalism in the workplace. Nurture relationships with your supervisor as well as your coworkers. Keep personal problems separate from work as much as possible. While it is acceptable to engage in casual conversations, keep the conversations positive and brief.

Social Media Slipup

A well-liked server at a popular restaurant was hard at work, serving customers and taking orders. She liked her job and worked hard and relied heavily on the gratuity she received from her customers.

One afternoon, a party of five arrived for the lunch hour. At the end of the meal, she left the check with the host of the lunch party. The check that was given for their meals automatically generated suggested gratuities as dollar amounts. Most customers appreciate this service as it helps them calculate a tip without having to do the math. Most servers appreciate the service because it helps them get a fair tip for their work.

When the diners had left and the server picked up the credit card receipt, she noticed that the diner had crossed out the suggested gratuities and totaled the bill without a tip. The waitress was angered by the lack of gratuity. In her anger, she took a photo of the receipt with her cell phone and posted it to the social-news-and-media-aggregating site Reddit noting how selfish and rude the customer was not to leave a tip.

zhu difeng/Shutterstock.com

Later, a person who was clearing the tables brought a sizable amount of cash to the server that he found on the table under a napkin. The server was humiliated. The customer had left quite a generous tip in cash rather than including it on the credit card.

She immediately removed the photo from the site. Luckily, the photo had not been shared anywhere else. If it had, the consequences could have been devastating. She, or the restaurant, could have been in legal trouble for slander and violation of privacy laws. Also in her favor, neither her employer nor coworkers saw it.

She learned a lesson that changed her life and career from this incident. Social media and lack of emotional control can be a dangerous combination in the workplace. Creating a digital imprint is something that normally cannot be retracted. Luck was on her side that afternoon, and she was able to preserve her future.

Conscientious employees maximize career retention by exhibiting effective leadership skills, even when they are not in a leadership position.

Be wise with your money, and start saving for your retirement as soon as possible. Saving money early can make your retirement years more comfortable and easier to attain. Research the retirement benefits your new employer offers, and take full advantage of them.

Grow and maintain your professional network as you progress in your career. The individuals you meet and work with along the way can help you throughout your career in many different ways. Additionally, being in touch with other professionals in your field will make you aware of new developments and opportunities in your career field.

Continue your professional development by staying up to date in your field. Successful employees continually seek opportunities to improve their career skills. **Professional development** is training that builds on skills and knowledge that contribute to personal growth and career development. There are many options for professional development. Many businesses are willing to pay to provide professional development training for their employees. By keeping abreast of the most current expectations in your field, you can earn success in the workplace and exhibit leadership qualities.

CONNECT TO YOUR CAREER

Complete 14-2 Take Charge of Your Career, pg 232

Career Portfolio

VGstockstudio/Shutterstock.com

Presenting the Electronic Portfolio. After your print portfolio is assembled, decide how to present your electronic portfolio. Just as you did for your print portfolio, review the digital files you have collected. Select the ones you want to include and remove those you do not. Decide how you want to present the materials. For example, you could create an electronic presentation with slides for each section. The slides could have links to documents, videos, graphics, or sound files. You could use a CD or a flash drive to present the material. The Internet also provides ways to help you present and store materials for an electronic portfolio. You could create a personal website with links to various sections. The method you choose should allow the viewer to navigate and find items easily.

Your electronic portfolio will contain documents you created digitally as well as documents that you have in hard-copy format that will be scanned. It will be necessary to decide file formats to use for both types of documents. Before you begin, consider the technology that you might use for creating and scanning documents. You will need access to desktop publishing software, scanners, cameras, and other digital equipment or software.

For documents that you create, consider using the default format to save the files. For example, you could save letters and essays created in Microsoft Word in the default DOCX format. You could save worksheets created in Microsoft Excel in the default XLSX format. If your presentation will include graphics or video, confirm the file formats that are necessary for each item. Use the appropriate formats as you create the documents.

Hard copy items will need to be converted to digital format. Portable document format, or PDF, is a good choice for scanned items, such as awards and certificates.

Another option is to save all documents as PDF files. Keep in mind that the person reviewing your electronic portfolio will need programs that open these formats to view your files. Having all of the files in the same format can make viewing them easier for others who need to review your portfolio.

1. Create the slide presentation, website, or other vehicle for presenting your electronic portfolio.
2. View the completed electronic portfolio to check the appearance and functionality.
3. Write a short summary about the format of your electronic portfolio. Include brief instructions on how to navigate or view the portfolio.
4. Give the portfolio to an instructor, counselor, or other person who can give constructive feedback. Review the feedback you received. Make necessary adjustments and revisions.

Summary

 Define professionalism.
Professionalism is a soft skill that includes the judgment, character, and behavior expected of a person who is trained for a given job. In addition to basic skills, thinking skills, people skills, and personal qualities, professionalism also includes self-management skills. Self-management skills include punctuality, dependability, time management, and emotional regulation.

 Identify various generations that make up a multigenerational workplace.
Five generations most common in the workforce today are the Silent Generation, Baby Boomers, Generation X, Generation Y (Millennials), and Generation Z.

 Cite actions that ensure a successful career.
The easiest way to ensure a successful career is by being a good employee. Other actions include taking work seriously, maintaining professionalism in the workplace, nurturing relationships with supervisors, keeping personal problems separate from work, and pursuing professional development, among others.

Glossary Terms

dependability	professionalism	time management
generation	punctuality	
professional development	self-management skills	

Review

1. What is *professionalism*?

2. List examples of self-management skills.

3. Aside from it being rude and unprofessional, being late or unexpectedly absent can lead to what?

4. What does it mean to be dependable?

5. What is the difference between average and excellent workers?

6. What generations are likely to be encountered in the workplace?

7. Describe the differences among the generations you may encounter in the workplace.

8. Describe actions that ensure a successful career.

9. Why is it important to start saving for retirement early?

10. How can professional development help achieve success in a career?

Application

1. How would you describe your personal level of professionalism? Provide examples of situations in which you presented yourself in a way that reinforced your professionalism.

2. What does "work smarter, not harder" mean to you?

3. To what extent are you a dependable employee? Cite examples to support your answer.

4. On a scale of one to ten, with one being the weakest and ten being the strongest, rate your top ten time-management or prioritizing skills. Describe how this information can help you improve your time-management skills.

5. Explain how you will successfully regulate your emotions in the workplace.

6. Of the generations listed in this chapter, which do you think you are most likely to encounter in your industry? Which are you least likely to encounter? Explain your answer.

7. What do you think causes the changes in how the value of work is viewed and treated from generation to generation?

8. Casual conversations in the workplace should be positive and brief. How do you know which topics of conversation are suitable for the workplace and which topics are inappropriate?

9. List types of professional development that are important to your career and explain their necessity.

10. How can you connect to your career?

CONNECT TO YOUR CAREER
Workplace Connection

14-1 Multigenerational Workplace

Each generation you encounter in the workplace has developed and adheres to expected behavior while at work. Conduct an Internet search for workplace characteristics common to your generation and list examples in the left column of the following table. Then, in the right column, list your personal workplace characteristics. Note any similarities.

My Generation	
My Generation's Workplace Characteristics	**My Workplace Characteristics**

To what extent would you agree or disagree that you are similar to the workplace characteristics of your generation?

Agree:

Disagree:

14-2 Take Charge of Your Career

Taking charge of your career includes accepting responsibility for your role in the company, taking necessary steps to improve and grow professionally, and planning for your future. It also includes personal financial management. Once you start earning a regular paycheck, it is important to create a budget so you can manage your money wisely. Your budget should include living expenses as well as paying off school loans and saving for retirement. Conduct a search on the Internet using the phrase *personal budget* to research various methods and formats for the creation of a budget. Select a method that works for you, and use the following space to help organize your budget items.

Expenses (monthly):

Savings (how much you can afford to save):

Discretionary Spending (surplus money for wants, not needs):

Professional development is an important aspect in one's career as it can affect a career path. In Chapter 1, you learned how to write SMART goals that are specific, measurable, attainable, realistic, and timely. Write one short-term professional development goal for your career and one long-term goal. Implement the SMART model in the creation of these goals by ensuring each one is specific, measurable, attainable, realistic, and timely.

Short-term goal:

Long-term goal:

Now that you have a job, it is time to update your personal career plan. Revisit the career plan you created in Workplace Connection activity 1-2. Throughout this chapter, you learned how to use job-search strategies to connect to your career. Based on what you have learned, update your career plan.

Career Plan: Year 1			
Career Item	**Specific Action to Take**	**Target Completion Date**	**Actual Completion Date**

Career Plan: Year 2			
Career Item	**Specific Action to Take**	**Target Completion Date**	**Actual Completion Date**

Career Plan: Year 3			
Career Item	**Specific Action to Take**	**Target Completion Date**	**Actual Completion Date**

Career Plan: Year 4			
Career Item	**Specific Action to Take**	**Target Completion Date**	**Actual Completion Date**

Punctuation

Terminal Punctuation

In writing, **punctuation** consists of marks used to show the structure of sentences. Punctuation marks used at the end of a sentence are called *terminal punctuation*. Terminal punctuation marks include periods, question marks, and exclamation points.

Periods

A **period** is a punctuation mark used at the end of a declarative sentence. A *declarative sentence* is one that makes a statement. A period signals to the reader that the expressed thought has ended.

> The final exam will be on May 26.
> Alma traveled to Lexington to visit her friend.

A period can be used within a quotation. A period should be placed inside a quotation that completes a statement. If a sentence contains a quotation that does not complete the thought, the period should be placed at the end of the sentence, not the end of the quote.

> Jacobi said, "The project is on schedule."
> She told me, "Do not let anyone through this door," and she meant it.

Question Marks

A **question mark** is punctuation used at the end of an interrogative sentence. An *interrogative sentence* is one that asks a question. A question mark can be used after a word or sentence that expresses strong emotion, such as shock or doubt.

> Will the plane arrive on time?
> What? Are you serious?

A question mark can be part of a sentence that contains a quotation. Place the question mark inside the quotation marks when the quote asks a question. Place the question mark outside the quotation marks if the entire sentence asks a question.

> Teresa asked, "Will the work be finished soon?"
> Did he say, "The sale will end on Friday"?

Exclamation Points

An **exclamation point** is a punctuation mark used to express strong emotion. Exclamation points are used at the end of a sentence or after an interjection that stands alone. An exclamation point can be used at the end of a question rather than a question mark, if the writer wishes to show strong emotion.

> Ouch! Stop hurting me!
> Will you ever grow up!

As with other terminal punctuation, an exclamation point can be part of a sentence that contains a quotation. Place the exclamation point inside the quotation marks when the quote expresses the strong emotion. Place the exclamation point outside the quotation marks if the entire sentence expresses the strong emotion.

> All of the students shouted, "Hooray!"
> She said, "You are disqualified"!

Internal Punctuation

Punctuation marks used within a sentence are called **internal punctuation**. These marks include commas, dashes, parentheses, semicolons, colons, apostrophes, hyphens, and quotation marks.

Commas

A **comma** is a punctuation mark used to separate elements in a sentence. Commas are used to separate items in a series.

> Apple, pears, or grapes will be on the menu.

A comma is used before a coordinating conjunction that joins two independent clauses.

> The sun rose, and the birds began to sing.

Commas are used to separate a nonrestrictive explanatory word or phrase from the rest of the sentence.

> Gloria's husband, Jorge, drove the car.
> Yes, I will attend the meeting.

A comma is placed before and after an adverb, such as *however* or *indeed*, when it comes in the middle of a sentence.

> Preparing a delicious meal, however, requires using fresh ingredients.

When an adjective phrase contains coordinate adjectives, use commas to separate the coordinate adjectives. The comma takes the place of the word *and.*

> The *long, hot* summer was finally over.

Commas are used to separate words used in direct address. The words can be proper nouns, the pronoun *you*, or common nouns.

Quon, please answer the next question.
Everyone, please sit down.

Commas are used to separate elements in dates and addresses. When a date is expressed in the month-day-year format, commas are used to separate the year.

On December 7, 1941, Japan attacked Pearl Harbor.

When only the month and year or a holiday and year are used, a comma is not needed.

In January 2010 she retired from her job.

A comma is used after the street address and after the city when an address or location appears in general text.

Mail the item to 123 Maple Drive,
Columbus, OH 43085.

A comma is used to introduce a quotation.

The speaker attempted to energize the workers by saying, "The only limits are those we put on ourselves."

Dashes and Parentheses

A **dash** is a punctuation mark that separates elements in a sentence or signals an abrupt change in thought. There are two types of dashes: *em dash* and *en dash*. The em dash can be used to replace commas or parentheses to emphasize or set off text. To give emphasis to a break in thought, use an em dash.

My history teacher—an avid reader—visits the library every week.

The en dash is used as a span or range of numbers, dates, or time.

We won the baseball game 6–3.
Barack Obama served as President of the United States from 2009–2017.

Parentheses are punctuation marks used to enclose words or phrases that clarify meaning or give added information. Place a period that comes at the end of a sentence inside the parentheses only when the entire sentence is enclosed in parentheses.

Deliver the materials to the meeting site (the Polluck Building).

Use parentheses to enclose numbers or letters in a list that is part of a sentence.

Revise the sentences to correct errors in (1) spelling, (2) punctuation, and (3) capitalization.

Semicolons, Colons, and Apostrophes

A **semicolon** is an internal punctuation mark used to separate independent clauses that are similar in thought. A semicolon can also be used to separate items in a series. Typically, items in a series are separated with commas, but if the serial items include commas, a semicolon should be used to avoid confusion.

> Twelve students took the test; two students passed.
>
> We mailed packages to Anchorage, AK; Houston, TX; and Bangor, ME.

A **colon** is an internal punctuation mark that introduces an element in a sentence or paragraph.

> The bag contains three items: a book, a pencil, and an apple.

A colon is also used after a phrase, clause, or sentence that introduces a vertical list.

> Follow these steps:

An **apostrophe** is a punctuation mark used to form possessive words. It is most commonly used in conjunction with the letter *s* to show possession. Position of the apostrophe depends on whether the noun is singular or plural. If singular, place the apostrophe between the noun and the *s*. If plural, place the apostrophe after the *s*.

> Akeno's dress was red.
>
> The students' books were to be put away before the exam.

A **contraction** is a shortened form of a word or term. It is formed by omitting letters from one or more words and replacing them with an apostrophe to create one word—the contraction. An example of a contraction is *it's* for *it is*.

Apostrophes can also be used to indicate that numbers or letters are omitted from words for brevity or writing style.

> Leisure suits were in style in the '60s. (1960s)
>
> The candidates will meet to discuss activities of the gov't. (government)

Hyphens

A **hyphen** is a punctuation mark used to separate parts of compound words, numbers, or ranges. Compound words that always have a hyphen are called **permanent compounds**. Some adverbs, such as *on-the-job*, always have hyphens.

> The close-up was blurry.
>
> My mother-in-law made dinner.
>
> Their orientation includes on-the-job training.

Compound adjectives have hyphens when they come before the words they modify, but not when they come after them.

> The well-done pot roast was delicious.
>
> The delicious pot roast was well done.
>
> These out-of-date books should be thrown away.
>
> Throw away the books that are out of date.

In some words that have prefixes, a hyphen is used between the prefix and the rest of the word.

| My ex-wife has custody of our children.

When a word is divided at the end of a line of text, a hyphen is used between parts of the word.

| Carter ran down the hall-
| way to answer the door.

Quotation Marks

Quotation marks are used to enclose short, direct quotations and titles of some artistic or written works.

| "Which color do you want," he asked.
| "The Raven" is a poem written by Edgar Allan Poe.

A quotation need not be a complete sentence; it can be a word or a phrase as spoken or written by someone. See the examples that follow.

| When the mayor refers to "charitable giving," does that include gifts to all nonprofit
| organizations?

When writing dialogue, the words of each speaker are enclosed in quotation marks with the appropriate punctuation mark.

| Anna arrived at the office and greeted her coworker, Joan. "Good morning. You're
| getting an early start today."

Chapter or section titles within complete books, movies, or other artistic work are typically shown in quotation marks. The full title of the work is typically italicized.

| "Books and Journals" is the first chapter in *The Chicago Manual of Style*.

Quotation marks are used to enclose words that are meant to show irony.

| Although Connie had the afternoon off, she was too "busy" to help me.
| In a survey of small businesses, one in five managers said their companies are
| "sinking ships."

B

Capitalization

Capitalization

Capitalization is writing a letter in uppercase (B) rather than lowercase (b). Capital letters signal the beginning of a new sentence and identify important words in titles and headings. Capital letters are also used for proper nouns, for some abbreviations, in personal and professional titles, and for parts of business letters.

A sentence begins with a capital letter. Numbers that begin a sentence should be spelled as words, and the first word should be capitalized.

| Thirty-three students took part in the graduation ceremony.

Capitalize the first, last, and all important words in a heading or title.

| *Gone with the Wind*
| *The Adventure of the Hansom Cabs*

For numbers with hyphens in a heading or title, capitalize both words.

| *Twenty-One Candles*

Do not capitalize articles or prepositions within a heading or title unless it is the first word in the title.

| *The Finest Story in the World*

When a title and subtitle are written together, only the first word of the subtitle is capitalized regardless of the part of speech.

| *Presidential Priorities: College's 10th president outlines three campus goals*

Do not capitalize coordinating conjunctions (*yet, and, but, for, or,* and *nor*) in a heading or title.

| *Pride and Prejudice*
| *Never Marry but for Love*

Do not capitalize parts of names that normally appear in lowercase (Ludwig van Beethoven).

| His favorite composer is Ludwig van Beethoven.

Capitalize the first word in the salutation for a letter.

| Dear Mrs. Stockton:

Capitalize the first word in the complimentary close for a letter.

| Sincerely yours,

Proper nouns begin with a capital letter. Recall that a proper noun is a word that identifies a specific person, place, or thing.

| Joe Wong is the principal of George Rogers Clark High School.

Capitalize initials used in place of names.

| UCLA won the football game.

Capitalize abbreviations that are made up of the first letters of words.

| HTML stands for hypertext markup language.

Months and days, as well as their abbreviations, should be capitalized.

| Mon. is the abbreviation for Monday.

Abbreviations for names of states and countries should be capitalized.

| The price is given in US dollars.

Capitalize abbreviations for directional terms and location terms in street addresses.

| She lives at 123 NW Cedar Ave.

Capitalize call letters of a broadcasting company.

| My favorite television show is on CBS.

Abbreviations that note an era in time should be in capital letters.

| The article included a map of Europe for the
| year 1200 CE.

Capitalize titles that come before personal names and seniority titles after names.

| Sen. Carl Rogers called Mr. Juarez and Dr. Wang.
| Mr. Thomas O'Malley, Jr., spoke at the ceremony.

Capitalize abbreviations for academic degrees and other professional designations that follow names.

| Jane Patel, LPN, was on duty at the hospital.

Number Usage

Number Expression

Numbers can be expressed as figures or as words. In some cases, as in legal documents and on bank checks, numbers are written in both figures and words. When the two expressions of a number do not agree, readers are alerted to ask for clarification.

Number expression guidelines are not as widely agreed upon as rules for punctuation and capitalization. Follow the guidelines in this section for general writing. If you are writing a research report or an article for a particular group or publication, ask whether there are number expression guidelines you should follow for that item.

Numbers Expressed as Words

In general writing, use words for numbers one through nine.

| One dog and three cats sat on the porch.

Use figures for numbers 10 and greater. (See other style guides for exceptions to this guideline.)

| She placed an order for 125 blue ink pens.

When some numbers in a sentence are 9 or less and some are 10 or greater, write all the numbers as figures.

| The box contains 5 books, 10 folders, and 15 pads of paper.

Use words for numbers that are indefinite or approximate amounts.

| About fifty people signed the petition.

Use words for numbers one through nine followed by *million, billion,* and so forth. For numbers 10 or greater followed by *million, billion,* and so forth, use a figure and the word.

| Two million people live in this region.
| By 2016, the population of the United States had grown to over 300 million.

When a number begins a sentence, use words instead of figures. If the number is long when written as words, consider revising the sentence so it does not begin with a number.

| Twenty copies of the report were prepared.

When two numbers come together in a sentence, use words for one of the numbers.

| On the bus, there were 15 ten-year-olds.

Use words for numbers with *o'clock* to express time.

| Come to my house for lunch at eleven o'clock.

Use figures with *a.m.* and *p.m.* to express time.

| The assembly will begin at 9:30 a.m.

To express amounts of money, use figures with a currency sign.

| The total amount is $18,395.40.

Do not use a decimal and two zeros when all dollar amounts in a sentence are whole amounts.

| The charges were $5, $312, and $89.

For an isolated amount less than $1, use figures and the word *cents*.

| Buy a cup of lemonade for 75 cents.

When an amount less than $1 appears with other amounts greater than $1, use figures and dollar signs for all of the numbers.

| The prices were $12.50, $0.89, and $12.45.

For a large, whole dollar amount, use the dollar sign, a figure, and a word, such as *million* or *billion*.

| The profits for last year were $5 million.

Days and years in dates should be identified with figures.

| On February 19, 2015, the court was not in session.

Use words for fractions. Note that a hyphen is placed between the words.

| Place one-half of the mixture in the pan.

Use figures for mixed numbers (a whole number and a fraction).

| I bought 3 1/2 yards of red fabric.

When writing a number with decimals, use figures.

| The measurements are 1.358 and 0.878.

Use figures in measurements, such as distance, weight, and percentages.

| We drove 258 miles today.
| The winning pumpkin weighs 50 pounds.
| Sales have increased 20 percent in the last year.

Pages, chapters, figures, or parts in a book should be referenced with figures.

| Open your book to chapter 3, page 125.
| Refer to figure 6 on page 72 for an example.

Glossary

A

ability. Mastery of a skill or the capacity to do something. (1)

adware. Form of software that displays or downloads advertisement material automatically without the user's knowledge. (6)

application cover letter. Letter used to apply for and provide personal qualifications for a position that has been posted by an employer. (8)

aptitude. Characteristic that an individual has developed naturally. (1)

B

background check. Evaluation of personal data that is publicly available. (12)

basic skills. Fundamental skills necessary to function effectively in society. (2)

behavioral question. Question that draws on an individual's previous experiences and decisions. (10)

blue-sky question. Question where the interviewer describes a scenario that may or may not be related to the job duties and requires a response from the candidate. (10)

body language. Communication sent through gestures, facial expressions, and posture. (11)

C

career. Long-term progression in one particular field with opportunities for growth and advancement. (1)

career ladder. Sequence of work in a career field, from entry to advanced levels. (1)

career lattice. Series of lateral and vertical moves in one career field. (1)

career objective. Brief statement that explains an individual's career goals to an employer. (7)

career plan. Documentation of where a person is today in the job-search process and where he or she would like to be over the course of a career. (1)

career profile. Details an individual's accomplishments, skills, and current career level. (7)

certification. Professional status earned by an individual after passing an exam focused on a specific body of knowledge. (2)

collaboration. Act of working together with another person to accomplish a goal. (2)

compensation package. Everything an employee receives in return for his or her work. (12)

complimentary close. Sign-off for the letter. (8)

compromise. To come to a mutually agreed-upon decision. (2)

connection. Person in an individual's network on LinkedIn who is added only by invitation. (4)

cookies. Bits of data stored on a computer that record information about the websites a user has visited. (6)

copyright. Acknowledges ownership of a work and specifies that only the owner has the right to sell the work, use it, or give permission for someone else to sell or use it. (2)

cover letter. Formal written communication that accompanies a résumé or a job application to introduce an applicant and express his or her interest in a position. (8)

D

dependability. Person's ability to be reliable and trustworthy. (14)

digital citizenship. Standard of appropriate behavior when using technology to communicate. (2)

digital footprint. Data record of all of an individual's online activities. (4)

discrimination. Unfair treatment of an individual based on his or her race, gender, religion, national origin, disability, or age. (2)

diversity. Representation of different backgrounds, cultures, or demographics in a group. (2)

Note: The number in parenthesis following each definition indicates the chapter in which the term can be found.

E

emerging occupations. New occupations that have developed or changed due to technological or other advancements. (1)

employment verification. Process in which a job candidate's employment history is checked to confirm the accuracy of the information he or she submitted. (12)

ergonomics. Science concerned with designing and arranging things a person uses so they can be used efficiently and safely. (13)

ethics. Moral principles or beliefs that direct a person's behavior. (2)

etiquette. Art of using good manners in any situation. (5)

F

firewall. Program that monitors information coming into a computer and helps assure that only safe information gets through. (6)

follower. Twitter member who views another user's Tweets in his or her own Twitter feed. (4)

formal seated position. Entails sitting upright, with both feet on the floor and both hands comfortably resting either on chair armrests or in the lap. (11)

G

generation. Group of people who were born during the same time period. (14)

H

harassment. Any unsolicited conduct toward another person based on his or her race, gender, national origin, age, or disability. (2)

hard skills. Measurable, observable, and critical skills necessary to perform the required, work-related tasks of a given position. (1)

hashtag. Searchable keyword that links users to all Tweets marked with the same keyword. (4)

heading. Person's full name, phone number, e-mail address, and geographic location. (7)

hypothetical question. Question that requires a person to imagine a situation and describe how he or she would act. (10)

I

identity theft. Illegal act that involves stealing someone's personal information and using that information to commit theft or fraud. (6)

infographic résumé. Visual résumé in which the content is displayed using a combination of words and graphics to present information clearly and quickly. (7)

informational interviewing. Strategy used to interview and ask for advice and direction from a professional, rather than asking for a job opportunity. (5)

infringement. Any use of intellectual property without permission. (2)

inquiry cover letter. Letter written to learn if any potential positions are available for which the job seeker would like to be considered. (8)

intellectual property. Something that comes from a person's mind. (2)

Internet protocol address. Number used to identify an electronic device connected to the Internet, known as an *IP address*. (6)

J

job. Short-term employment for compensation. (1)

job application. Form used by employers to gain more information about a person applying for a job. (9)

job offer. Formal invitation to work under mutually agreed terms and conditions. (12)

job-search website. Website on which multiple employers post employment opportunities on a daily basis. (9)

K

keywords. Words that specifically relate to the functions of the position for which the employer is hiring. (1)

M

malware. Term given to software programs that are intended to damage, destroy, or steal data on a computer, short for *malicious software*. (6)

microblog. Short communication limited to a certain number of characters per post. (4)

multi-level marketing (MLM). Business strategy in which employees are compensated for sales they personally generate and for the sales of the other salespeople they recruit, also called a *pyramid scheme.* (6)

N

networking. Talking with people and establishing relationships that can lead to career growth or potential job opportunities. (4)

networking cover letter. Letter that introduces an applicant noting that a person in his or her network recommended he or she apply for the position. (8)

O

Occupational Information Network (O*NET). Occupational resource that provides descriptions of in-demand industry areas in emerging occupations. (1)

onboarding. New employee's introduction to a company's brand, mission statement, values, and practices. (13)

online job board. Website that hosts job postings for employers and allows applicants to apply for jobs seamlessly. (8)

online presence. What the public can learn about a person from viewing his or her Internet activities. (4)

P

panel interview. Interview in which a candidate talks with multiple interviewers in a room. (10)

people skills. Skills that enable people to develop and maintain working relationships with others, also called *interpersonal skills.* (2)

performance evaluation. Formal process designed to evaluate an employee's work with productive outcomes. (13)

personal brand. An individual's reputation. (3)

personal brand statement. One sentence that describes what a potential job candidate offers an employer. (3)

personal commercial. Rehearsed introduction that includes brief information about a person's background and a snapshot of his or her career goals, also known as an *elevator speech.* (3)

personal qualities. Characteristics that make up an individual's personality. (2)

personality. Unique blend of qualities that predict attitudes, values, and work habits. (1)

phishing. Use of fraudulent e-mails and copies of valid websites to trick people into providing private and confidential personal data. (6)

plagiarism. Claiming another person's material as your own, which is both unethical and illegal. (2)

portfolio. Compilation of materials that provide evidence of a person's qualifications, skills, and talents. (1)

professional development. Training that builds on skills and knowledge that contribute to personal growth and career development. (14)

professional network. Consists of people who support an individual in his or her career and other business endeavors. (5)

professional reference. Person who knows an applicant's skills, talents, or personal traits and is willing to recommend him or her. (5)

professionalism. Soft skill that includes the judgment, character, and behavior expected of a person who is trained for a given job. (14)

profile. Information that describes who a person is in his or her professional life. (4)

proprietary information. Any work created by company employees on the job that is owned by that company. (2)

punctuality. Being on time. (14)

R

ransomware. Software program that takes over a computer system and locks it until the owner pays a sum of money to regain control of the computer. (6)

respect. Feeling or belief that someone or something is good, valuable, and important. (2)

résumé. Written document that lists an individual's qualifications for a job, including work experience and education. (7)

S

screening interview. Preliminary, informal interview designed to determine if a candidate's skills qualify him or her for a formal interview. (10)

search engine optimization (SEO). Process of indexing a website so it will rank higher on the list of returned results when a search is conducted. (4)

secure password. Code used to access a private account or other private information. (4)

self-management skills. Skills that enable an individual to control personal habits and make the best use of his or her time and abilities. (14)

self-talk. Internal thoughts and feelings about one's self. (4)

signal phrase. Preplanned beginning phrase that enhances a question. (10)

signature block. Full name, phone number, and e-mail address of the owner of the account. (4)

skill. Something an individual does well. (1)

skills résumé. Résumé that lists work experience according to categories of skills or achievements rather than by employer, also known as a *functional résumé*. (7)

SMART goal. Goal that is specific, measurable, attainable, realistic, and timely. (1)

soft skills. Applicable skills used to help an individual find a job, perform in the workplace, and gain success in any job or career. (1)

software virus. Computer program designed to negatively impact a computer system. (6)

spyware. Software that spies on a computer. (6)

structured interview. Formal interview in which a predetermined list of questions is posed to each candidate interviewing for a position, also known as a *directive interview*. (10)

subjective element. Factor that contains bias and is more emotional than logical. (11)

T

thinking skills. Skills that enable a person to solve problems. (2)

time management. Practice of organizing time and work assignments to increase personal efficiency. (14)

timeline résumé. Résumé that emphasizes employers and work experience with each, also known as a *chronological résumé*. (7)

trending. Refers to keywords and phrases that have the highest number of online searches in any given day. (7)

two-step authentication. Process in which a host requires two identity verifications before granting permission to an account. (6)

U

unstructured interview. Interview that is less formal and may not necessarily consist of a specific list of questions. (10)

V

values. Principles and beliefs that a person considers important. (1)

visual résumé. Résumé that presents information in a graphically appealing format. (7)

Index

cookie hijacking, 90
cookies, 89–90
copyright, 28
cover letters, 125–134
  application, 125
  body, 129
  complimentary close, 129
  date, 128
  e-mail submission, 129, 133
  greeting, 128
  hard-copy, 134
  heading, 128
  inquiry, 125
  inside address, 128
  introduction, 128
  networking, 125
  parts, 126, 128–129
  submitting, 129, 133–134
  types, 125
  uploading to online job board,
    133–134
creative thinking, 25
cultural competency, 210
cursive, 129

D

decision making, 25
dependability, 225
desired qualification, 143
digital citizenship
  intellectual property, 28
  netiquette, 28, 62
  software downloads, 27
  use of company-owned
    equipment, 27
digital etiquette. *See* netiquette;
  online etiquette
digital footprint, 55
directive interview, 157
discrimination, 26
diversity, 26
downloads, 27
dress code, 207
Dropbox app, 182

E

education, 107–108
electronic portfolio, 13, 228

elevator speech, 42. *See also*
  personal commercial
e-mail
  cover letter submission, 129, 133
  professional account, 56
emerging occupations, 3
emotions, managing, 191–192, 225
employability skills, 8, 25, 43
employment forms
  benefit forms, 210
  Form I-9 Employment Eligibility
    Verification, 209
  Form W-2 Wage and Tax
    Statement, 209
  Form W-4 Employee's
    Withholding Allowance
    Certificate, 209
employment process, 192–196
employment scams
  recognizing, 87–88
  reporting, 89
employment verification, 195–196
endorse, 59
entry-level position, 11
equipment, proper use of company-
  owned, 27
ergonomics, 213
ethics, 26, 90
etiquette
  business, 76
  in person, 77
  netiquette, 28, 62
  online, 77
  workspace, 212
executive-level position, 11
experience, 107

F

face-to-face networking, 75
Federal Trade Commission (FTC), 89
file formats
  Microsoft Word document, 111
  PDF, 111
  plain text, 111
  saving résumés, 111
firewall, 92
first day of new job, 207–214
  employment forms, 209–210
  new-hire training, 210
  workspace assignment, 212

first impressions, 179–180
first-degree connection, 60
flexibility, 30
followers, 62
foreign language skills,
  documenting in portfolio, 181
formal aptitude placement tests, 6
formal offer letter, 195
formal seated position, 180
Form I-9 Employment Eligibility
  Verification, 209
forms
  benefit, 210
  employment, 209–210
  performance evaluation, 212
Form W-2 Wage and Tax
  Statement, 209
Form W-4 Employee's Withholding
  Allowance Certificate, 209
foundation skills, 8, 25, 43
freemium, 57
FTC (Federal Trade Commission), 89
functional résumé, 108

G

general information questions,
  160–161
generation, 225
  five generations in workforce,
    225–227
Generation X, 226
Generation Y, 226–227
Generation Z, 227
Glassdoor app, 3
goals, SMART, 10
Google Drive app, 125
grooming for job interview, 179

H

harassment, 26
hard-copy job application, 141
hard skills, 8–9, 43
hashtag, 62
heading, 105–106, 128
headshot, 59
Hootsuite app, 42
humility, 157
hypothetical question, 163